FRANK HARRIS

A portrait of Frank Harris in 1895, painted by
Sir William Rothenstein

FRANK HARRIS

THE LIFE AND LOVES OF A SCOUNDREL

by VINCENT BROME

921

NEW YORK • THOMAS YOSELOFF • LONDON

ILLUSTRATIONS

FOREWORD

No one more successfully mangled the facts about his own life than Frank Harris. The four volumes of *My Life and Loves* are—for half their length—a monument of profligacy, sexual swagger and distortion. I have tried to find my way through the labyrinth but there were times when the nature of the evidence blurred the truth almost beyond recovery. Whenever equally convincing evidence seemed to cancel fact beyond redemption, I have tried to isolate and present the stories of the two most important witnesses, side by side. In the hope that total contradiction is as entertaining as it may prove enlightening, there are some half a dozen examples within the present book. Similarly, many other statements had to be qualified. Despite these occasional checks on direct narrative I still hope that Harris— the true Harris—comes alive in these pages as a person.

It can be argued that the portrait which follows is a sad comment on one cultural prescription of his day. Among the complex values of the nineteenth century it was culturally prescribed that individuals should not only get on as individuals, and conform, outwardly, to a puritanical code of morals, but should strain towards the achievement of material wealth. It would be interesting to know what might have happened to Harris' talents in a society less money conscious.

Equally, from the portrait which follows, Harris can be described as a person who became a blackguard of the worst possible kind and who would, whatever the society into which he was born, have remained true to his blackguard's nature.

Somewhere between these extremes may lie the truth. In philosophical jargon any value-judgment on the facts of his life must take more account of the conflict between nurture and nature than is normal. It was commonly said that nurture did not stand a chance when confronted with the naked and unqualified nature of Frank Harris. This may be true. I must leave the reader to draw his own conclusions.

The last biography of Harris published in England was written in 1929. Since then new evidence from many important witnesses has become available: Enid Bagnold, Emma Goldman, Douglas Goldring, Augustus John, Chief Justice Kotze, Middleton Murry, Edward Pease, Hesketh Pearson, Reginald Pound, MacLaren Ross, Frank Scully, Bernard Shaw, G. S. Viereck and H. G. Wells. There are many other people who have helped me with this book. I would like to acknowledge the work of Miss J. Telford in detailed criticism of the manuscript at many stages of its preparation. Montgomery Hyde provided invaluable material about the rival claims of Harris and Wilde to the play *Mr. and Mrs. Daventry*, and Frank Scully gave me permission to quote from his fascinating picture of his collaboration with Harris.

I must particularly thank Mr. E. Gertz—co-author of *Frank Harris* with Dr. A. I. Tobin—for his long and patient help and for access to many unpublished letters and some documents. Indeed this book could not have been written without his assistance. Reginald Pound also very kindly made available a collection of Harris' letters to Arnold Bennett. Hesketh Pearson gave invaluable help, not least in personal memories of Harris. He also took considerable trouble to read and criticize the first draft of the book. Middleton Murry and Enid Bagnold also made available important evidence. There were many lesser sources of letters and details given in the bibliography, and I must not forget Hugh Kingsmill's excellent study of Harris which first inspired this one. For the rest, very clearly, this is no definitive life of Harris—if such a book were possible. It is an interim portrait. Some personalities lend themselves to solid, traditional biography in three dimensions with every detail in place. I have written such a biography of Havelock Ellis which will be published in due course. With a man like Harris this approach seemed to me out of place. By his nature, and the nature of the evidence, it called for something far more impressionistic. This, then, is an interim portrait.

I am very grateful to the following authors and executors for permission to quote from books and letters: The Public Trustee and Mr. Norman Croom-Johnston, letters from Arnold Bennett to Harris; E. Gertz and A. I. Tobin, *Frank Harris*; Vyvyan Holland, *Son of Oscar Wilde*; Augustus John, *Chiaroscuro*; Dorothy Hopkinson, *Frank Harris*; J. Maclaren-Ross, *The London Magazine*; Hesketh Pearson, *Thinking It Over*; Frank Scully, *Rogue's Gallery*; The Public Trustee and The Society of Authors, letters of G. B. Shaw; the Executors of H. G. Wells, *Experiment in Autobiography*.

VINCENT BROME

CHAPTER ONE

At the window of the beautiful apartment on the sixth floor in the rue de la Buffa, the old man sat brooding over the sixty-five tattered pages of a manuscript which he had re-read for three months without adding a word. It was to become a big book. It would pour splendidly from his pen, startle the critics, sell in tens of thousands and at last convert these clamoring creditors into the admirers they had once been.

The sun came swiftly up the boulevards. The morning promised another day of burnished gold as the old man swept up the worn pages, shivered in his thick underclothes, and climbed painfully back into bed again. With a cap placed in reverse on his head to protect him against draughts, and his Imperial moustaches supported by metal clips, he tried once more to write, but nothing would come.

One hour later his wife Nellie knocked on the door. Frank Scully had arrived, she said. By now the old man was up once more and sitting in a chair, the woollen underclothes discarded and drying over the radiator. The Master suffered from some mysterious form of sciatica and in the sun-drenched climate of Nice, he slept in these overwhelming garments which, in the morning, needed what was understated as— airing.

Frank Scully, an American journalist, automatically expected a long wait. It had been arranged that Scully should assist Frank Harris in writing what Harris freely referred to as THE life of Bernard Shaw, but familiarity with the sixty-five worn pages of manuscript had taught Scully, over many beautiful and

I

completely idle mornings, that Harris' industry did not match his enthusiasm.

While Scully settled back to wait, somewhere behind deeply closed doors Harris moved through the elaborate ritual of washing, shaving and dressing. His broad shoulders sunk in a forward stoop, his step shuffling but still rapid, his voice a ghost of its former self, a transformation had to take place before the outer world was permitted to see the resurrected man. Every sign of age and decay had to be diminished. The clothes must be immaculate, the moustaches waxed, the tie, the diamond tie-pin, the stick, all perfectly in place; and if Harris was now, unmistakably, an old man, the result was sometimes startling. Carried out with a total disregard for the rest of the household, the ritual took small account of Frank Scully waiting outside. Fragment by fragment, Frank Harris tried to resurrect the dark, flashy, Napoleonic personality which had once thrust its way to the highest peaks of society, journalism and literature.

It was 11.30 when he at last emerged. Striding into the room he boomed at Scully in a voice reminiscent of its old thunder, 'Just time to go down to Nats.' This was the Palais de la Méditerranée where, every morning, Harris repaired for coffee and cognac. Scully hesitated, was about to say something and thought better of it. 'You go, Frank,' he said, 'I'll get on with this.' He vaguely indicated the papers in his hand. Harris waved his cane gaily and said, 'I'll be back very soon,' and strode away into what remained of the morning. Passing through the door the effect was superb—the shoulders back, the step springy, the eyes alight, but five minutes later, outside, small relapses began to overtake him.

Another hour went by. Harris returned to the sixth floor flat and instantly his voice began booming, 'Nellie—Nellie. Come on, old girl, where's lunch.'[1]

Once an auburn-haired beauty with very white skin and large brown eyes, Mrs. Nellie Harris showed signs of the appalling mission to which she had devoted a large part of her life— marriage to Frank Harris—but she continued to produce, with little money and no help, excellent luncheons, fully

[1] Frank Scully, *Rogue's Gallery*, pp. 223 (Murray and Gee, 1943).

aware that they were yet another part of the face-preserving ritual.

Harris summoned Scully to lunch with the air of a man who had been kept waiting rather too long. In the early stages of lunch he was liable to bad temper, but once through the *hors d'oeuvre* and two glasses of wine, a hint of color came back into his mottled cheeks, his voice once more recovered something of its power and he began to talk vividly. Scully would turn the conversation to Bernard Shaw searching for those devastating reminiscences which Harris constantly said—with knowing chuckles and highly expressive gestures—were only waiting the appropriately inspired moment to emerge in full flood. Sometimes he did talk about Shaw; sometimes he repeated himself hopelessly, memory playing endless tricks; sometimes Nellie intervened to cover faulty recollections or to check the flow of invention; sometimes she beamed when Frank recovered his old powers and carried a story with tremendous verve to its climax, only to give way to a paroxysm of coughing as he looked into Scully's eye trying to detect whether he had said it all before or not.

Scully had once imagined that with lunch over, real work might begin. He had not then quite grasped the masterly way in which Harris rose from the table, took three powerful steps to a chaise-longue, and dropped abruptly from eating, talking, gesticulating, into the profoundest sleep.

The period of unconsciousness varied. If it ended at 3.15 there might be a note of irritation when Harris woke because he had not drawn deeply enough on the new life which sleep could give. If it continued until 3.30 he rose all eagerness to grapple not with Bernard Shaw or Frank Scully, but with the business of finding a taxi to drive him round the hills of Nice while his brain mulled over the sentence which might yet extend the sixty-five pages to sixty-six.

Tea time at 4.30 was not tea time. Something far stronger kept Harris on the verge of entering the creative state. Skirmishing dangerously with work he contined to find alibis until at last he could claim that the day was too advanced and dinner imminent. Sometimes he ate richly and recklessly at dinner and his stomach, ruined by a mysterious episode in some primitive

3

region of Africa, rebelled. Turning a pale green he left the room, but the ghastly ritual of the stomach pump quickly restored his spirits. An india-rubber tube was pushed down his throat, a quart or so of warm water poured through a funnel into the stomach and . . . well the rest is best left to the imagination. Once through dinner, if in good spirits, Harris might wrap himself up to read Balzac, or, if he felt unwell, turn to the cheapest French fiction with the sauciest spice.

Day after day it went on. The great collaboration to produce the definitive life of Bernard Shaw became more and more a series of evasions; the attempts to recover the brash splendor of the once formidable Frank Harris continuously revealed a man grown old, tired, and incapable even of concentration.

Sometimes Nellie would come unexpectedly into the drawing room in the evening and find Harris turning the sixty-five tattered pages of manuscript again, a manuscript he had written and published ten years before but now dimly saw as a fresh contribution to the life of Shaw which Messrs. Simon and Schuster in New York and Victor Gollancz in London, impatiently awaited. How many times he re-read the pages no one ever knew. The manuscript was like a talisman from an irrecoverable past . . . .

A past when Frank Harris had lorded it over literary London, as a friend of Bernard Shaw, H. G. Wells, Oscar Wilde, Max Beerbohm, Aubrey Beardsley, and half the famous hostesses of the time. Barely 5′ 5″ high he wore 'cuban' heels to increase his height, and compensated for other inferiorities with a voice like thunder and a Napoleonic vehemence which few could resist. In many physical respects he seemed unfortunate, but there were some who saw him as they might a prize-fighter with his 40″ chest, 14″ biceps and 12″ forearms. His swart body he clothed with ornate waistcoats, butterfly collars, spats and gold watch chains, the total effect sometimes carried off by the swashbuckling air of the greatest literary tycoon which nineteenth century England knew. His face dark and tough, his ears ugly, his hair coming down low on his forehead, gave him an almost Neanderthal appearance, but he looked and played many roles.

At the height of his fame Bernard Shaw wrote to him:

4

'People whose curiosity is roused by your writings ask what was wrong with Frank Harris? Wasn't he a Jew or a financial blackmailer, journalist or another Verlaine or a German spy or something? It is necessary to reply No! he was simply the most impossible ruffian on the face of this earth.'

Oscar Wilde said of him: 'Frank Harris has been to all the great houses of England—once!' Wilde claimed to know Harris better than most. 'He has,' he said, 'no feelings. It is the secret of his success just as the fact that he thinks other people have none either is the secret of the failure that lies in wait for him somewhere on the way through life. . . .'

In his hey-day Frank Harris' behavior reinforced the legend of the total ruffian. He seemed not to understand the consternation he caused when his voice boomed out at a brilliant gathering of London's élite, 'Rape! Any sensible woman would relax and enjoy it!' But very complex forces were at work behind the façade and there were long periods of his life when he was a quite different person.

In his hey-day, he brilliantly edited the *Saturday Review* and the *Fortnightly*, wrote two collections of short stories, two novels, and bombastically launched on the world a book about a man with whom he had a tendency to confuse himself— Shakespeare.

It was in the Café Royal one spring day in 1896 that his love of Shakespeare broke through dramatically. Fifty guests had arrived for a luncheon party the invitations to which were sent on telegrams as large as letters, but Harris, in his grand manner had either forgotten or not bothered to book a table. He was the Great Frank. Luncheon tables of any required proportion sprang up at his bidding, restaurants brushed aside lesser mortals to meet his requirements. The manager did not disappoint him. An enormous table was inserted into the center of the main dining salon, the fifty guests settled down and lunch proceeded, until suddenly Harris' voice roared out above the hubbub. 'Homosexuality! No, I know nothing of the joys of homosexuality. My friend Oscar can no doubt tell you all about that.'

These were the days when people recoiled from the word as the devil, and Oscar Wilde's name carried Satanic implications.

It was Harris himself who broke the immense silence which had fallen on his guests. Once more his words echoed round not merely their table, but the whole restaurant:

'But I must say that if Shakespeare had asked me I should have had to submit.'[1]

Astonishingly, throughout the height of his career, the man who looked like the owner of a circus, continued to find identities between himself, Shakespeare and Christ, and he would say with all the quietness of understatement: 'Christ goes deeper than I do but I have a wider experience.' Or, if someone risked introducing Shakespeare into the conversation: 'When it comes to those things in Shakespeare I couldn't have written myself . . .' Happily free from anything so depressing as modesty, he boomed his way through the literary London of the nineties overwhelming anyone so foolish as to question the absolute rightness of anything he said, with a lion's roar, but the single picture of a brassy, boasting Harris handed down by his contemporaries, was subject to serious qualification. There were many Harrises. There was the serious writer and editor: there was the man who could play the lover, politician, actor and man of action, when he chose, with equal conviction, and when he chose, above all he could enthral an audience, pouring out wit, ideas, comments, throwing off long quotations from the poets and the Bible in a voice which, if it did not please everyone, could not be ignored. It was an extraordinary voice. It reminded one famous author of the rustling of iron leaves. Harris could sing two tones lower than the written scale. For many women, to hear it was to feel a primeval thrill as if someone had spoken out of the darkest depths of the forest and stirred their very roots. It was the voice which gave such force to his personality, the voice which talked his way into such high places, the voice which carried him to the verge of the House of Commons and made one man remark: 'With Frank it is as if he had been granted an extra organ.'

Harris never failed to exploit the last drop of his varied talents: with his voice he abused its power endlessly; but 'abuse' to him was the wrong word. In his hey-day he lived by that law which required complete freedom from normal conventions

[1] A. I. Tobin and E. Gertz, *Frank Harris*, p. 18 (Madelaine Mendelsohn, 1931).

for anyone resembling a genius, insisting that his own genius gave him 'divine' rights. He lied and seduced, drank and deceived, drained every cup to the dregs because he drew special sanctions from the gifts entrusted to him—or so he claimed. It all tended to overwhelm the Harris he did not particularly want known. In the end he could not recall the person he had once been. In his seventies his memory blurred and he slowly lost track of the details. . . .

In his seventy-fourth year, Frank Scully continued to arrive in the mornings, bursting to work on the Shaw biography, and Harris continued to disappear for his long apéritif, elaborate alibis protecting him against the too serious proximity of a pen.

Sitting at his favourite café in the sunshine, he looked out on the blazing sea and bleached beaches of Nice, his chin sunk on his hands, his homburg hat still at a jaunty angle, his Eton tie perfectly knotted, his Queensberry waistcoat crossed by the gold watch chain, and his eyes still flickered as he dimly followed the swish of a skirt and the flash of silk-stockinged legs.

Sometimes in the shade of his umbrella he drifted away with the heat into reverie and more and more to friends he spoke of what he called 'the big things'; he could no longer remember the details, but the big things were still there. He liked to remember the days as a bootblack in the United States when he squatted with scorn before every kind of boot and shoe; the days when the cowboy rode the range surviving ambush and Indian assault; and the ambitious young writer who forced an entry into editors' private rooms and literally browbeat his way to the editorship of the *Evening News* and the *Fortnightly Review*. He could still remember that final heady rush along the heights when the author, editor, celebrity, had not entirely succumbed to the ways of Horatio Bottomley, and the dark goddesses he came to love so much.

It was all dead, gone, done now. It was lost in a maze of less reputable memories. People did not bother to recall what he—Harris—thought he had done for the world or how it had made him suffer. He was old and he did not want to be old. The beautiful Laura seemed half a world away and the wild

7

CHAPTER TWO

F RANK HARRIS was born in two different countries on three
different dates and his name was not Frank Harris. Any confusion in these statements is due to the pleasure which Harris
took in deliberately creating new origins for himself according
to the company which he kept. Unravelling lie from truth it is
possible to say that he was almost certainly born on February
14th, 1856, in Galway, the far western seaport of Ireland, and
that he was baptized James Thomas Harris.

In those days Galway was a seaport still used by sailing ships,
its narrow streets dangerous after dark, its quayside harbors
neglected, reflecting the decay of its mercantile life. It was a
place of crowded stone houses, narrow streets, horse traffic and
peasants who clearly remembered the famine and the emigration
which followed. Memories of that part of the Spanish Armada
once wrecked on its shores were also evident in the houses
built like fortresses with low doors and central courtyards.

At night, there was little lighting in the streets of Galway,
and the Field of Mars still knew duels to the death, Irish feuds
continuing to be fought with a bitterness abandoned in England. Men with strange tongues brought strange cargoes into
the port and a whole rich variety of color, smells, activity,
fascinated the boy. Harris remembered the smell of tar, of tea,
of tallow and coal, and the groaning of ships straining at
anchor, far into life.

In the wild variety of origins with which he endowed himself, he spoke with equal conviction of his Welsh and Irish
roots, but having some resemblances to what is commonly

supposed to be a Jew, flatly denied Jewish origins. Certainly his father was a lieutenant in the Royal Navy commanding a revenue cutter with the tough efficiency which he later brought to educating his son. Welsh by birth and a self-made man, Thomas Harris had fought his way from cabin boy to officer and at forty-two presented a rugged exterior of oaken strength, preserving, in every inch of his life, the puritanism from which James (alias Frank) Harris was so quickly to recoil.

To the seaport of Galway, with the hard bitten Lieutenant Harris still in command of his cutter, there came one day in the 1860s, a very important gentleman dressed in braided uniform and a cocked hat, who saw over the ship on behalf of the Admiralty. Suddenly he noticed the small boy. Proud of his son and anxious to display a skill he had by no means perfected, Thomas Harris ordered James to plunge overboard and swim round the ship. It was a cold October day with a moderate sea running and as the boy came blue and gasping through one wave top after another, My Lord of the Admiralty indicated his astonishment that so small a boy could perform such a feat. Whereupon the pride of Thomas Harris swelled to the point where he roared: 'Again! Again!' Reluctantly the blue-cheeked boy fell back into the water and began, with steadily growing difficulty, to circle the ship. For the second time, cold and breathless he came back to the rope, grasped it and was about to haul himself aboard with what remained of his strength when—'Again!'—the dreaded word came booming down. As the beginnings of panic seized James Harris, the man from the Admiralty intervened. He was impressed, pleased and full of tolerance. The boy had done enough. James Harris never forgot that episode.

If memories of his father were vivid and very often bitter, it was otherwise with his mother. Born in a beautiful Welsh valley, Mrs. Harris was as frail as her husband Thomas was tough. She had that Welsh pallor which went with dark watchful eyes and mystical beliefs. Tuberculosis continuously drained her strength, and she was troubled by the long lonely stretches when her husband was away at sea and she tried to support a family on limited money. She seemed, to her son James, as gracious as Thomas Harris was rough, and he remembered her taking her husband's arm for support as she coughed her way down the streets. Mrs. Harris preserved a conventional interpretation of good behavior, but she understood that there was something beautiful in the world around her, and she helped to redeem for James Harris a childhood he regarded as embittered.

Partly it was embittered because, beyond all reclaim, his face was ugly. There were two brothers and two sisters all better looking than James and their early affection was qualified as the 'main ugly' lad showed signs of a temperament of his own.

'Main ugly' . . . it was a phrase from one of his stories. In the story one woman remarked to another that a certain 'child was too weak to live' and a third commented 'A good thing too; it's main ugly.' Whereupon the mother of the child clutched the child to her and said: 'No baby's ugly that has all its features.' [1]

Whether Harris' mother did in fact protect him in this way remains obscure, but she always glowed in his memory and among the welter of his brutally frank writing, mothers sometimes emerged beatified. Her death came quite unexpectedly. Just four, and dimly aware that he was different from his brothers and sisters, different in a way which sometimes made him feel more like a girl than a boy, James Harris ran in at dusk one day to his mother's bedroom, saw her lying on the bed, and went to whisper in her ear. He received no response. He reached out a hand and brushed her forehead. She always awakened when he did that, but now, she did not stir. Suddenly afraid of something he could not understand he touched her lips, and still there was no response. He stared for a moment frowning. Then something about the utter stillness of her body struck into him and he turned and fled screaming from the room. Life, after that, was never quite the same again.

In his Autobiography, Harris implied that he was detached from the death of his mother and that she did not very much matter to him. Later, he gave Nellie and others a very different account of what was undoubtedly a powerful memory. Curiously undemonstrative for a Celt, his father could never replace the affection the boy had once drawn from his mother.

[1] Frank Harris, *Great Days* (John Lane, 1914).

There were also long stretches when he remained at sea and left James to the mercy of his brothers and sisters.

Whenever he was home on leave, Thomas Harris applied naval disciplines to his family. He seems almost to have enjoyed punishing the children whenever their behavior 'justified' it. Sometimes he had such an effect upon James that the boy went in 'sick fear' of his father. From Thomas's point of view it all had one object: to create complete self-reliance in his son. Whether this sometimes became an alibi for far harsher and less respectable impulses no one will ever know, but he certainly tried—with disastrous results—to produce adult behavior in a person still a child.

The Ugly Duckling. That was the title of a story written much later in life by Harris and said to disguise some of the realities of his early days. In the story, the Ugly Duckling finds himself driven by eccentric urges, and warnings from his mother are quickly overwhelmed by punishment and blame. He wanders off on his own, he does daring things and finds himself ostracized by the family. In real life, it was his father who continuously put James in his place, and if, in the beginning, he retaliated with the courage of unwary childhood, as his father snapped back at him still more fiercely, his courage began to fail and 'in my wretchedness I would wander away from the others'.

Soon that aching sense of isolation which childhood alone can bring to its full pitch, had James Harris in its power, and he went off to play his own imaginative games alone. He fought many battles from the twisted corners of Galway streets, a solitary, stubby little boy, rather dirty and distinctly furtive, reaching his desired victories by cunning, the kind of cunning he sometimes used against his brothers and sisters, and later in life brought to such perfection.

Presently the whole family travelled widely—from Galway to Kingstown, Kerry, Belfast and Armagh— as Thomas Harris' ship was stationed at different ports. Schooling was various and constantly changing. James Harris came top in arithmetic at Carrigfergus, and found some masters pleasantly disposed towards him, but against all his adult reputation Frank Harris, as a boy, was a sensitive child, moved by some of the finer emotions and tending to identify his feelings with those of a girl. When he was forced to attend a girls' school in Kingstown, accompanied by his sister Annie—because he could not be left alone when his father went to sea—it may have prematurely developed one side of his nature. He could not be the only boy in a girl's school without an attempt to see himself in their likeness. Similarly, the tenderness, the sensitivity to beauty, and the apparent search for a love equivalent to his mother's which he never, after his mother's death, found, were all stimulated by the girl's school. Later there were moments of revelation when he saw, as if for the first time, the beauty of sunlight playing on water, an old bridge across a river and a thick, dark wood beyond; there were spontaneous responses which seem to have been warm enough to a number of playmates; there was also the first awareness of the music of words which could, later in life, so easily move him to tears.

And then, slowly, over the next few years came the change. When he found that other people did not consider him he decided that he would consider them even less; when other people mangled his finer feelings he determined that theirs too should be brutalized. Sensitivity, he decided, was a mistake and must be suppressed; the small, ugly frame must be blown up in size and power to realize whatever desire most dominated his day. First dressed in the extraordinary ambition to become an athlete, these impulses were given very physical expression. Vernon, his brother, was a considerable boxer and despite his short sight, James presently managed to hold his own in a few brief and sometimes bloody exchanges. He boxed, he ran, he jumped, slowly hardening his body, but whatever potential his toughening body revealed, the life of the athlete was hopelessly wrecked by his short sightedness. It was difficult for a boy who wanted to distinguish himself at games to justify his ambition when a ball simply, at a certain distance, vanished from his ken. But he persevered; he ran, boxed, walked and fervently tried to control the rubber ball as if dominance over these skills would enable him to reduce the harsh outer world to similar disciplines.

The world in which James Harris spent his boyhood was a world torn and divided by the Irish troubles, by memories of the great famine and stirrings of revolt against what was freely referred to as the despotism of England. In England, Queen Victoria reigned supreme and four years after his birth, a British General Election brought Lord Palmerston back into office as Prime Minister, with Lord John Russell as Foreign Secretary. In Ireland, in the town of Skibbereen, a small body, with the deceptive title of the Phoenix National and Literary Society, came to life, and presently fathered the revolutionary Fenian Brotherhood. Widespread death from sheer hunger and the ravages of typhus had left bitter memories, the talk of open rebellion against England had grown, and a small group of mistaken idealists prepared for action. The dark Gaelic soul of Ireland was stirring as it had not stirred for years and experiences regarded as belonging to the primitive past, threatened to engulf her. Against this somber back-cloth, heroes of almost sword and cloak caliber made the young heart of James Harris leap with excitement. Gladstone was to dis-establish the Protestant Church of Ireland in 1869, Home Rule came in 1870, but Harris in his early childhood was absorbed in the colorful figures of the Fenian Brotherhood and far more personal matters.

With that precocity which marked his developing brain he had already found and explored certain sexual experiences without clearly knowing their significance. First it was his sister Annie, awed by the strange way in which her body changed, who decided to share the magic with her brother and sister and covertly, one day, bared her half-formed breasts to them. Then an expedition in the early dawn to steal bread and jam, brought him up short at the nurse's bedroom where he could dimly discern, beside the plump, comfortable nurse he knew so well, another form which seemed to him to be that of a man.

Presently, furtive gropings into the mysterious taboos and reticences which in those days made up no small part of the life of women, were reinforced by an experience which might have set fire to the dullest imagination. For a solitary young boy, placed in a girl's boarding school, sheer difference in dress must have forced upon his immature senses an awareness of feminity out of all proportion to their natural growth. What he saw is not recorded; what acts he witnessed unknown, but the attention of the girls too must have focused upon this phenomenon in their midst. Harris, propped in his high chair and subjected to glances, giggles and hints, quickly decided, with a mind already adventurous, that he must know more about these creatures. The technique was simple. A pencil dropped on the floor and kicked a little distance, justified his roving on all fours amongst the forest of plump young legs, until some instinct drew him to a particular pair, and he carefully rolled the pencil close enough to brush them with his hands as he sought to recover it. Sometimes the legs recoiled, sometimes a muffled shriek necessitated explaining the loss of his pencil, sometimes the legs simply quivered and remained still. Freud has since reduced such events to commonplaces and infantile sexuality has become a considerable cliché, but in the third quarter of the nineteenth century, the act of reproduction itself remained an unfortunate necessity, and everyone recoiled from sexual associations in the child with horror. When the still very uncertain boy found himself surrounded by temptations far beyond the normal, he determined to yield to each new impulse as it arose, but never dared to breathe a word of the tumult set loose inside him.

If free discussion of sexual matters was rigorously excluded from the family circle, talk about the revolutionary Fenians was not. It is possible that this had considerable influence on him. Sufficient talk of rebellion against England might condition a boy to rebel against all forms of authority.

Whatever happened, within a very short time the scene changed. At the age of 12 Harris was sent from Ireland to England to complete his education, and the abrupt change unsettled him still more. Completely lacking the spontaneous warmth of the Irish schools which he had so far known, Ruabon Grammar School in Denbigh, on the Welsh border, employed a brand of teaching not calculated to enlighten James Harris about the more important issues of the day. He quickly came to hate the system of fagging, the brutality, the implied or practised homosexuality, and above all a certain boy named Jones, Captain of the cricket First Eleven. Hatred grew as he ploughed his way through mathematics, English, geography and elementary science, and became aware that the fascination of words was even greater than he had at first imagined.

The ageing Harris in America, was very fond of telling the story of the revolt he organized among the fags, its dramatic sequel and his partial liberation from the bullying Jones, but his skill in re-arranging facts to justify his own claims to courage, was matchless. As the story went, someone informed against him, his rebellion was quelled, and the Monitors gave him a severe beating, Jones, the Captain, taking the leading part. According to Harris he then waited his chance. It came one day when a visiting cricket team from another school challenged the Ruabon team of which, by now, Harris was one of the more ferocious bowlers. The day of the match was a beautiful summer day and the white-flannelled figures stood about, idly throwing the ball while the rival captains span the coin. The ball came to Harris. He kept it, waited until Captain Jones had lost the toss and was moving down the pitch. Jones had hardly taken two paces when a flushed, determined Harris drew himself up to his full 5′ 5″ in front of him and said: 'You are a common bully.' For the first time the voice achieved something of its true depth. Jones could not have been more stunned. Then he saw Harris' hand raised, the red cricket ball whizzing towards him and dropped his head to one side as it hurtled past, grazing his cheek.

Harris had committed the unforgivable sin. Physical assault was of small moment, but to expose, to a visiting school, domestic feuds carefully concealed even from their own masters —nothing could be more dishonorable.

However dubious the details, the spirit of the story adequately expressed Harris' hatred of these first years at Ruabon Grammar School. If he saw, in Captain Jones, the substitute for a disciplinarian father figure and at last stood up to his father at one remove, the cost threatened to be high. It might mean expulsion from the school which would bring down on his head untold horrors from the very person whose despotic rule he was now driven to challenge. But no one expelled him. No one beat him again. He was simply left more and more to his own devices and at last the story of the Ugly Duckling repeated itself. Once more he came near to being an outcast among some of the boys and the great lesson which his father had tried to inculcate from very early childhood—self-reliance—reached ironical fulfilment. There were compensations. Some masters did help him, some boys remained friendly, but the short-sighted, stocky little boy, useful with his fists, and so capable of threatening to knife anyone foolish enough to abuse him, turned more and more to books, to lonely walks and communion with himself. He missed the Gaelic legends, the stories of Irish heroes, which had enthralled his early childhood, and now he turned to equivalent stories to compensate, losing himself in the colored worlds of Captain Marryat, Mayne Reed and Sir Walter Scott.

When the Christmas holidays came around at last, after an interval which seemed one of the longest in his life, he decided that Ireland was too distant and the thought of his father too depressing to face. Instead, with considerable initiative for a boy of his age, he decided to go with a school friend to North Wales. There, at Rhyl, two things happened. He met a girl whose name was probably Mary Montgomery, and witnessed an accident which left far deeper impressions than he could bring himself to admit. Mary and James had wandered off together one evening and the first clumsy passions of a young boy and girl were beginning to express themselves when a tremendous explosion came up from the direction of Rhyl.

It was a disaster which filled the newspapers the following day, and gradually the story unfolded of a goods train, carrying oil barrels, slipping down a gradient to crash into an express train travelling at full speed from London. The boy and girl, breaking away from a clumsy embrace, were suddenly aware of a great shock passing through the earth, and then a flicker of flame which spread until it lit the whole night sky, dazzling their eyes. Torn between two excitements, they at last rushed down to see what had happened and suddenly, were forced to negotiate a fence. It was at this fence that Harris tried to become still more intimate with Mary, and his exploring hands were severely rebuffed.

The picture which confronted them when they reached the railway line, remained vividly in his mind for many years. Half the train was a blazing wreck, fire engines, ambulances and police were everywhere, and intermittently another shapeless, smoking huddle was dragged, with great difficulty, from the twisted carriages. It was reported later that thirty-five people died in the accident. But if the horror of burning flesh, the smell of oil fumes and the hopeless struggle to reach people trapped beyond rescue, remained powerfully in Harris' mind, so did his experience with Mary Montgomery.

Not many more details of that Christmas holiday are available. Back once more in Denbigh, outwardly the ways of Ruabon Grammar School continued to dull and depress him but by now internal combustion had fired off a dozen new interests. He read T. H. Huxley and flirted with agnosticism, he read Shakespeare and found a wonderful exaltation in the rhythms of blank verse, he read Scott and dreamt of a chivalry which he saw denied in the life around him. Presently his awakening brain could not reconcile itself to the limitations of the school, to the isolated life he led and a growing sense that he was meant for something different. He determined, when next he saw his father, to take his courage in both hands and beg him to let him leave this black, benighted, abominable school and—nothing could have been more remote from the Harris he became—join the Royal Navy. The hope of realizing this dream sustained him through many weary months. What followed has been recounted in A. I. Tobin and E. Gertz's biography of Harris, and seems more reliable than the extraordinary contradictions which appear in Harris' autobiography.

According to the autobiography there was a stand-up fight at the school with Jones the bully, in which James performed considerable feats, eventually knocking his opponent to the ground, but this was probably an imaginative extension of the cricket ball episode. Similarly, the very curious affair of the withheld prize took the form, in the autobiography, of James winning one of the school's annual scholarships to Cambridge and simply, because he was too young, having it denied him by the visiting Cambridge professor who thought the second prize of £10 more appropriate for such a young person. It is more probable that Harris, to his own chagrin, did in fact win the second prize and later convinced himself that he had raced away with the first.

Now a boy of fifteen, continuously hungering for the magic summons from the Royal Navy which never came, disappointed that a £10 prize had been substituted for more ambitious dreams, and depressed by the dull grind of Latin and Greek, games and abuse, he determined that there was only one way to cope with such a blackly hated world—to run away. He had done well in mathematics and English, he had certainly won a prize of some distinction, but this miserable school and some of its toadying teachers had most foully misused him and must be abandoned. The pattern had repeated itself. The discipline, loneliness and abuse of family life had been reaffirmed, in part, by school. And one wild spring day, with the sun slanting through the clouds and the buds beginning to burst, he ran away. He pretended to the school authorities that he was going to see his father and ran away to—'freedom, to the ends of the earth'—he did not mind where, so long as Jones and all he stood for was forgotten.

In the event it was Liverpool which he reached first. There, excitement knew no bounds. Alone in a city teeming with every kind of life, he brushed shoulders with the strangest men, watched the swaying hips of women walking the gas-lit streets, and every so often glanced over his shoulder as if pursuing vengeance in the likeness of Jones might still overtake him before the beautiful dream of freedom came true. In reaction against the puritanical codes of the day, the music-halls were frankly bawdy and in the dim streets he tried not to stare at garish posters representing scenes from the Can-Can. He knew the theater to be the abode of the devil. He knew that the circle of dirty plush seats and the platform where men and women exhibited themselves, was a place of wicked abandon. His father had not merely told him so; he had driven it home with vivid illustration. The pale young boy walked the streets looking for a theater which he dared to enter, still frightened by the thought of what his father might do if he pursued and cornered him. Two, at least, of many parental taboos had been broken, and now, very rapidly, another one succumbed. If the evidence given to Hugh Kingsmill meant anything, the result was unexpected.

Imagine the small boy with large ears and ugly face sitting forward on the edge of his seat, gazing from the rather smelly pit at the gas-lit stage, totally enraptured as the heroine of the play, *The Two Roses*, revealed herself not as a sulky trollop but a rather lovely young person, capable of common affection and no small degree of loyalty. He had seen many little girls, he had observed adolescents maturing into young womanhood, and he had watched women reduced to tawdriness by the pressures of living in the city streets. But not this, not a beautiful woman, beautifully clothed, with large, sad eyes and a capacity to convey real feeling. He went out into the night with his head swimming and his first taste of something dimly remembered from the days of his mother. Throughout the remainder of his life, whenever that romantic streak in his nature, capable, in these early years, of poetic· expression, struggled against the swashbuckling person he was to become, something of the feeling of that first night in the theater and the enchantment of the gas-lit box returned to him.

In the morning the mood was gone. He had to get away from Liverpool, to make sure he could not be dragged back to school or his father. A gigantic plan matured in his mind. With the remainder of his £10 prize money, the following morning he made his way to the offices of a certain shipping company whose advertisements for steerage passages abroad had set his mind aglow. Joining the queue outside, his heart beat fast. Standing as he was between two tall gentlemen, he knew that his pathetic fifteen years, his small figure and painful inexperience of the world, must be very apparent, but he avoided their stares and preserved a tense silence.

Reaching the ticket office window he thrust his money through, blew himself up like a bull frog, and in a voice of thunder said: 'I want a ticket to America.' [1]

Telling the story Harris added the usual embellishments. According to him the gentlemen behind him took a step back at the sound of the great voice coming from the small frame and said: 'Bless me—I thought it was a giant talking.'

Whereupon the fifteen-year-old Harris coolly eyed the stranger from head to foot and answered—if the testimony of his fully adult self means anything—'So we're both mistaken. I thought you were a gentleman.'

[1] A. I. Tobin and E. Gertz, *Frank Harris*, p. 37 (Madelaine Mendelsohn, 1931).

CHAPTER THREE

In the wealth of fact and fancy which later confused Harris'
memory of the voyage, it is certain that the romantic beauty of
The Two Roses quickly faded. An elderly and wealthy passenger
talked to the boy at some length during the voyage and offered
to adopt him; a gale one night frightened Harris and convinced
him that the ship must capsize; but Jessie, the daughter of the
Chief Engineer, remained most vividly in his memory because
she represented his first serious attempt at seduction, an
attempt surrounded by every kind of hazard. He described the
two young people, still in their teens, meeting by stealth of
night to make love in one of the ship's boats, and Jessie resisting
his advances with the constantly repeated words, 'Not here—
later—later.' There was something pathetic in the picture of
their two figures dwarfed by the vast Atlantic, clutching each
other in clumsy passion, but the story as Harris told it many
years later, to Hugh Kingsmill, quickly lost any pathos it may
have had. Overwhelming curiosity and exploding passion combined in a boy of fifteen to produce a fairly commonplace
exhibition of lust. Later in life, Harris held that lust was as
much a reality as love, and it was far better to accept it than
to disguise it under other and more acceptable names. Certainly
the voyage across the Atlantic failed to revive any of Harris'
finer feelings, not only because of Jessie. He also came under
the influence of a cynical young man who regarded all women
as legitimate sexual prey to be exploited to the full.

The voyage took twelve days. When the ship at last arrived
there is no record of what he thought as he stood on deck

watching the first haze of New York sharpen into an outline so different from today. There were no skyscrapers, no deeply caverned streets, no berths for ocean liners, no bronze figure emphasizing liberty. New York was still a city dominated by racketeers, political buccaneering and graft, and the immediate past had seen a number of riots. On one occasion partisans of the American actor, Edwin Forrest, had laid seige to the Astor Place Opera House where Macready, the English actor, played, and the governor had been forced to call out the militia; on another occasion two rival police organizations in New York decided that it was time to establish ascendancy over one another and had fought it out with guns until the militia was once more involved. By 1872, the year following Harris' arrival, the *New York Times* was busy exposing the activities of Boss William Tweed whose skill in negotiating corrupt contracts for public building had netted him a sum approaching one hundred million dollars, and Vanderbilt, Gould and Fisk were manipulating a very effective gold rush which carried the price of gold to astronomical heights and threatened to topple the whole economy in confusion. Out West the Comanche and Sioux Indians were still a considerable trouble, fighting with superb horsemanship and the courage of annihilation, the Union Pacific railway forged its way towards completion, cattle had begun to crowd the bison from the central plains, troops tried to keep law and order over vast territories, mills, mines and roaring camps were everywhere and the whole powerful scene beat to the giant cannon-pulse of emerging America.

At the Northern end of this scene, the stocky little English boy walked, one beautiful May morning, through the streets of New York and wondered at the zest and liveliness which made England seem to him a land of tired people. There was a soft bite in the air, a wonderful optimism and an apparent indifference to the complications of a gigantically growing city.

Perhaps because romantic legend required it, Frank Harris always said that he first worked as a shoe-black in New York. Certainly the profession was an obvious one for any very young, very impoverished and adaptable young man with no special training, and it may quite easily have happened; there is far more evidence to support the second phase of his career in America.

He became, in a sense, one of the pioneer builders of Brooklyn Bridge. In other words he was employed as a sand-hog working in the underwater muck of the East River which was to take the foundations of the Bridge. Every morning at nine o'clock precisely, he entered the airlock compartment of a huge iron caisson and the taps controlling the compressed air were turned on until the pressure became acute, he covered his ears with his hands, and the process was slowed to accomplish the final stage. There was a method of continuously swallowing the air which helped to slacken pressure on the ear-drums, but very often partial deafness followed compression. Once the pressure in the lock and the caisson was roughly the same, everyone climbed down the long narrow ladder to begin work on the river bed fifty feet under water. [1] Wearing only trousers, the gang of workers shovelled sand from the river into tubs which carried it to the surface. The caisson was artificially lit and a ghoulish glare of green from protected lamps gave the whole black apparatus the appearance of a particularly nasty hell. The men worked with their feet in ice-cold water which was prevented from filling the compartment by the compressed air. They worked for fifteen-minute stretches and then rested while the air grew fouler, the sweat poured down and the close quarters of one man to another encouraged quarrels. Two hours was the maximum of any one shift, and by then men were troubled by headaches, buzzing ears and a curious dragging of the limbs as though leaden-weighted. De-compression involved far worse horrors. Wet with sweat the sand-hogs climbed back into the airlock, the panel was shut and the cocks opened. The hissing jets poured in air which seemed, to the overheated men, ice-cold. They went blue, felt sick and unsteady on their feet, and reached the outer air weak and exhausted. Any attempt to hasten the process could lead to appalling results in which a man fell semi-conscious to the floor, blood seeping from ears and nose, his limbs writhing in agony and sometimes remaining twisted for life.

With the morning shift over and the lunch interval finished,

[1] Frank Harris, *The Bomb*, p. 33 (John Long, 1908).

23

the thought of penetrating the black slime again in the afternoon was sometimes more than men could bear, and time and
again the gang went down one man short. Harris was paid five
dollars a day. It was princely. It meant that he could live for
ten days on one day's pay, but he hated the work, loathed, with
growing passion, the iron monster which engulfed and spewed
out mud, sand and human beings indiscriminately. An unending
vista of shoes to clean had been bad enough, he later said;
however, judging people by their shoes as he cleaned them had
passed the time reasonably, in fresh air and sunshine; but here,
in the black waters, under the earth, with men who black-
guarded all day long and drank to dull their pain . . . this was
horrible. He, Frank Harris, was made for different things. On
the other hand if he endured the ordeal for only two months
he knew he would have enough money to support himself for
a year. A whole, free year to make his choice, to pick his way
as he pleased: that was what he dreamt of. In the event, after
three weeks, he gave up the job of sand-hog and went back to
shoe-shining.

And then one day, cleaning the expensive shoes of a Mr.
Kendrick, Harris absent-mindedly quoted something from a
classical author, and Kendrick, struck by the words, took a
deeper interest in the thin, rather ragged young man who
shone his shoes with near ferocity. Before he walked away, he
had offered Harris the job of night clerk in a Chicago hotel
which he owned. That, at least, is Harris' story. Certainly the
brawling city of New York did not yield the prizes which Harris
had decided were his by right, and even the glittering pay of
the sand-hog had not compensated for the horrors of the river
bed. Just as certainly, some days after meeting Mr. Kendrick,
he left New York one night and made the long journey to
Chicago, to Mr. Kendrick's hotel.

*   *   *   *   *

When Frank Harris, aged seventeen, first stepped down from
the old horse buggy he had hired to take him from the station,
the Chicago he saw around him had every characteristic of a
raw, explosive city, trying to reconcile the more civilized life
of the East with the primitive West. It was eight o'clock of a

24

winter evening, rain had reduced the outlying streets to mud, a giant wind was blowing, horse-cars swayed alongside concrete side-walks, and a thousand gas lamps hissed and spluttered. Already there were fine hotels, offices and banks, new avenues and houses, but every contrast appeared in a metropolis which seemed to expand overnight. There were cowboys in from the West, occasional mounted troopers, saloon bars choked with all kinds of people and soberly dressed citizens driving past in fine carriages in the centre of the city.

The Fremont House Hotel was not then a very significant part of the bursting life of Chicago, but for Frank Harris it became the center of a new career. From eight at night until six o'clock in the morning, he sat at a small reception desk behind a hissing gas burner dealing with every kind of late-comer, as night clerk. There were stretches in the middle of the night when a hush descended on the whole building and alone, beside his gas-lamp Harris read, steadily becoming more aware of the fascination of literature; but the work was hard and sometimes exhausting.

He threw tremendous energy into it. He bowed people in, he rang for porters and bellboys, he poured out information, he began to take an interest in the hotel accounts, he met and charmed difficult customers from the West, and presently Mr. Kendrick heard someone say: 'That's a smart night clerk you have—quick as a knife—yes sir!'

By now, every nerve in Harris was ready to seize upon the first big opportunity. When it occurred his reactions revealed the struggle between the two developing sides of his nature. Luck had not so far shown any disposition to favor Harris. The triple disadvantage of an authoritarian father, difficult family and bullying school had reinforced the effects of his ugliness to prematurely toughen and harden him. In the early years, the developing process did not quite overwhelm the other side of his nature. There was a struggle, if not very prolonged, between the Jekyll and Hyde in his character. Thus when he discovered that the book-keeper of the Fremont Hotel had taken to drink in an effort to forget the ordeal of his unhappy marriage, Harris did not disclose the fact to the proprietor. He kept it dark for some time and it must have been a considerable effort because the removal of the book-keeper might have opened the way to swift promotion. True, the book-keeper later had to confess; true, by that time, Harris had learnt to manage the books and was able to take over the work in a glow of disinterested glory; but the first protective gesture was undoubtedly made. Unfortunately the 'Hyde' always in such close attendance on his somewhat flagging 'Jekyll', quickly thrust forward again. When Payne, the steward of the hotel, in turn revealed to him that he 'received a commission from the butcher who supplied the hotel with meat' [1], Harris at once disclosed the fact to the hotel manager. The cold-blooded 'Hyde' who had learnt that everything was designed to embitter his life, suddenly and deliberately disavowed the 'Jekyll'. Within a few weeks Payne, exposed by Harris, was sacked, and Harris stepped into his shoes.

As the struggle between different elements of his character intensified it was interesting to reflect that another two inches in height, a less austere father and happier school, might have corrected the balance and rendered the remainder of this steadily more extraordinary story, quite different. It is commonly supposed, in modern thinking, that nurture and nature are indivisible, one continuously reacting upon the other from birth to produce the adult individual; but the caprice of inheritance not merely played pranks with Frank Harris' whole appearance; environment, too, made havoc of his attempts to cope with life. In the early and very influential years he was doubly unlucky.

He remained nearly twelve months at the Fremont Hotel, becoming a familiar figure to many customers, he learnt many sides of the hotel business, he pleased Mr. Kendrick 'mightily' and steadily saved money; but the limitations of hotel life were too cramping for him, and it could not last. One day three cattlemen came into the Fremont Hotel and proceeded to drink far into the night, telling one story after another. Harris listened enthralled. Presently he joined in the talk. The three men, Dell, Ford and Reece, told him how cattle bought in Texas for two dollars, could be driven over the trail for hundreds of miles and sold in Chicago for twenty dollars. These men

[1] Hugh Kingsmill, *Frank Harris*, p. 25 (Jonathan Cape, 1932).

represented to Harris that tough ideal which had become, in his mind, invulnerable to the shocks and troubles still threatening his not yet secure self. He had saved 1800 dollars with scrupulous care, each dollar representing another step towards the total independence which he so much desired to possess; he had come to hate the stale servility of hotel life almost as much as boot blacking, and he had learnt something of horses and horsemanship.

Before the men left, he decided to throw in his lot with them. It was a dramatic move—the townsman risking the rough life of the open plains—but Harris smelled many of the things he coveted in the stories which they had recounted so vividly.

*　　*　　*　　*　　*

In the year when he left Chicago and plunged hundreds of miles into the 'Wild West', it was still a land of pioneers, adventurers, and desperadoes, a rough place where justice sometimes went with a shot in the dark. Indians scoured the countryside in marauding bands and the handful of troopers stationed at key points throughout vast territories were inadequate to preserve law and order. Every kind of activity went forward by day and night, carrying a tide of flotsam across the countryside; reservation boundaries were continually broken and Indians, who went stoically to their death in bloody battles, were still capable of outwitting the white man. Harris always remembered and thrilled to the story of General Custer and his men who were mown down, one by one, until Custer himself, shot through the temple, collapsed in the confusion.

Out into this Wild West, Harris rode one day, the clerk-book-keeper-steward transformed into a cowboy. It was a burning hot day with the dust blowing through the outlying streets of Kansas. Feeling very odd in chaps, high-heeled boots and a flannel shirt, he set out into a series of adventures which cannot escape the most sceptical examination. The torture which overtook him in the saddle before he learnt to 'fry' his hips in salt water and whisky every night was commonplace to every cowboy. So was the episode of buying the first horse he ever owned—Moll—and discovering her powers. Later came the 'cowboy circus' when he tried to ride an innocent-looking broncho, and in the best Western tradition, discovered that she could perform maneuvers unknown to nature while the onlookers spat, and grunted with expressionless faces: 'Quiet to ride ain't she?' The first sight of Reece's ranch, too, had nothing remarkable about it. Reece's ranch—like so many others—was a one-storey frame building set high off the ground on stilts with cattle, fowls and dogs roosting under-neath when the prairie wind did not make that impossible. There followed a number of brawls and encounters with hostile strangers inevitable in that part of the country, but Harris claimed in a book, the origin of which I shall presently examine, that bigger things happened to him; much bigger things.

He spent the winter months on Reece's ranch. There he met the legendary Bill Hickok, learnt to break in horses, en-countered Indians, branded cattle, saw saloon fights and according to his own account, shot up a number of Mexicans. He also became familiar with the yellow-eyed beauties who smelt at a distance of some yards and were liable to leave more than memories of passion among their customers. A whole medley of strong smells which went with the West—horses, cattle, women, leather, wood-smoke, raw beef, and sometimes blood—remained powerfully in his memory. But it was Bob, a five feet nothing, dried up nut of a man who first introduced Harris to the big set piece of his cowboy career—cattle rustling. What would he give, Bob said to Harris one night, for two thousand head of cattle of his own? [1] Harris was more amused than interested, but presently it became clear that Bob had devised an ingenious brand of rustling which made the question very real. Whatever remnants of European culture rose to resist this plan, the smell of big and easy money, the thrill of driving by night a herd of stolen cattle, became quite heady. In the purely physical life of the prairie he had tried to keep alive other sensibilities. He carried Mill's *Political Economy* and Carlyle's *Heroes and Hero Worship* in his saddle-bag; he returned, sometimes, with a wild flower in his hand anxious to determine its name; and he tried to preserve other depths of awareness in a world where drink, women and hard riding

[1] Frank Harris, *On the Trail*, p. 129 (John Lane, 1930).

28

made up the greater part of life. But freedom and power; freedom to do what the moment dictated and power over his own future; these were the goals he desperately needed to reach. In cattle rustling, he suddenly saw them coming within his grasp. So it came about that a handful of men deployed across a river one moonless night, entered Mexico and succeeded in heading off a number of cattle from a wealthy hacienda.[1] It was understood that they should press slowly and silently back towards the ford which crossed the river boundary, providing no emergency occurred. According to Harris: 'for the first half-hour, all went according to program. Charlie and I moved the cattle together and drove them over the waves of prairie towards the river; it all seemed as easy as eating and we had begun to push the cattle into a fast walk when suddenly there was a shot in front and a sort of stampede.'[2]

Immediately Harris rode out to one flank of the herd, and Charlie to another, their long whips driving the cattle into a canter. The murmur of hooves became a thunder, and then they were pouring over the prairie with every kind of animal noise loose on the air. Bullets hissed over Harris' head, and suddenly he turned and there was a man riding at breakneck speed down towards him. He swung his revolver up, took whatever aim he could, and pulled the trigger. The man slumped forward in his saddle and that was the last Harris saw of him.

Whether he had killed or wounded the man did not greatly interest him. The excitement, the tension and the struggling black mass of animals needed all his attention, and again and again he brought the whip down, dashing around the stragglers with near professional skill. Slowly they drew away. But late that afternoon twenty Mexicans overtook them, and at last, they were forced to turn and fight it out. It was, according to Harris, a short sharp battle with several Mexicans killed and the rest retiring in confusion.

In the end they drove the cattle safely to Reece's ranch. There they rested a week, branded the cattle and began the

[1] Frank Harris, *On the Trail*, p. 132 (John Lane, 1930).
[2] Ibid.

long, hazardous trek north towards whichever market town offered the biggest price and the most anonymous sale. Several days hard driving brought them to an oak forest, and there came news that a number of Indians were in the neighborhood. They decided to lay up in a bay created by the forest. What followed was described in detail in Harris' book . . . . The Indians circling the camp, thinning out and making a classic assault upon the eight men who first lay firing with deadly accuracy, and then came to their feet firing from the shoulder. With a remarkable access of modesty, Harris claimed no part in the actual shooting which at last threw the Indians into confusion and forced them to retreat. The firing followed mercilessly, mowing down every Indian straggler. But this was not the end.

The battle went on for days. Again and again the Indians attacked at night, cutting out a few hundred head of cattle, and sometimes horses, until the men were awake at all hours. The Indians grew in number as news of the great prize spread, and it became clear that the cattle rustlers would never reach the north without help. Two men must try to break through the growing bands of Indians and reach Fort Dodge. Which two should it be? Inevitably the choice fell on the worst shots, Harris, and 'Peggy' the cook, but everyone agreed that the cook could not be spared, and in the end Reece himself set out with Harris.

Half-an-hour after sundown they filed silently away, 'taking advantage of' every 'dip in the ground.' [1] It was a beautiful night, the stars shining, the air crisp and clear, but if it was not a night for violence, almost at once, somewhere to the left, something stirred and cracked in the darkness. Reece sheered sharply to the north and a moment later another shadow flitted across his path and was gone. Reece whispered at Harris— 'They've picketed every inch . . . .' [2]

Five seconds later they spurred into an open gallop, ignored all precautions and were dashing away, Harris dragging out his revolver, and desperately trying to penetrate the darkness, his heart racing more with excitement than fear. A shot came,

[1] Frank Harris, *On the Trail*, p. 172 (John Lane, 1930).

[2] Ibid., p. 173.

something seared the darkness and they were tearing on. Then the quick patter of hooves, many hooves, broke the silence and they knew that the Indians were already mounted and in pursuit. Neither spoke for over an hour. By then, both horses had begun to show serious signs of strain, but there was that in the movement of his new horse Blue Dick, which told Harris that something more than exhaustion troubled her. She did not pull as he knew she could pull. And then a very nasty thought suddenly gripped him and his mouth went dry. Had that first single shot hit her? An extraordinary streak in Harris' nature became apparent. He loved animals. The hard-bitten cowboy, already deeply indoctrinated against pity and convinced that feeling was a sentimental indulgence, could not bear to see an animal suffer. Presently, as Blue Dick's pace slowed, he was anxious to throw himself off to relieve what had clearly become her agony. Reece would not hear of it. He must ride her to death. Then Reece would 'take him up behind'. But, Harris wrote, with that streak of sentimentalism which marked all his writing about animals: 'I could not bear to press her . . . who galloped on, in spite of everything, in spite of the pain. . . .'[1] Presently she was down to a canter. At last, very swiftly, Harris dismounted and slipped his hand under her barrel. It was wet with blood. He stood there for a moment hesitating and uncertain. Then he kissed Blue Dick's head as it drooped and the blood dripped away. Harris was considerably moved. He knew the horse was finished.

In the confusion of truth and lies surrounding this episode, the worst doubts might have dissolved if Harris had not insisted on pouring into it sufficient highlights to enrich Metro Goldwyn Mayer's shooting schedule for years to come. For now, instead of taking his place behind Reece on his horse, Shiloh, Harris insisted that he should hold Reece's stirrup leather and urged Reece to put Shiloh at full gallop. He then proceeded to run on flying feet, for one whole hour, without visibly tiring. No more fleet-winged mercury ever soared across rough country with such indelible purpose, his courage seriously challenging the best examples of film heroism.

But something of the story remained true. Something of the

[1] Frank Harris, *On the Trail*, p. 178 (John Lane, 1930).

great ride across the prairie to bring help to the beleaguered cattle thieves remained, in the book at least, real. Supremely unaware of the irony of U.S. troopers coming to the rescue of cattle thieves, Harris did catch on every other page the tension, the atmosphere, and a sense of elemental forces contending with one another. There were the nights of hunger and thirst, of Harris' feet torn and swollen, of Shiloh's joints gradually filling, and Reece beginning to look haggard and ghost-like. There was the first desperate sight of the fort splendid in the grey before the dawn. Inevitably the American soldiers gave them a great welcome, news was rapidly exchanged and almost at once the break-neck ride back to the beleaguered men began. Sixty troopers of the U.S. 3rd Cavalry set out with Harris and Reece but they seemed to take far longer to cover ground which Harris and Reece had covered in five nights. Inevitably the sight of the scarlet uniforms and the cavalcade of galloping men sent the Indians scuttling away. There was much embracing and congratulation when they reached the rustler's encampment. A young cow was killed, a feast ran far into the night and the last cask of whisky was drunk in the next few hours. Then began the arduous business of bringing the cattle safely into the nearest town.

Many details of the story as Harris unfolded it were totally unconvincing, but the raw life, the danger and the Indians, were all, in reality, there, and Harris had known at first hand an experience similar to this one. In his book he was driven to romanticize. Driven by what? Continuously, in the last quarter of his life, when he was said to have written *On the Trail*, sheer poverty drove him to write and sponsor exaggerated books some of which he later regretted.

Yet something came out of the western prairies which he never forgot. There were times, he confessed to Bernard Shaw, when his still youthful mind was moved by the vast poetry of the open prairie and he rode his horse, singing Shakespeare at the top of his great voice, aware of a wild grandeur in his veins as if the spirit of that gigantic landscape had entered into and possessed him.

It remained unfortunate that when the American critic Dobie came to compile his *Guide to Life and Literature of the South-West*, he referred to Frank Harris' *My Reminiscences as a Cowboy* as 'a blatant farrago of lies'. Nor did the story stop there. The American journalist, Frank Scully, has since revealed that he became the official ghost-writer for Harris towards the end of his life. He claimed that it was he who took a fragment written by Harris called, *On the Trail* and transformed it into the book *My Reminiscences as a Cowboy* which sold 30,000 copies.[1] [2] But that was not yet.

[1] Frank Scully, *Rogue's Gallery*, p. 212 (Murray and Gee, Inc., 1943).
[2] Tobin and Gertz state that the success of *My Reminiscences as a Cowboy* was due to the efficiency and generosity of Arthur Leonard Ross, Harris' friend and legal advisor.

CHAPTER FOUR

Harris rapidly tired of the range and the roaring camp life. No one with his brain could tolerate for long the intellectual limitations of Reece and Charlie, even if Dell and Bob had revealed a surprising knowledge of literature and economics. Once Harris tried his hand at writing to relieve the tedium and the results were very successful. He wrote a series of sketches of saloon keepers, range-riders and travelling salesmen which the editor of an obscure but enterprising local paper, the *Groveville Herald*, published. The break in the monotony was brief. City life, with its richer culture, exercised a steadily more powerful attraction until the rancher's life bored him unutterably. And then one hot afternoon he rode into Kansas City, doffed the chaps, the check shirt and the high-heeled boots, and set out by train for the small city of Lawrence in the state of Kansas. This was to become the scene of the second great watershed in his early life.

Lawrence stood astride the Kansas river, a broiling new city thrusting out in all directions with splendid banks, offices and railway lines, but its people were very aware that not more than ten years before Harris arrived, a band of Missouri bushrangers had ridden in at dawn one morning and murdered 150 sleeping citizens. The air was still thunderous with pro and anti-slavery campaigns. People could not remember the immediate past without brutality and bloodshed. A pattern which repeated itself more violently in a dozen emerging cities of the South, drove the people of Lawrence to defend what they regarded as the dwindling rights of the whites, ferociously.

Harris was not concerned with minority rights. He came tough, bronzed, full of physical confidence into a city where horse-buses plied, women wore skirts reaching to the ground, and the scene was still alive with the spirit of bush-ranging pioneers, but he was quite oblivious to social injustice which did not touch him personally. He went straight to the most famous hotel in Lawrence, the Eldridge House Hotel, a 'magnificent building' with its four brick storeys reaching high into the sky and a service which included running cold water in all rooms. One reason why he had chosen Lawrence was the totally unexpected appearance of his brother in that city. Tired of England and what he described as its crippling limitations, William had set out for America, dimly aware that Frank had broken into the vagabond life of the American plains and made some undefined fortune involved with cattle. Now a handsome, dark-haired man of 23, William was suddenly confronted with an apparition which bore no resemblance to the fat, well-dressed rancher he had expected to meet and he could not conceal his surprise when first he set eyes on Frank. He hardly recognized in the wiry, alert person with the almost yellow face, the young brother he had known what seemed all those years ago. They talked; they compared news; they drifted away into that hesitation which marks conversation between two alien temperaments. William had already started, with some success, a real estate agency in Lawrence, but it was not William or his agency which gripped and held Frank's attention in the growing city.

Over the next few months he saw less and less of his brother. They did not get on well together. Meanwhile Harris moved from job to job. An interval when he ran a butcher's shop saw him hacking up bloody carcasses and selling joints of meat; he also became, for a time, a bouncer in a gambling den, but no details of his performance as a chucker-out are available. Selling space for an advertising agency kept him alive for another few months, but none of it—not even William who faded away as rapidly as he had come—mattered very much beside Professor Byron Smith. If something beyond all normal scepticism must be brought to bear on the first volume of Harris' Autobiography, there remains, in the chapter describing his first meeting with Professor Byron Smith, that glow, almost exaltation, which sometimes overtakes one human being when moved by the discovery of nobility in another.

It happened, Harris said, one evening when Senator Ingalls addressed a political meeting at Liberty Hall, on the growing restlessness between Wall Street, the western farmers and the northern industrialists. Full of sentimental appeals to free, white and democratic Americans, Ingalls claimed in his speech that they could not deny the right of farmers to organize against Wall Street. Cries then arose for Professor Byron Smith to speak, and a man who had already attracted Harris' attention rose, walked to the platform, and delivered himself of the most revolutionary doctrine. The 'Federal Government,' he said, 'should take over the railways', run them on behalf of the farmers and wait until competition among the manufacturers of the north began to reduce prices.[1] According to Harris, he himself now rose, deliberately dressed in his old cowboy clothes and was greeted by bursts of laughter. He demanded a hearing which was at once given him. Of course he made a tremendous speech, adorned with quotations from John Stuart Mill, full of economic wisdom, and the audience rose to him. 'Senator Ingalls came over and shook my hand saying he hoped to know me better, and the cheering went on until I had gotten back to my place.'[2] Later, Harris said that Professor Byron Smith, struck by his speech, invited him to his rooms.

Unfortunately, Kate Stephens—Byron Smith's fiancée—was driven, for reasons which will presently appear, to produce a chain of the most damning evidence to show that Harris' power of invention had excelled itself in this account. 'There never was such a meeting,' she wrote. 'There was a Liberty Hall in Lawrence. In this Hall political meetings sometimes convened. Frank may have been at such meetings. But he sets down the time, September 1872. He says Senator Ingalls was going to speak—did speak. An impossibility. John James Ingalls was not chosen United States Senator until 1873. . . .

'In staging his story Frank tells—cries arose from all parts of the hall for Professor Smith. Impossible—Nobody knew him

[1] Frank Harris, *My Life and Loves*, Vol. 1, p. 196.
[2] Ibid, p. 198.

in September 1872. He was an utter stranger. He was not at the Hall. He never talked at a political meeting in Lawrence. Frank adds that he had a thin tenor voice. His voice was low and mellow. . . .

'Swinging along in his narrative Frank says that Professor Smith invited him to his rooms and 'day dawned before we had done talking.' From the time he went to Lawrence in 1872, until the next spring, Professor Smith lived in a cottage with his invalid mother. He never invited Frank to his rooms after any meeting. . . .'(1)

Set large in the center of this argument, everything turns upon the date, and if Harris had mistakenly written 1872 instead of 1873 many of Miss Stephens' objections might have collapsed. Indeed, there is some evidence to show, in the sequence of events, that his meeting with Byron Smith could have taken place in 1874.

Whatever invention went into Harris' account, there is no doubt that he did in fact meet Byron Smith and there is no questioning the effect upon him of this brilliant young Professor. Dr. Kellog described Byron Smith in *A Young Scholar's Letters* —'Tall and slender of figure, he moved with the grace and elasticity of an athlete. His dark and lustrous eyes told of the man's enthusiasm and quick perceptions . . . Dark brown hair, tinged with auburn, clustered in ringlets about his head and the fair skin and mantling blood of his face. People turned to observe him twice, for the beauty of youth and intelligence were upon him. His voice was low and mellow . . . his bearing so modest that he seldom opened conversation and seemed to be led rather than to lead. . . . Of ambition he displayed nothing. The pre-eminence that came to him seemed unsought.'

In their excellent study of Frank Harris, A. I. Tobin and E. Gertz claimed that it was at the Free Congregational Church in 1874 that Professor Smith delivered the lecture—on culture as a creed—which left such an indelible impression on Frank Harris. Later in life, Harris spoke of few people without contempt or indifference, but until the end a certain reverence always informed his words whenever Smith's name occurred,

(1) Gerrit and Mary Caldwell Smith (Editors), *Lies and Libels of Frank Harris*, with Arguments by Kate Stephens, pp. 105-6 (Antique Press, 1929).

and he could write movingly of the man who hallowed for him those difficult days in the city of Lawrence. It was Professor Smith who encouraged him to enrol as 'a special student in a select preparatory group under the name of James F. Harris of Tenby, Wales. . . .'[1] F. took the place of the legitimate J. for the first time, the Christian name Frank coming into use. It was Professor Smith who talked philosophy to him, who analyzed literature with him, introduced him to the visual arts, and responding to the leap of his mind, encouraged him to discover its full powers.

Hannah Oliver has left this picture of Harris as a student: 'James Harris was a brilliant youth with a remarkable power of absorbing knowledge. He was a great reader and an eloquent, fascinating talker. He was self-confident and sometimes showed an extraordinary youth's lack of respect for the opinions of others and this I think won him . . . dislike.'[2]

Now boisterous, now arrogant, now deeply aware of his academic inferiority, Frank Harris summoned all his growing brassiness, his big voice and personality, to assert himself against more fortunate fellows in the University. He was not a student in the ordinary sense. He loafed and read, speculated and philosophized and whenever confronted by someone better equipped with facts that he was, fell back on his Irish eloquence and sheer force of personality.

Kate Stephens remembered the day she was examining some chemical specimens in the laboratory at Fraser Hall, and heard voices growing louder as they approached until no one could escape them. An elderly voice broke in asking for directions. 'Three doors down on your right, Judge,' came the answer from Harris with ironic emphasis on the invented title. Another question from the elderly voice and this time Harris completed his reply with 'Colonel'. It underlined age, disrespect and student arrogance in a way which discomfited both Kate Stephens and the subject of his remarks.[3]

Harris exhausted, in his own distinctive way, the pranks of the young student finding his feet in University life, but the

[1] A. I. Tobin and E. Gertz, *Frank Harris*, p. 55 (Madelaine Mendelsohn, 1931).
[2] Ibid., p. 56.
[3] Ibid.

38

College magazine still carries a reference to him which reveals him in a revolutionary light. He had delivered a carefully prepared oration in the school chapel, and the magazine commented: 'According to Mr. Harris, this extortion, the not giving of just and due equivalent for what one obtains, is taught in every school, legalized by long custom, justified by special statute and is the self-same fraud for which a thief is hunted from society and deprived of his natural liberty. Mr. Harris as an advocate of Communism, looks forward to the time when all men shall have one creed, self-control, and one God, a perfect and symmetrical development of the whole man.'

Communism . . . self-control . . . one God. . . . The egomaniac atheist may have sprung, by some law of opposites, from these roots, but this remarkable passion for Communism, long before it became poison to the United States, need not be dwelt upon. It never really conditioned his outlook or behavior. If he anticipated Shaw's socialism and sometimes spoke like a Fabian tract, Marx was not then translated into English and it seems likely that his Marxism was acquired once more from Professor Byron Smith, himself very deeply left of center. Whether Harris' convictions were genuine at the time, or were simply used as a banner to draw attention to himself, does not gravely matter. Nor shall I comment here upon the consistency with which a man said to be utterly selfish concentrated so much attention on big social issues; the extraordinary relationship with Byron Smith is of far more importance for the moment.

Young, brilliant, and frustrated by very bad health, there is, in every photograph of Byron Smith, that nobility of which Harris spoke. Appointed professor at a very early age simply because he 'seemed to know everything', he brought Plato and Socrates to life for Harris, illumined the classical poets in quite a new way and gave him glimpses of a philosophy which crystallized for Harris the life he would so much like to lead if only it could be led in luxury. It was a philosophy aware that the pain, confusion and injustice everywhere evident in society might be remedied if men would abandon self-interest, break away from certain traditions and take their destiny into their own hands. It was a way of life, Byron Smith said, where the sordid scramble for profit, position and power would be superseded by beauty, security and undreamt of satisfactions beyond the common range. This way of life was so nearly within our grasp it needed no more than a million men of good will to give the dream substance. . . . Harris floated for days on words like these, delivered in Byron Smith's low voice which never asserted itself but compelled attention.

It was not only Harris who found himself magnetically drawn to Byron Smith. A relationship of considerable intensity had developed between Kate Stephens and Byron Smith before Harris appeared upon the scene. It was a relationship more beautiful because of its fragility, more vivid because continually threatened with extinction. Even when Miss Stephens, desperately anxious to cherish Smith's frail person, wanted to marry him, he gently refused her, afraid that he might become a burden to her. Every advice was sought, every cure for his complicated illness tried, but slowly the beautiful young man grew paler and thinner until presently it seemed that only a spiritual glow kept him alive.

One day he left for new treatment in Philadelphia and Harris wrote to him saying how empty Lawrence seemed without him. He had come to the conclusion, Harris added, that he must leave America and return to Europe to develop his studies, but he needed Smith's reassurance that he had the capacity to do something striking before he wasted further years on scholarship. Smith gave him this reassurance in a reply which Harris promptly talked about, exaggerating the intimacy of their relationship, until rumors came to Kate Stephens' ears. She thereupon wrote to Byron Smith, and he replied:

'I must offer what reason I can for my writing the letter to Harris. You saw it of course and will therefore be able to judge the value of my plea.

'You know I have no confidence in or respect for the moral character of the man and could not therefore dream of making him a confidential friend. He had however been so persistently kind to me, and seemed to build so much upon my good opinion, and besides wrote me so ardent and eloquent a letter, that I could not find it in my heart to answer in terms not somewhat touched with warmth. But I was careful to express only that enthusiasm for humanity which is natural with me and goes out to everyone who appeals to it—without meaning to establish relations of personal confidence. Doubtless he understood me in a personal sense. I wished also to benefit him by pointing out that the only foundation of friendship which I recognize is that of personal honor and devotion to great and worthy aims. I overdid the matter and felt that I had before your letter brought it home to me with so much force. . . .'

Later in life Kate Stephens had good reason to be angry with Harris not merely because of this episode. 'With an ease more facile than usual,' she later wrote, 'he refers in the Autobiography to associations he pretends he had with me and with relatives of mine. He knew nothing of me except by means of the floating gossip of a small town. I rarely saw him. . . . His overweening assertions are too ludicrous to contradict. . . .'[1]

By now, the sensualist in Harris was not only released in full flood, but given every encouragement which a highly purposeful imagination could devise. He referred to himself as 'a rattlesnake striking at everything that moves, even the blades of grass'.[2] The merest sight of an attractive young woman was enough to bring about a complete transformation of his person—parching his mouth, setting his pulses pounding, fixing his eyes in passion. He was 19 and his hot blood would brook no check.

In a torrent of sensuality which sometimes plunged into animal indulgence, sometimes paused breathless before the beauty of a lovely body, the driving purpose to display his powers as a lover makes it difficult to disentangle truth from lie in his record of what took place. Harris surrounded every detail with crude excitations, but underneath the narrative the same old impulses were at work. The short, rather ugly young man had to exaggerate his capacities, to strike at every woman within reach, to prove that he was better than the six-foot well-to-do young gentlemen, with their polished manners, who lorded it among the university students. And the names of the women said to have succumbed to him—Kate, Lorna, Rose,

---

[1] Gerrit and Mary Caldwell Smith (Editors), *Lies and Libels of Frank Harris*, with Arguments by Kate Stephens, pp. 105–6 (Antique Press, 1929.)

[2] Hugh Kingsmill, *Frank Harris*, p. 32 (Jonathan Cape, 1932).

Lily—multiplied. Some surrendered quickly, some positively enjoyed the blunt methods he employed to rouse 'the animal dormant in women', and some resisted. At least one among these myriad early conquests remained warm in his memory for years to come. A cloud surrounds Sophy in the first volume of the Autobiography. Every step in the narrative can be seen as a concession to the romantic picture of a husky voiced child whose responses were as uninhibited as the mulatto blood in her veins made natural. Sophy had a slight, girlish figure, a golden brown skin, lustrous eyes and a natural grace. Her first meeting with Harris set his senses aflame. There followed— according to Harris—his noble restraint when he turned away from her with mixed motives, only to have Sophy arrive, immodestly, at his room one night, with the words 'I'se tired of waiting.' She didn't like colored men, she said, and white men despised her but Harris . . . well . . . she loved him. Thereupon she buried her face in his shoulder and a tumult of passion broke loose. As the picture emerges from Harris' pages she presently made good her statement that she could 'love better than any white trash', erotic inspiration leading her into highly sophisticated acts which could hardly have been learnt by a child still in her teens. Harris was ravished out of his senses. Temporarily he abandoned his other loves. Within the whirl of fact and lie which characterized the first volume of the Autobiography, there remained a feeling for Sophy's beauty which removed this affair, at least, from the completely animal.

*   *   *   *   *

Harris did not remain long at Lawrence University. Enrolling in 1874 he had left again by 1875. In that time, he not merely read deeply in English literature and the Greek classics; he mastered the rudiments of law and was able to talk glibly about legal procedures. So it came about that immediately he left university he applied for one job after another in lawyers' offices, and each time he bluffed his way to within striking distance of some very interesting work. It was, in 1875, according to his account, that a Mr. George Barker of the legal firm of Summerfield and Barker died from hiccoughs and Harris received an invitation to take his place. Mr. Barker did not, in fact, die until 1912, thirty-seven years later, his death was not caused by hiccoughs, and he was never a member of the firm of Summerfield and Barker. Extending the simple fact that a lawyer named Barker represented him in two small lawsuits, Harris quickly transformed himself into the brilliant law student irresistible to a company needing a new partner. Extraordinarily, it remained true that Harris was admitted to the bar of Lawrence on June 22nd, 1875, although there is no evidence to show that his qualifications to practice were any more impressive than those of an inspired amateur.

Certainly his legal 'work' did not provide enough fees to carry out a plan which was now becoming more and more persistent in his mind. Leaving the University had not freed him from the influence of Byron Smith. It was almost as if he knew that without this guiding star the evil in his own nature might overwhelm and suffocate so much that was still struggling towards quite different ends. Every remnant of warmth and feeling of which he still remained capable, went into the description he later gave of the man he now desired to follow to Philadephia, where he was still undergoing treatment. Byron Smith seemed to Harris 'the most wonderful creature in this strange, sunlit world. I used to hang entranced on his eloquent lips. I never found a fault in him of character or of sympathy . . . . He was the dearest, sweetest, noblest spirit of a man I have ever met in this earthly pilgrimage.'[1] [2] Despite the flamboyance, Harris, for once, really meant what he was saying.

He broke away, at last, from the city of Lawrence and the law, and left for Columbia, Ohio. There an old American acquaintance, Ned Bancroft, offered to help him on his way. Bancroft provided Harris with a railway pass and he travelled on to Philadelphia to meet once more the man still haunting his imagination.

What precisely took place between Harris and Smith when they met again, no one knows, but Harris' lofty preoccupations with the beauty of Byron Smith's personality, quickly drifted down to far more practical matters. He was determined now to

[1] A. I. Tobin and E. Gertz, *Frank Harris*, p. 50 (Madelaine Mendelsohn, 1931).
[2] Frank Harris, *My Life and Loves*, Vol. 1, p. 317.

CHAPTER FIVE

ONE day in the spring of 1876 a young man of 20, totally different from the boy of 15 who had run away from Ruabon Grammar School, approached England in a ship which still labored to complete the voyage in twelve days. With a facility characteristic of his more venomous moods, the land which had once held such golden promise for him—America—had become a black pit of materialism where only the Philistine flourished. Harris did not go straight to England to see the family he had neglected for seven years. Sporadic correspondence between them had, on his side, quickly collapsed into prolonged silence and he had no great regard for any member of a family which he still remembered for its abuse of crucial childhood years. He went instead to France.

There is some evidence to show that in Paris he attended the lectures of Taine in what was then known as the University of Paris, improved his French and explored the more obvious byways of French literature, but his money quickly ran out, and presently he was driven to risk reunion with a half-forgotten family.

How drab, limited and utterly depressing he found the small-town life of Tenby in Wales, he later explained to Hugh Kingsmill. If Tenby lacked what the Americans referred to as 'drive', the graces of Paris were also painfully absent. According to Tobin and Gertz, Harris' gloom in Tenby was somewhat relieved when he became reconciled with his father, and for the first time appreciated the attempts his father had made to give him a good education. This was followed by a 'year's' [1] teaching as an assistant master at Brighton College, which ended abruptly for reasons never fully explained.

The famous and hotly disputed Carlyle interview followed. Carlyle had now become an important part of Harris' thinking and he read and re-read every word written by him. It was natural, in consequence, that Harris, still in a confused state about his future, should search out when the opportunity occurred, a man whose blending of the rhetorician and prophet he so much admired. He wanted advice very badly, and particularly he wanted it from a famous writer. According to Harris, the opportunity did occur in the most prolonged, revealing and intimate manner. Precisely how he first introduced himself to Carlyle it is difficult to establish, but later he drew a vivid picture of the old man, who was then 83, walking through the rain at Hyde Park Corner accompanied by Harris and pausing suddenly to doff his hat at the spot where Mrs. Carlyle had died. This seemed flamboyant enough, but later in their walk a still more astonishing thing occurred. Carlyle gradually spoke more and more intimately of his wife until suddenly, carried beyond his intent by an upsurge of emotion, he revealed to Harris that he had never consummated his marriage. [2] Describing Carlyle as deeply guilt-ridden by this memory, Harris said he did his best to reassure the famous writer, but Carlyle remained glum and uneasy throughout the rest of their talk. [3] Whether or not Carlyle was impotent, whether he did in fact walk beside Harris in the rain, or make any such astonishing confession, led to a quarrel many years later, when Harris published an elaborate account of the meeting. For the moment it is worth recalling his comment to Hugh Kingsmill. 'They say I never saw Carlyle. The fools don't see that when they call the portrait imaginary, they're praising it. Any damned son of a bitch can put down what he's heard. I'm an artist, not a reporter.' [4]

[1] Some said it was a few months.
[2] In letter to me 3.8.57 Hesketh Pearson said: 'Harris pinched the story of Carlyle's relations with his wife from a publication called *My Relations with Carlyle*, by J. A. Froude, which was published after Froude's death by his executors in 1903.'
[3] *English Review*, February 1911.
[4] Hugh Kingsmill, *Frank Harris*, pp. 50–1 (Jonathan Cape, 1932).

Something far more dramatic now intervened. News of the Russo-Turkish War had just reached England and within a few weeks it so fired Harris' imagination that he determined to rush off there and then half across Europe to the scene of battle. But how? Where would the money come from and what exactly would he do when he got there? Crosland later said of Harris—'he refuses to be poor'—and now, with serious impoverishment threatening him, he splashed down a number of letters to the editors of American newspapers, suggesting that his intimate knowledge of American psychology made him the obvious choice as a war correspondent. Cautiously, two or three replied that they would pay him so many dollars in proportion to what they used of any copy, and one agreed to help him with expenses. Full of excitement he rushed about London making preparations for the vast journey and was suddenly as alive with talk about the splendors of the Russian way of life as he had once been about the American.

Somehow Harris, with very little money and no influence, made his way across Europe to Moscow, and within a week was in the neighborhood of Plevna where fierce fighting had developed. Within two weeks he had met the colorful, chivalrous and now long forgotten figure of General Skobeleff. Tremendous things were to do and Harris tried to catch the chaotic landscape, the smoke, flame and confusion of old-fashioned battle in a number of dispatches written at white heat in great discomfort. By the time the full-scale attack on the Plevna redoubt began, Harris had become a familiar of General Skobeleff, notorious for his liking for war correspondents. Once more, on Harris' testimony, the General was drawn into that kind of sexual indiscretion which Harris infallibly aroused in the memory of men never before known to expose their private lives in public. Skobeleff, he said, confessed that at 14 or 15 he was after every pretty girl and now, at 40, was almost impotent as a result of over-indulgence. 'Good God! What a dreadful fate!' Harris cried and made a private resolution to husband his resources. [1] The description given of the General by *The Times* correspondent did not tally with

[1] Hugh Kingsmill, *Frank Harris*, p. 55 (Jonathan Cape, 1932).

these words—a broad, powerful man with a strong nose, thick beard and vibrant virility.

General Skobeleff's attack on the Plevna redoubt began at four o'clock one afternoon. He 'brought down twenty pieces of artillery to the spur of the ridge overlooking Plevna, and with these opened fire on the position which he had to attack. . . . His force consisted of four regiments of the line and four battalions of sharpshooters. Having formed his attacking column in the little hollow below the redoubt, he caused his artillery to cease firing and ordered the advance. With music playing and banners flying, but without firing a shot, these devoted men moved towards the opposing walls. In a little while they wavered and hung back. Skobeleff, who was close at hand, immediately supported them with a fresh regiment, when the advance was resumed with renewed spirit and force, but only for a little while. The fire from the Turkish redoubt was so terrific that flesh and blood could hardly endure it. Another regiment was sent up to give additional impetus to the assault, and again the line advanced, getting nearer to the fatal position. Every man of Skobeleff's escort was either killed or wounded; but, by some extraordinary fate, the General himself was untouched. Still it was doubtful whether the fort would be taken; for again and again the momentum of the attacking force flagged, or was broken by the deadly fire of the Ottoman soldiery.

'Presently Skobeleff had only two battalions of sharpshooters left, the best of his detachments, and putting himself at the head of these, he dashed forward on horseback and carried them forward with a rush and a cheer. The redoubt was a mass of flame and smoke, from which screams, shouts and cries of agony and defiance arose, with the deep-mouthed bellowing of the cannon, and above all the steady, awful crash of that deadly rifle fire. Skobeleff's sword was cut in two in the middle. Then a moment later, when just on the point of leaping the ditch, horse and man rolled together to the ground; the horse dead or wounded, the rider untouched. Skobeleff sprang to his feet with a shout; then, with a formidable savage yell, the whole mass of men streamed over the ditch, over the scarp and counterscarp, over the parapet, and swept into the redoubt like a hurricane. Their bayonets made short work of the Turks still remaining and a joyous shout told that the redoubt was captured, and that at last one of the defences of Plevna was in the hands of the Russians.'[1]

Such was the opening phase witnessed by Harris. Skobeleff lost two thousand men killed and wounded and it quickly became clear that his victory was fraught with every kind of hazard. Harris, dashing about on horseback, had a wonderful view of traditional battle in all its horror, chivalry and glory, and it is difficult to believe, at a time when war correspondents were sometimes taken for combatants, that he did not continuously face some very dangerous situations.

But Skobeleff's triumph was short lived. In the murky dawn which followed the night, the Turks opened fire from all sides. Harris, once again present at the scene, claims that the attack did not take place until afternoon. Whatever the time, Skobeleff at once demanded reinforcements, confident that he could hold the redoubt, granted more men. The first attack by the Turks he repulsed. A second, third and fourth followed. Dead, dying and wounded were everywhere. Literally hundreds of men were mown down where they stood as the Turkish attacks grew in ferocity, until Skobeleff's companies were dwindling away. Weaving through them with great daring and a complete disregard for the hail of bullets, Skobeleff kept rallying his men. His broken sword waving, his eyes agleam with the excitement of battle, he dashed between the companies urging them to hold on at any cost because reinforcements were coming.

They never came. Skobeleff and his broken remnants were driven back and back until a terrible rage overtook the General. 'He was in a fearful state of excitement . . . His uniform was covered with mud and filth, his sword broken, his cross of St. George twisted round on his shoulder; his face black with powder and smoke; his eyes haggard and bloodshot and his voice quite gone. He spoke in a hoarse whisper. I never before saw such a picture of battle as he presented.'[2] Even for Harris, involved in what must have been a horrifying slaughter, his

[1] Cassell's *History of the Russo-Turkish War*, p. 413.

[2] Mr. MacGahan. *The Times* Correspondent.

modest assertion that, 'Naturally I was at [Skobeleff's] heels,' became a little masterpiece.

When it was all over and the General safely away from the battle, Harris asked him why reinforcements had not arrived and the General answered because 'the Grand Duke hates me'.[1] This did not remotely accord with other accounts.

It needed a remarkable combination of courage, audacity and talent for any young man to make his way to Plevna, face such conditions and plunge into a career for which he had no training, but it all led nowhere. A few dollars trickled in from America and then dried up. Harris never saw any of his work printed. He spent some days after the battle hanging around General Skobeleff and the remnants of his staff, and then tired, disillusioned and horrified by what he had seen, he decided that this was no place or profession for him. He came away from Plevna uncertain and depressed. One day, very soon afterwards, he bade farewell to the defeated Skobeleff and set out, first, for Moscow.

The influence of Byron Smith once more became apparent. Smith had once undertaken a long European pilgrimage which included Moscow, Heidelberg, Göttingen, Berlin, Munich, Vienna and Athens. Harris now followed a similar course. Once again, energy, enterprise, audacity, were of the very essence of the undertaking. Without any serious academic training he entered Heidelberg University in 1878, registered in the Department of Philology and spent approximately a year in a number of ill-defined activities. Within a few months of his enrolment he had annoyed at least two of the professors. First he interrupted and attempted to correct statements which the famous Kuno Fischer made about Shakespeare, and then, hardly recovered from this skirmish, plunged in to enlighten none other than Lotze, the philosopher, about a man Lotze had spent his life studying, Aristotle. Quite unmoved by the hostility he aroused, he continued to give Fischer's lectures the closest attention and presently, Fischer succeeded in firing his imagination about Shakespeare to such a pitch that he stayed up far into the night reading one play after another. For the first time, a quality few noticed in a person overwhelmed by

[1] Frank Harris, *My Life and Loves*, Vol. 1, p. 28.

such startling characteristics—the ability to appreciate and convey greatness in others—became evident in Harris.

His study of Shakespeare was thorough. He re-read passage after passage, analyzing and committing it to memory. Sometimes, walking the streets of Heidelberg with another student he would quote, without pause, for ten minutes in a powerful bass voice which made people stop and stare. A phenomenal memory enabled him to master ten pages at a stretch, and once, when an incredulous student doubted his prowess, he gave a public performance with less than four major mistakes in ten pages. But his interests were much wider. It was not merely analyzing and memorizing the plays which stimulated his imagination: behind the plays, already he was groping for the personality of the poet, an investigation later to be carried into some highly original places. Harris would also have us believe that during his short stay in Heidelberg University he performed the astonishing feat of lecturing to the students on the virtues of chastity, but even if there was a very marked diminution in his own love life at this period, it is difficult to visualize him in the role of moralizer. Tobin and Gertz also state: 'Swallowing his pride, he shaved off his moustache, and entered the gymnasium in which young boys were enrolled, to take the task of really learning Latin and Greek. A little later, however, he was incarcerated in a student prison and expelled from the University as a result of a false assault charge lodged against him after he had felled a German corps-student with a blow of his fist for an insult.' [1]

Leaving Heidelberg somewhat hurriedly, Harris proceeded to Göttingen, and there once more entered the University. This time a self-imposed educational program gave as much attention to Money and Credit, Historical Methods and Laws of Production, as to Literature. He remained at Göttingen for two semesters from October 1878 to August 1879. In that time he developed his command of the German language, but much later in life when his studies were long over, Hugh Kingsmill wrote: 'Except to persons not interested in books, he never gave the impression of a man widely read in German or any other literature. While he assimilated knowledge easily, he lost

[1] A. I. Tobin and E. Gertz, *Frank Harris*, p. 79 (Madelaine Mendelsohn, 1931).

it, as he says himself, with equal speed. Still, some of his reading, in the ten years between his arrival in Lawrence and his first London editorship, stuck. . . .

Some twenty books and authors really shaped his thought in that time. 'The Bible headed the list, followed by Shakespeare, Emerson, Goethe, Balzac, Heine, Dante, Montagne, Cervantes, a volume of English and a volume of French lyrics, Schopenhauer, Charles Reade, Flaubert, Turgenev, Dostoievski, Browning. . . .'[1]

Certainly there was much in Heine's thought which later appeared in Harris' 'philosophy of life'—bitterness, cynicism, sophistication and sensuality—but it was remarkable that Carlyle did not occur in the list. It was to Carlyle that the young Harris, still very unsure of his future, still the victim of half a dozen conflicting impulses, now poured out a long letter.

It was a very odd letter. Part sycophantic, part arrogant, it confessed to bombast in the writer and yet gave an overall impression of modesty. This young man really did want advice about the possibilities of making writing his career. He had already, the letter said, launched into a skeleton novel which he enclosed, in the hope that Carlyle might be prepared to read it. This was probably the manuscript, never published, which Frank Scully later took as the basis for *My Reminiscences as a Cowboy*. Harris' long letter to Carlyle ended sycophantically with 'a reverence too deep for words'. So far as I can trace, Carlyle never replied.

Another and very different person next intervened in Germany itself to leave a far deeper impression on Harris. It was a Germany lately ablaze from end to end with the Franco-Prussian War, a Germany where the upsurge of Socialism had been met and absorbed by Bismarck, and the man of blood and iron had launched a program of social legislation which was to make Germany a great modern state. Harris never forgot a glimpse he had of that remarkable gentleman riding by in a carriage, bolt upright, with an air of fixed purpose which conveyed itself to the young student as a highly desirable condition. In Germany, the socialistic theories of Byron Smith

[1] Hugh Kingsmill, *Frank Harris*, p. 56 (Jonathan Cape, 1932).

had seemed much more feasible to Harris, and he was aware of historic changes going on almost within personal touch. But the figure of the Iron Chancellor quickly overwhelmed Socialist theory in his ambitious brain and Bismarck became, for him, an idol. This was the kind of man into whose likeness he desired, at the earliest opportunity, to step. Years later he still hankered after the power, eminence and life of action which Bismarck represented. A romantic glory surrounded the military moustaches and long afterwards Harris cultivated his own moustache to a tremendous pitch.

For the moment he still did not know where he was going. A recurring restlessness drove him from one place to another searching for . . . but how could he define what it was he wanted when he did not know its nature? One day he left Göttingen abruptly for Berlin, but finding that 'provincial', pressed on again, after a short interval, to Munich. Wherever he went he never failed to search out any possible university and with a remarkable flair for ingratiating his way into circles normally closed to everyday people, took a bohemian interest in studies of one kind or another. Presently, all over again, his restlessness drove him out of Munich and this time he set out for the land which Byron Smith had brought so beautifully alive in his writings.

Harris left two accounts of what followed in Greece, accounts which contradicted one another with familiar consistency. In the *Saturday Review* he recorded that he and two friends, moving northwards from Thebes to Orchomenous, stumbled on the famous archaeologist Schliemann, directing a 'dig'. From Schliemann they learnt that a young Greek colleague working nearby, had just uncovered the bones of the Sacred Band, said to have been wiped out defending Thebes against Macedon over two thousand years before.

By the time he came to write his Autobiography thirty years later, Schliemann and the young Greek colleague had disappeared from the narrative. Harris himself led the expedition to the Chaeroneia, and it was under his brilliantly intuitive direction that the barrow of the Sacred Band came to light. 'At a big meeting of the Classic Greek Society, I declared my belief that the lion at Chaeroneia was an excellent specimen of antique work carved in classic times. I believed it had been erected over the barrow of the Sacred Band and if excavations were carried out I felt sure that the grave of the heroes would be discovered. . . .' [1] Reckless psychological compulsions had driven him over the edge into lying of such extravagance that it could only be admired. It could not alter the fact that Harris did not discover the barrow.

From Athens, Harris presently made his way to Vienna, from Vienna to Salzburg and there in that land of snowy mountain peaks and blue lakes occurred an idyll which touched even his prematurely hardened heart. When Harris later spoke of the girl, Marie Kirschner, and those wonderful summer evenings looking out across the lakes, his eyes always brightened. Marie Kirschner was a café dancer by profession, a girl he claimed to have 'a piquant, intelligent face,'[2] hazel eyes and a figure preserved in all its boyish grace. Bred in the sophisticated ways of Vienna she had two other qualities which made her irresistible to Harris. She was quite uninhibited about retailing her earlier sexual life, and she understood erotic inspiration in a manner so much more subtle than his own. On their second evening together she divulged to him that she had lost her virginity to a Hungarian banker at the age of thirteen. Simultaneously she brought Viennese skills to the preliminaries of love-making and enraptured him. She would tell Harris what a beautiful voice he had, how she listened enthralled to his quotations, how his face had an 'amazing life in it,'[3] and his virility approached the phenomenal—and he loved every word of it. No one had spoken to him quite like that before. No one had shown such spontaneous understanding of what he regarded as his own unique talents. For seven magic weeks they were lovers. But it could not last. He had drifted for four years through Europe, picked up a wide range of knowledge in one university after another, mastered a cosmopolitan culture, and learnt to speak German and French with some fluency. Now he desired, above all, to find some means of making his mark on the world as rapidly as possible.

[1] Frank Harris, *My Life and Loves*, Vol. 2, pp. 104–5.

[2] Ibid., p. 113.

[3] Ibid., p. 115.

An early photograph
of Harris

Harris towards the
end of his life

Not even the rich wines, the mountain air, the blue lakes and a beautiful young dancer in his arms could quite hold the impetuous, hot-blooded and determined Harris for long. One night he left her without a word and fled away to Italy, *en route* for England.

CHAPTER SIX

The young man who returned to London in the early 1880s was 26 years old. He had no degrees, no friends, and fewer prospects than thousands of others who had been wise enough to stay at home and accept the limitations of a conventional career, but whatever commonplace advantages Harris lacked there were characteristics in his make-up which could rise and perform astonishing feats, in any emergency. Within two years of his arrival he had become a distinguished editor. Within two and a half years he was the talk of London.

It was a vanished and incredible London where Gladstone and Queen Victoria dominated the scene, men still rode iron bicycles, telephones were unknown, and horse traffic cluttered narrow streets. A very considerable culture sometimes went cheek by jowl with poverty, fine carriages at one extreme were matched by slums at the other, and the threat of unemployment had become considerable for thousands of workers. Kipling caught and developed the spirit of Empire in books and poems which found a lofty destiny in colonial outposts, and the mid-Victorians could not doubt that right would prevail so long as their gods—Dickens, Darwin, Gladstone—remained in the ascendant. But clashes between workers and employers had grown; Blatchford's *Merrie England* sold a million copies; the Fabian Society appeared in 1884 and a ferment of revolutionary thought disturbed a number of middle class intellectuals. H. G. Wells, wearing a violent red tie, hurried through the gas-lit streets to hear William Morris on Socialism, Bradlaugh on Atheism, Gladstone on Home Rule and that raw, aggressive

Dubliner, George Bernard Shaw, on everything. Sometimes, it seems, Frank Harris was present at the same meeting as Shaw and Wells, but he did not speak to either.

In his own strange way Harris learnt to love London. He saw the city as a woman who responded to those who understood her and spat upon those who didn't. Any hot June day, in the Mall, with the carriages rolling by and St. James's Palace agleam in the sun, London was to him a royal city full of the richest variety, a city alive with treasures and beautiful houses and the means of living in taste and luxury. Many years later he revealed his powers of descriptive writing and the depth of feeling which places could evoke in him, when he wrote: 'London, to me, is like a woman with wet draggled, dirty skirts (it's always raining in London) and at first you turn from her in disgust, but soon you discover that she has glorious eyes lighting up her pale wet face . . . And if you admire her eyes and tell her so passionately one mid-summer evening, when the sunshine is a golden mist, she will give you her lips and take you to her heart, and you will find in her spirit, depths undreamed of, passionate devotions, smiling self-sacrifices and loving, gentle tendance till your eyes dim at the sweet memory of her. And ever afterwards you, the alien and outcast and pariah of this all-hating world, will have a soft heart for London. You will find magic and mystery in her fogs, as Whistler did, and in her gardens some June morning you will wake to find her temperate warmth of desire more enchanting than any tropic heat. . . .'

But this description of London was not the result of Harris' first year in the metropolis. In the first year he became a clerk in the office of a stockbroker called Klein, loathing every minute of the day. His income was given variously between £1 and £3 a week, and he rented a dowdy bed-sitting room in a Bloomsbury back street. If work in the stockbroker's office depressed him, sometimes at night, walking in the West End, he saw the rich carriages and fine houses, watched elegant men entering luxurious hotels, and determined that he must be absorbed into this glittering scene at the highest level, no matter what the cost.

The first step in the desired direction began with a letter

from Carlyle. According to Harris, very soon after his arrival in London, he somehow came by a letter of introduction from Carlyle to Froude the historian, which said: 'I expect more considerable things from Frank Harris than from anyone I have met since parting with Emerson.' [1] No trace of this letter remains and it is difficult to believe that even in his eighty-fourth year Carlyle would have committed himself quite so extravagantly when he had read nothing whatever of Harris' writing beyond, possibly, the outline of the novel sent to him from Germany. False or true, nothing stopped the vigorous, thrusting young Harris from calling on Froude and presenting —was it Carlyle's letter? Perhaps the young man with the craggy jaw and big voice proved as irresistible to Froude as, later, he proved to so many others; perhaps Froude did, in fact, see in Harris something of that remarkable potential which was indeed there; at all events, by the time Harris left Froude's house on that first day, the historian had asked to see some of his work and invited him to dinner.

If we accept, for the moment, Harris' narrative—a procedure rapidly becoming more dangerous—it is clear that he did not expect Froude to provide any very dramatic change in his fortune. Instead, while waiting for the day of the dinner, he walked boldly into the offices of the *Fortnightly Review* one morning, and demanded to see Mr. Chapman of Chapman and Hall, who then published the magazine. Waiting two hours he eventually saw Mr. Chapman, was told that the *Fortnightly* had no work for him, and promptly demanded to see the acting editor. Mr. Escott gave him the same answer in less polite terms. Quite undismayed Harris at once conceived the idea of arriving every morning at the offices of the *Fortnightly* and sitting in the outer office, patiently waiting all the morning, in case, as he said, some small task within his wide capacity might occur. Day after day he arrived and settled down in the outer office. Day after day Mr. Chapman entered at 10.30 and was embarrassed to find the young man continuously there. Far less troubled, Mr. Escott went striding past Harris and up the stairs as if he did not exist.

Perhaps it was one week, perhaps two, before he decided to

[1] A. I. Tobin and E. Gertz, *Frank Harris*, p. 92 (Madelaine Mendelsohn, 1931).

change his tactics and widen his activities by going across to the offices of the rival *Spectator*, and asking to see the editor, Mr. Hutton. An appointment, it seemed, was a vital preliminary to entering such an august presence, but Harris slipped a sovereign into the hand of the clerk and whispered fiercely, 'Where's his room?' A long moment's hesitation, the golden sovereign turned over and then instructions were whispered back. Harris strode up the stairs, knocked on the door and walked in. A thick-set man, bent over proofs, heard Harris cough, turned in surprise and asked who the devil he might be. There are various accounts of the conversation which followed, but the facts seem fairly clear. Harris introduced himself and presently said he wanted to write for the *Spectator*. Hutton gently explained that there were, already, far too many people anxious to fill the columns of the *Spectator*. When Harris replied that he was quite prepared to enter into competition with them, Hutton asked whether this casual intruder regarded himself as a better writer than the great names who wrote for the paper. Harris replied no, but he felt that he was better equipped to write about certain subjects—which was, for him, a very modest claim. It transpired that Hutton had a book about the Russo-Turkish War awaiting review and when he heard that Harris had been in Russia with General Skobeleff, he promptly gave it to him. In the end, Harris left the office with two books, but it was some time before he settled down to write his reviews. First he took the precaution of going to the British Museum and reading all the books which Hutton had written in order to gain some insight into the nature of the editor of the *Spectator*. Then he deliberately set out to write the kind of review which he thought matched Hutton's tastes. It was received warmly. Reviewing was not the only form of writing to which he quickly turned his facile pen. There remained long evenings sitting alone in his bed-sitting room when he tried to forget his loneliness by writing occasional poems.

The dinner party at Froude's house proved unsuccessful. A dazzling affair, attended by the editor of *The Times*, Austin Dobson the poet, Mr. Longman the publisher, and a number of other highly influential people, Hugh Kingsmill has given a succinct account of what took place. Froude himself '. . . read out a poem of Harris', and asked Austin Dobson for his opinion. . . . Harris slipped out to search in his overcoat pocket for his latest sonnet. Returning, he heard Austin Dobson's verdict; good knowledge of verse form, genuine feeling, but no new cadence; and when Froude called to him to come over and be introduced to Mr. Longman the publisher, he stammered a refusal.' What followed was remarkable. Hugh Kingsmill wrote: 'How he left the room he had no idea. Shamed to the soul, he wanted but one thing, to be alone, to be by himself— alone!' [1] Nothing could more flatly contradict the swashbuckling picture of Harris so often drawn at this stage of his career. The dividing line between sensitivity and vanity is often very hard to draw but Harris clearly regarded Dobson's comment as shattering and retired from the party badly shaken. However the world of writing and editing had become irresistible to him and presently he proved as resilient as he was sensitive. If he wasn't a poet he would be something else, no less important.

Returning to his vigil in the offices of the *Fortnightly* he revealed to Chapman that he was reviewing for the *Spectator* and within a few days was asked for his opinion on a book which Chapman and Hall thought of publishing. Giving a quick and downright view of the book brought another manuscript into his hands. His ambitions widened. Within a few months he not merely bounced in and out of newspaper offices with new confidence, but began, behind the scenes, to maneuver towards work of greater interest. He had bought and read the *Evening News* with steadily increasing scorn, convinced that what was to him dull and unoriginal beside the vivid newsheets of America, could be transformed overnight. He determined that he must, somehow, make contact with the men on the *Evening News* who had the power to dispense the kind of privileges he sought.

What really happened then? A book appeared some years later called *The Adventures of John Johns* by Frederic Carrel, which was said to be a very close picture of Harris himself at this time. 'The sketch of Frank Harris in *John Johns* is superb,'

[1] Hugh Kingsmill, *Frank Harris*, pp. 62–3 (Jonathan Cape, 1932).

Oscar Wilde wrote in a letter to Robert Ross in July 1897. If one can believe the story of Frederic Carrel's novel, a meteoric change overtook Harris' fortunes within a few years of his arrival in London. By a series of ingenious maneuvers he met and gradually worked his way into the confidence of none other than the proprietor of the *Evening News*, Lord Folkestone. Many others who knew Harris well at the time, saw close identities between the book and Harris. In the book Johns (alias Harris) becomes involved with two women, Mrs. Weber and Mrs. Lucy Dawson, and the husband of Mrs. Dawson is the proprietor of the *Planet* [alias *Evening News*]. In the book, the circulation of the *Planet* has dwindled away week by week from the double attrition of a rival paper and an inadequate editor, a situation closely resembling that of the *Evening News*. Johns, like Harris, quickly achieves an interview with the proprietor and the whole chapter brilliantly catches Harris at this time; a Harris diamond hard once more and no longer sensitive to simple rebuffs about his poetry. In the book the interview reaches a climax where Johns realizes that he can talk better standing and rises from his chair. I now quote from the novel: ' "Listen, Mr. Dawson," he began, "*I* offer myself as editor."

' "You?" said Dawson, with astonishment.

' "Yes, I! I am ready to guarantee that, if you appoint me editor, your circulation will not only regain its former figure in three months' time, but will go beyond it. The paper wants fresh blood, fresh life. It has been going too long upon its old lines, and the public has found something better for its money. I'll turn you out the smartest thing in London, sound, bright, written by younger men, and a thousand times more interesting. . . ."

'Dawson stared at Johns.

' "Do you mean to say," he said, "that you think you could edit the paper with the experience you have?"

' "I don't *think*; I'm sure."

'Dawson smiled.

'Johns said sharply—"I've made an offer, Mr. Dawson and a serious one. It's for you to consider whether you accept or not. All I can tell you is that if you don't I'm going to start a paper of my own. I'm promised strong support from Australian business men."

'And seeing that Dawson still looked sceptical, he continued—

' "You think perhaps that is a mere boast, but you'll find it's not, and to be frank with you, if I have not already closed with them, it is because I don't consider there is room for another evening paper. I would prefer to edit yours, which is properly established." Then bringing his fist down upon the desk with a loud thump, he said—

' "By God, sir, I'm the man you want. . . . I'm not one of those kid-glove journalists with their academic snobbery, but a man who knows his public and how to please them. I've taken the measure of every available editor in London, and there isn't one, not one, that is of any value who would leave to come to you unless you offered him the salary of an ambassador. If you got in one of those sublime arses from the universities who imprison journalism within the bounds of their own narrowness, the fate of the *Planet* would be sealed.". . . .

' "But you have no plan to offer, no program?"

' "No program!" Johns repeated. "Haven't I?" And then he proceeded to unfold a whole scheme of ameliorations, partly drawn from his imagination. He continued to develop his ideas for at least ten minutes. . . .'

In the novel, after the interview, Johns spends a very restless day. He knows that Dawson is worried about the *Planet* and thinks that he has made a very good impression. The following day the impossible happens. He is offered the editorship for a trial period of three months. There follows a wonderful description of what it feels like for a fledgling journalist, entirely new to the profession, to find himself suddenly become no less than editor of a considerable London paper.

'Editor! He, John Johns, was editor of a London "daily", with that delicious sense of power, and more than two sovereigns a day! How easy it was, after all, to make the world believe in you! How men, and women too, were influenced by talk! As he drove along, the shops, the people in the street, even the autumn sky, seemed to smile on him. There was a glamor of success in everything. An editor! There was an editor driving in that hansom, and he almost felt that the people in the streets should know it. Now that he had got his foot in the stirrup in real earnest, a hundred new horizons revealed themselves to him in the rosy future. His life seemed suddenly to have a higher value in the world's plan. He was a master now in one of the fields of intellect. He was a personage; he was somebody. . . .'

So ran the story in Carrel's novel *The Adventures of John Johns*. Harris himself gave an account which was similar in spirit and very different in detail. In his account the same dazzling leap occurs—a leap not easy to believe. One moment Harris is seeking books to review and the next achieving the editorship of a big London newspaper. There must have been a period when he did odd jobs, worked at other forms of journalism and slowly equipped himself with some pretence of editorial ability; he makes no reference to it in the Autobiography. He simply represents himself overhearing Escott say to Chapman in the offices of the *Fortnightly*: 'I think your protégé will get the editorship of the *Evening News*. I gave him a warm letter to Coleridge Kennard the banker who I understand foots all the bills. . . .'

This was followed by some advice from Escott to Harris: '. . . get Hutton of the *Spectator* to write about your editorial qualities and see Lord Folkestone about the place: for though Kennard pays, Lord Folkestone is really the master. . . .'

Hutton, like Escott, did not it seems, hesitate to write a glowing letter highly recommending him. Harris sent off the two letters and quickly made enquiries about the nature and standing of Lord Folkestone, the man he so much desired to meet. Among many discoveries, what seems to have impressed Harris most, was the imminent inheritance by Lord Folkestone of a rent roll in the neighborhood of £150,000 a year. Lord Folkestone, he said, met him at the offices of the *Evening News* and he was quickly shown over the whole building from the machine to the composing and editorial rooms. It seems feasible that Lord Folkestone might, without further investigation, have offered a journalistic fledgling some minor job on the paper, but that he should return to his own office and thereupon discuss Harris taking over the editorship becomes absurd to anyone familiar with the hard-headed realism of newspaper barons. When an offer to support Harris for the editorship was made in the face of a confession from Harris to Lord Folkestone that he had not 'the remotest idea how to make a daily paper a success', one can only marvel at anyone believing a word of it.

One fact in the confusion remains certain. Harris was unquestionably appointed editor of the London *Evening News*. It is equally clear that he brazened his way into the job with all the brassy glory of his fast developing personality. The details do not gravely matter. He had got there on talk, bluff and bravado. As to seducing the wife of the proprietor. . . .

Simultaneously with rocketing to the editorship of the *News*, a tumult of affairs broke loose, affairs which, with one exception, were no less practical than they were passionate. Life had changed dramatically. Smartly dressed in close-fitting check trousers, an Edwardian jacket, a cravat with an artificial tie-pin, and a hat with a curling brim, every morning he walked part of the way from his rooms in Gray's Inn Road, a tense young man, pale and pre-occupied with the enormous responsibilities he had so glibly assumed. Regularly, at a certain point, he raised his cane, summoned a hansom and underwent a complete transformation by the time he arrived at the office. It was the masterful editor who bounded out of the cab, flung twice his fare at the driver and dashed up the steps.

Within a few weeks one of the old staff had gone, sacked out of hand by Harris as 'an unnecessary driveller of a dead way of life'. A new young man devoted to the person who had given him his chance, received him in the mornings with that blend of reverence and fear proper to a freshly risen god of Fleet Street. Quickly he learnt how to lift the news from the early editions of the *Telegraph*, blend it with agency reports, re-vivify it and serve it piping hot to midday audiences. He learnt from his newsboys how to prepare good news bills. He even found a secret source of intelligence inside the *Telegraph* office which enabled him to rival its early morning editions with 'late special' stories taken from the original copy of the *Daily Telegraph*. This was said to have been done by the brother of one of the news boys then working at the *Telegraph* office. An underground liaison fed the material via the brother into the offices of the *News*, and a specially summoned, early morning staff, worked like fiends to get editions of the paper into circulation before the late-morning editions of the *Telegraph*. Things had certainly, in the phrase of one of the old members of the staff, 'got lively'.

A struggle now developed between the tough, barrel chested person from the American plains, liable to knock down one of his staff in a burst of rage, and the Editor, covering his prize-fighting appearance under elegant clothes.

Sitting at a scarred wooden desk under a gas-lamp, the continual traffic of people was controlled by the stentorian voice bellowing 'Boy!' in exactly the same tone as he bellowed 'Jones!' for his chief reporter; he was liable to turn up at eight in the morning and set the dim old office quaking with a life it had rarely known; he sometimes bullied people with twice his years and experience, and would literally hiss into the mouthpiece by which he communicated instructions to the 'subs', when the sheer power of his voice did not reach them unaided.

These were to be great days and whenever they threatened to slacken he did not hesitate to re-awaken them. He laid about him gloriously. For the first time in his life money, power, prestige, were in his grasp and he lunched and wrote, entertained and blasphemed, sacked and employed, never for one minute forgetting that he lived or died by the paper's circulation. It was at this period that he bought a new pair of boots the heels of which were reinforced by an extra two inches, and one morning his Chief Reporter became uneasily aware that overnight the Editor had suddenly grown. It was no more than a natural part of the miraculous changes which were overtaking the *Evening News*, stirred in its bumbling traces to the most astonishing performances. No mistake must be made about it, Frank Harris was destined to become a great editor and already, a mere 28 years old, he revealed a brassy originality.

He claimed in the Autobiography that he met, in his early journalistic days the great Labouchere, which may be true, but if what he claimed to have said to Labouchere was never, in fact, said, it brilliantly summed up his journalistic principles: 'I edited the *Evening News* first as a scholar and man of the world of twenty-eight; nobody wanted my opinions but as I went downwards and began to edit as I felt at twenty, then at eighteen, then at sixteen, I was more successful; but when I got to my tastes at fourteen years of age I found instantaneous response. Kissing and fighting were the only things I cared for at thirteen or fourteen and these are the things the English public desires and enjoys today. . . .'

Kissing and fighting. It combined sentiment with love, sex with adventure and violence with drama. Over the whole field of human endeavor a newspaper can be very wrong about politics, international affairs and the prospects of war, but its circulation may continue to progress towards astronomical figures providing kissing and fighting play a considerable part. Harris did not reach astronomical figures. In those days, technical limitations restricted circulations; but he raised the circulation from 7,000 to 70,000, and as the graph crept steadily up he arrived at the office each morning freshly jubilant.

No one will ever know the full extent of the devices used by Harris to increase the circulation of the *Evening News*, because his more daring schemes were cut short by the law or the proprietors. He pioneered the human story, as it is known today in modern newspapers, he took long, dull reports and interspersed bright paragraphs, he used knowledge acquired from American newspapers to bring cold news alive. When he learnt that a Conservative peer was being sued for breach of promise he sought out Miss Fortescue, the lady involved, won her sympathy and printed her story under the headline Beauty and the Peer. When the Oxford and Cambridge boat-race came round he consulted the experts, took a chance, printed a large edition with the headline—Oxford Wins—and released the edition immediately the news came through that Oxford had indeed won.

Later he discovered that thousands of workers reconciled their drab lot with horse-racing and investigated a jungle of starting prices, odds and runners until he had devised a means of printing two entirely different starting prices from two rival newspapers, thus giving a better service than either. He changed the staff of the machine room, reduced the time required for making stereos, tried to re-organize the system of delivery by cart and steadily 'stepped up' headlines until the once staid and very Conservative *Evening News* carried titles like—Assault on an Austrian Girl—Extraordinary Charge Against a Clergyman—Gross Outrage on a Female.

It was a pity that sheer opportunism overwhelmed many of his fixed convictions and drove him deeper and deeper into journalistic sympathy with the masses he so much despised. The conflict remained. The necessity to increase the circulation of the *News* was inhibited by the desire to make himself acceptable in the highest Tory circles. As Hugh Kingsmill pointed out in his admirable study of Harris: 'The Victorian love of peace was being challenged by the Imperialists, their belief in the industrial system by the Socialists and their reticence in literature by the disciples of the French novelists. On all these points Harris was anti-Victorian; yet while the *Pall Mall Gazette* was, throughout the eighties, the diary of Stead's social and political passions, the *Evening News* reflected little but Harris' adroitness as a sensational journalist. . . . It was not only to make quick profits that Harris exploited the popular taste for scandal, but also to revenge the uneasiness which afflicted him in his Tory environment. He had become a journalist to make money but a Tory journalist in order to rise in society. . . . His keen desire to entertain (the upper classes) in a Park Lane palace conflicted with an equally keen desire to send the lot of them to the guillotine.' [1]

Extraordinarily, during his first year in London, the impoverished Harris had in fact joined the Social Democratic Federation, an organization which preached a gospel very close to revolution. He became one of the Federation's most powerful and persuasive open air speakers, his big voice carrying to the fringes of the largest crowd, but once the *Evening News* had set him on the road to wealth and affluence his interest in the Social Democratic Federation diminished, and the Socialist in him quickly came to terms with the ruthless egoist.

His leaders in the *Evening News* reflected the Tory hatred of

[1] Hugh Kingsmill, *Frank Harris*, pp. 70-1 (Jonathan Cape, 1932).

CHAPTER SEVEN

S EE him now, brash, strident, successful, his power of talking
at last fully realized, his voice deep as a Russian choir. See him
the center of gatherings in a Fleet Street tavern, quoting whole
pages from the Bible or Shakespeare, his audience violated or
enraptured according to persuasion. See him before the mirror
in his new and far more sumptuous bedroom, brushing his
dark hair desperately back as if, with enough persistence, he
could broaden the distance between it and his nose and cease
to have a 'brutish low forehead'; see him curling the already
immaculate moustache, fastening the bright new spats, and
with cuffs shot out to the right distance, taking up his cane
and sallying forth with a vigorous stride and a voice booming
for a hansom. He boomed his way into great houses and often
became invisible because of his short stature, but he would
talk in a roomful of people until heads turned and the whisper
went round: 'It's Frank Harris . . . What do you make of him?
Vulgar? Oh, worse than that. But a coming man . . . a coming
man. . . .'

He was approaching 30 and he had taken the measure of
his powers. If it seemed to him, as it undoubtedly did, that
most things were within his reach, his old sense of inferiority
still drove him into rude, thrusting behavior. He was a great
newspaper editor. His name was spreading in those London
circles which mattered. He wrote leaders of national consequence. But he still lacked any of the graces. Women, once
attracted by the great voice and sheer virility, were now interested in him as a professional man of power and stature, but

the world he was creating in the *Evening News*, the world of vivid and sensational journalism, brought him favor with the masses and notoriety with that class of wealthy and distinguished men and women into whose ranks he so much desired to step. He edited the *Evening News* for four years, became a member of several famous clubs, asserted himself brassily in whatever company surrounded him, and still felt frustrated.

In the many careers he now examined with the cool certainty that he could succeed in any, the one where his virtuosity was already beyond question—acting—did not occur to him. Harris, when put to the test, could acquit himself as well in the role of the sensitive, poetic spirit as he could in the role of a rampaging realist. He could browbeat, ingratiate, dominate, devour, reverence, ridicule, all with extraordinary conviction and it is possible that, granted the final crown of his remarkable voice, the world lost a great actor, but acting at this stage seemed small beer to him and his restlessness grew. The skies shone, his salary increased, life was full, rich and varied, but a growing conviction that he was made for far greater things drove him on. Success, glittering and undeniable, carried him into speculations about far more ambitious schemes and he began to look avariciously towards no less than the editorship of *The Times*, then held by Buckle. Simultaneously the bush telegraph of Fleet Street spread ugly rumors about the methods of Frank Harris. Sharp practice, it said, had become second nature to him; lying, a convenience to be used whenever it served his purpose. Far worse devices, it was whispered, might be brought to bear against those who threatened to interfere with his ambitions. Buckle for instance. . . . Harris had succeeded in releasing subtle undercurrents of scandal vaguely connected with Buckle, and for the express purpose of developing these he had taken over a small news-sheet called *The Hawk*, then owned by Jimmy Glover.

It was the big, gurgling, happy-go-lucky Glover who said to Hugh Kingsmill one day: '. . . I'll tell you a story about Frank Harris. He bought *The Hawk* from me, paper I used to own, lively little sheet . . . huh! . . . His idea was to make it hot for Buckle, you know editor of *The Times*. Spicy past . . . something Harris had nosed out about Buckle . . . I dunno . . . . Any-

Oscar Wilde in 1893

way Buckle didn't give a damn for it . . . Why should he? . . . different public. . . . After a year or so Augustus Moore (who edited the paper) came to me, said Harris wanted me to take the paper back. . . . I was agreeable and went along with my cheque. Harris was there with his partner. I handed him the cheque. Bit of a silence. Moore asked Harris what he (Moore) was getting out of it. "Nothing," said Harris. Moore got wild, said Harris had promised him his whack for fixing up the transfer.'

' "You've got the editorship," said Harris, "what more do you want?"

' "I want what you promised," said Moore.

' "I'm not giving you anything," said Harris.

'Moore picked up his hat and looked at Harris and the other chap. Harris asked him what the hell he thought he was looking at. "I'm looking at you two," said Moore, "and thinking that if you got a cheap Christ and put him between you what a damn fine Calvary it would make. . . ." '[1]

Buckle remained quite untouched by all this. Meanwhile the struggle between different elements of Harris' personality was forcing a new pattern upon him. Naked, unashamed ambition had begun to drive him over the edge and as success went with each fresh outrage a malignant glee became apparent in some of his actions. It would nonetheless be a mistake to assume that all finer feelings were automatically swept away. The struggle was sometimes prolonged and bitter.

The story of Laura revealed a capacity for romantic love still untouched by his exploits in journalism and big business. He had met Laura during his first impoverished year in London and the sight of her chestnut hair, broad forehead and beautiful figure had made a sudden silence in his mind. He fell in love with her and for six long years, with marked fluctuations, his love continued. If he thought quickly of marriage and wanted to carry her off into that world of sensual abandon which he now understood so well, either sheer poverty made marriage impossible, or poverty became an excuse to escape a commitment still terrifying to him. Uneasily they agreed, that they must wait—and wait apart. For months Harris looked for

[1] Hugh Kingsmill, *Frank Harris*, pp 78–9 (Jonathan Cape, 1932).

reasonable work and then, when the *Evening News* had opened the treasure trove of London at his feet and his eyes were suddenly feasting on undreamt of prospects, he saw Laura, one evening, with another man. A fever of jealousy, totally unexpected in the calculating young editor, seized and tore him.

Later he met Laura's mother who disliked him. Later he persuaded Laura to come to his room in Gray's Inn Road and they became lovers. They continued to meet several times a week over the next few years, he paid her an allowance, she became, in effect, a kept mistress and still he hovered uneasily on the verge of marriage. She held him, he later said, because she added intelligence to beauty, five languages to the conversation and a continental disdain to the English scene; but there was also a considerable emotional awareness and, undoubtedly, passion. In the man represented by gossip and rumor as a monster who devoured every woman's body and ignored her spirit, it is interesting to find love brought to that pitch where it sometimes broke in a fever of jealousy. On a second and to him unforgettable occasion, he found Laura with yet another man in a private salon of the Charing Cross Hotel. He exploded. A mad rage drove him back to his rooms alone. True he had taken girls to private salons himself in the interval, but now, suddenly, he was afraid of the violence to which jealousy might drive him. Wild schemes came up at the back of his head and were suppressed. Laura never knew how close to violation of a quite different kind she came; and even if vanity or self love played no small part in the outburst, it was vanity qualified by a form of feeling far more powerful than anything he had yet known.

Nothing conveys what Laura meant to Harris, better than his words to Hugh Kingsmill. Late one night, in advanced years, he recalled for Kingsmill the beautiful eyes, the chestnut hair and the times when he used to take her to the theatre . . . '. . . and there, in the darkness at the back of the box, she gave herself to me. Again and again. Ah, what hours! But she resented my dislike of her mother. We were always quarrelling about the wretched creature. And at last I had had enough and more than enough. She came to my room while I was packing. "Where are you going?" she cried. "Away," I answered and

72

lit a cigarette. But it drove me to the verge of madness. At Basle I weakened. There was a train back in half an hour. But I held to my resolve and went on home. I used to see her in the mirror. In the corners of the room. But I wouldn't go back. I had suffered too much. There was a woman, a widow, who was sympathetic. I used to talk to her about Laura, ease the pain in words. . . . Then Laura came back. She was always slow to passion, very hard to rouse. But now she tore her clothes off to show herself as I loved to see her best, naked before the mirror. But . . . I don't know. . . . Our love cooled. One day she came to me, said a Mr. Hodge wanted to marry her, a millionaire. A good name and a good sum, I said. We never met again. Later I was hard up. I had given her thousands and wrote to her. But she replied that she couldn't help.'

Harris finished his story in a voice charged with emotion: 'Oh, if I could see her again, so splendid and shameless.' [1]

* * * * *

TWO reasons were given for Harris' dismissal from the *Evening News*. The first came from the late Edward Pease, one time secretary of the Fabian Society. It had been bad enough, he said, when sensational headlines in the *Evening News* shook that hushed complacency in which one at least of its backers, Coleridge Kennard, lived; it had been disturbing to read the story of Beauty and the Peer, and shocking to observe some of the more extravagant stunts; but when Harris proceeded to print intimate details from the Colin Campbell divorce case and it led to an indictment for obscene libel, retribution became inevitable. In those mid-Victorian days one could go nobly to the gallows as a murderer, embezzle, with some semblance of dignity, the life savings of the workers, or deliberately sit on the board of a fraudulent company, but to be brought before the law courts for printing obscenities . . . The directors decided that Harris must go.

The second account says that Harris overstayed his holiday in Rome and was told that the assistant editor could run the paper without him. Both events probably combined to cut short his career on the *News*. It is a remarkable tribute to his

[1] Hugh Kingsmill, *Frank Harris*, pp. 83–4 (Jonathan Cape, 1932).

73

resilience and reputation that within a very short time he had switched his whole personality to quite a different class of reader and almost overnight became editor of the *Fortnightly*. No adequate record remains of how he won the editorship, but it is not difficult to imagine the man who had multiplied the circulation of the *Evening News* by ten, meeting the directors of the *Fortnightly* and talking them into believing that he could perform precisely the same feat for their own paper. They offered him, he claimed, £500 a year and a ten per cent share of any profits.

Journalism had first promised him power and money. Now, in a different category of the same profession, he sought to rise in society. Despising his own middle class origin, Harris was at once fascinated and repelled by the English upper middle class. He coveted their assurance and powers, but he was infuriated by their 'undemonstrative acceptance of themselves as the only people that mattered'. The aristocracy might be justified in its conceit, he thought, but the judges, the dons, the periodical journalists, the solicitors, and clergymen seemed to him to claim a prestige out of all proportion to the lives of deadening respectability which they led.

Asked once, whether he had ever met Leslie Stephen, Harris answered: 'No—Stephen and that set looked on me as a cad. They didn't want to know me.' [1] But now he believed that he was not only going to know them; free from the necessity of a wide circulation in his new journal, he was going to enter and dominate the class which he had so long coveted. Scholarship did not mean anything to him; social birth was of no consequence; respectability he hated; but to people with just such distinctions as these he now addressed himself in the *Fortnightly*.

In the complicated motives which made the *Fortnightly* more important to him than another popular paper, he now cherished political ambitions. It was freely bandied about in journalistic circles that the dazzling young editor of the *Fortnightly* might soon be seen in the House of Commons, but few were aware that Harris himself had set the rumor moving. Clearly editorship of the *Fortnightly* was worth its weight in political gold;

[1] Hugh Kingsmill. *Frank Harris*, p. 53 (Jonathan Cape, 1932).

74

it remains a mystery how the directors continued to sleep soundly in their beds at night when the man who had once been charged with obscene libel took over and edited their so much more solemn journal.

At the outset his office methods were not reassuring. There were the days when the walls seemed to tremble and shake as his bass voice boomed out: 'Somebody bring me a whisky and soda!' There was the occasion when Mr. Chapman observed him, from the end of the passage, propelling an old contributor towards the door with words which sounded blasphemous. There was the old and battered tin box left behind by John Morley, a previous editor, which Harris ruthlessly looted, sending back all but two of the manuscripts, one from a quite unknown writer called H. G. Wells, and the other from a novelist Mrs. Lynn Linton.

On close examination Harris discovered that 'The Rediscovery of the Unique' by H. G. Wells was a very odd document. He read the manuscript again, fell into a fury of incomprehension, bellowed for his secretary and demanded that she get this fellow Wells to come and see him at once. The invitation disturbed Herbert George Wells. He was still very inexperienced in journalism, still inclined to regard editors as gods and totally unaware what would be the correct garb for such an occasion. Eventually he wore his best suit and a top hat which he had carefully cleaned with the aid of water.

'Highly self-conscious, he arrived at the *Fortnightly* office, and was further put out by having to wait half an hour before Harris would see him. Then he was shown in and advanced across the room to a large desk where the figure of Harris sprawled with the cultivated ease of a distinguished editor. He had almost reached the desk when he became aware that the hat, which he held in his hand, was beginning to curl and warp from the water, and suddenly to his terrified eyes, looked oddly reminiscent of a bankrupt undertaker. He colored and fidgeted. Harris fixed a basilisk stare on this strange buckled object. Two of his satellites also concentrated their gaze. There was a long pause which all but paralyzed Wells. Then, condescending to notice the thin form beside the hat, Harris suddenly threw the manuscript across the table and demanded in a voice like Irish thunder: "So it was *you* who sent me this Universe R-R-Rigid? Tell me what you *think* it's about. Before Gaard what in the name of heaven is the bloody article trying to say? What's it mean? Who will read it?"

'Nobody ever did read it in the end. The type was broken down and distributed because Harris could not make head or tail of it. . . .' [1]

But Harris remembered Wells. The born editor carefully noted the skills he had observed in the writing of an article which, from its very nature, should have been dull, but was in fact brimming over with life.

Within certain closely defined limits, Harris did attempt a dash or two of originality as editor of the *Fortnightly*, but the daring editor of the *Evening News* seemed sadly inhibited by social climbing and his new board of directors. He was one of the few who quickly detected the 'winkings of that new . . . and distinctly cheeky star . . .' H. G. Wells, but he was sparing in his encouragement. He had to be. If the Board's desire to stimulate the *Fortnightly*'s sluggish circulation stopped short at anything resembling originality, it regarded the socialism of Shaw and Wells as dark corruption. With Harris 'in the chair' everyone had looked for sparkle and explosion from the 'good old *Fortnightly* slowly dying of dignity', or at least a flare of brilliance which would dazzle everyone.

Instead, at dinner one night, Whistler was driven to say to Harris: 'But no! You've done it in the . . . way of genius; every month the *Review* appears regularly, just what one looks for, a work of high-class English mediocrity; lamentable, you know, quite lamentable.' [2] [3]

When a banker-proprietor of the *Evening News* had objected to Harris' policy once before, Harris had simply ignored him, but now, when the price of entry into the upper middle class was conformity, Harris conformed. Fascinated by Shaw, he dared not publish him, attracted by Henley's *Song of the Sword* he had to reject it, and even Oscar Wilde received something dangerously close to a rejection slip. Not that Harris was

[1] Vincent Brome, *H. G. Wells*, pp. 60–1 (Longmans, Green, 1951).

[2] Hugh Kingsmill, *Frank Harris*, pp. 62–3 (Jonathan Cape, 1932).

[3] Frank Harris, *Contemporary Portraits*, p. 73 (Methuen, 1915).

entirely subdued. According to the late Edward Pease there were days, in the offices of the *Fortnightly*, when he sat growling and grumbling in the oaken chair, suddenly overtaken with a sense of intolerable humility. That he should be forced to toady to these dummies of respectability drove him into bursts of anger when he would take up a poem by Verlaine, carry it like a live bomb to the outer office, and say in a voice of thunder— 'Put that in the next issue at any cost.' Half an hour later he would appear again. 'Don't tell anyone about Verlaine. If they want to know what's in the next issue refer them to me.'

By some such means, Verlaine, Pater and even an ode by Swinburne praising tyrannicide appeared in the *Fortnightly*, to the manifest discomfiture of Mr. Chapman who began to wonder whether Frank Harris had the 'taste' without which editorship of the *Fortnightly* was impossible.

'Taste', to some extent, Harris acquired in the eight years he edited the *Fortnightly*, and no small part of it was acquired for the satisfaction of the woman who came into his life to over-whelm Laura. Mrs. Lynn Linton first introduced Harris to the wealthy widow Mrs. Edith Mary Clayton. Mrs. Lynton was the writer of the second article, 'The Modern Girl', which Harris had retrieved from the old box of manuscripts. He had written to her about the article and their correspondence led to a meeting which, in turn, brought about an introduction to Mrs. Clayton. How this correct and respectable lady ever came to think of marriage to Frank Harris, remains something of a mystery. W. L. George, the short story writer, met him at this time, and recorded: 'One doesn't meet Harris, one collides with him. What an impact of personality. His voice seemed to me like the ruffle of the leaves of a brass artichoke. He told me of a story he would write. I remember how he placed his right hand on my shoulder. I couldn't feel the palm of his hand, but the grip of his five fingers. I was under his spell, a sinister spell. He upset me but attracted me most strongly. . . .'

I was under his spell. He could now exercise an extra-ordinary fascination on many women and some men. It was as if, one woman later said, 'his great voice penetrated your personality, vibrated inside you, and his boldness, the swift stroke towards the very heart of you, got you in its grip and from then on you were hypnotized and there wasn't much choice. . . .'

Mrs. Clayton was not a woman to be hypnotized. Sexuality, if it existed for her, was a subdued activity carried out after dark in near anonymity, but if she epitomized the correct restraints of an upper middle class desperately anxious to avoid direct contact with the raw material of living, and faithfully fulfilled an elaborate social round in the right hat, gloves, state of mind and morals, she was wealthy, she had a house in Park Lane, she was received by Royalty and—after her own fashion—overwhelmed by Frank Harris.

The *Fortnightly* represented one half of the golden key which could unlock the social power and privileges which Harris so much desired to possess and Mrs. Clayton, when he married her on November 2nd, 1887, completed it. Her age was not known. On the marriage certificate, with that combination of modesty, dignity and deception which characterized much of her behavior she wrote: 'full'.

In one sense, Harris blazoned forth into the social life of London with a roar which should have warned anyone within earshot that this could not possibly last. In another, remarkable restraints occurred. There were periods of near conformity. Periods when he sat on his stool and waved his paws as his new wife required, but he remained a lion, and once or twice over the next year, a wicked and powerful claw raked open a convenient back and Mrs. Clayton suddenly shuddered to think what manner of man she had married.

Their luncheon parties in 'one of those funny little squeezed houses in between the big ones in Park Lane', [1] became famous. Oscar Wilde was often there, friends of the Prince of Wales came, Margot Asquith and Sir Harry Johnston were old friends of Mrs. Clayton, and one luncheon included the Duke of Cambridge, the American Ambassador, Beerbohm Tree and John Burns.

Harris quickly asserted himself at any gathering; indeed, he usually assumed a Napoleonic dominance over any party he was generous enough to grace; but now, in the presence of his simple, warm, middle-aged wife he contrived to preserve

[1] Sir Harry Johnston, *The Story of My Life*, p. 225 (Bobbs-Merrill, 1923).

certain restraints—for a time. It was vital to his career. The third string to a bow which was steadily becoming more complicated had drawn the attention of the Conservative party managers, who had their eye on him as a possible candidate. He must, for their sake, remain respectable.

If he talked and dazzled, drank and argued, and never hesitated to challenge the most celebrated wits at the multiplying parties, the obscene outbursts and the great rages were carefully subdued. Soon, on the mantelpiece there were invitations to far more house parties than he could ever attend, but within a few weeks of their marriage, Mrs. Clayton revealed herself as an insanely jealous woman.

Sir Harry Johnston said of Frank Harris and his wife: 'I could see they were not a happily matched pair, though the wife struck me as a nice kindly woman. I understood she . . . came from Yorkshire. . . .' [1]

Her methods of holding Frank in check were extravagant. She would walk out of an hotel if his eyes became too attentive to a pretty girl, she would deliberately choose the corner of an expensive restaurant where two blank walls confronted him, and she was liable to burst into tears if other young women so much as wrote to him. Paradoxically, Harris, prevented by vanity from wearing spectacles, was so short sighted that all women at a distance were a blur to him, and in the street, her jealousy could not have been more misplaced. In private . . . There is no documented evidence of his extra-marital love life at this period, but sexual restraints had become something he regarded as an interference with the laws of nature.

In due course, he became Conservative candidate for Hackney, nursing the constituency hard, spending his wife's money lavishly and trying to keep within the bounds of what Hackney regarded as respectable. It was a considerable effort. Lavish living and aristocratic company pleased and flattered him for a time, but as his political ambitions hardened they were confused by doubts about the way of life to which he had committed himself. Did the men and women he met in these big houses want to know Frank Harris as Frank Harris? Or were they interested in him because he had married a wealthy

[1] Sir Harry Johnston, *The Story of My Life*, p. 225 (Bobbs-Merrill, 1923).

woman, was a coming politician and editor of the *Fortnightly*? Exasperatingly, people who were stupid, somehow contrived to have a quiet assurance which Harris, with all his brains, wit and eloquence, could never achieve. It was infuriating to discover comparative simpletons, caught off their guard, with a look of near condescension in their eyes. He could trust Mrs. Linton with her flowered cap, grey hair and kindliness to speak her mind, but what lay behind the smiling mask of all those famous people who passed through the dining-room of the Park Lane house and so often remained remote and self contained. Was he the intellectual clown jumping through the hoops to show his cleverness and did they see something rather vulgar in the display? Over many months the conflict grew in Harris while his wife's modesty and respectability began to close around him in a suffocating cloud. Once she said to him: 'Frank—you know I don't want to interfere . . . but I wish . . .'

'Wish what?'

'Oh, it doesn't matter.'

'Come on—out with it.'

'Well, I wish, Frank, that you could manage to lower your voice a little more, over dinner sometimes.'

Suddenly using its full force so that Mrs. Harris (Clayton) shot back in her chair he boomed: 'My damned voice was given to me by your God and he intended me to use it . . . What can I do if your namby-pamby milk-sop lot think a lowered voice a fine thing? They haven't got any voice worth raising. . . .'

Scenes were now inevitable. Soon, with some regularity, Mrs. Harris disappeared behind a screen of hurt tears and flawless scraps of cambric, sobbing in the low manner required by her station.

It is possible to see Harris at this stage of his career as one fiery particle in a tide which was gathering considerable force in late Victorian England, a tide represented by Havelock Ellis, H. G. Wells and Bernard Shaw at one level, and thousands of thinking men and women at another. They saw that half the conventions of the day were shams and challenged them with great courage, but where others were prepared to compromise, there were times when Harris wanted outright destruction. Particularly he wanted destruction in the well-bred hush of a dinner party consisting of nothing but friends at one, two or three removes from Royalty, which did not permit him to repeat the slightly *risqué* stories told him by his journalist friends.

Moving between the Park Lane house, the offices of the *Fortnightly* and his constituency, he would sometimes arrive at the office at eleven in the morning to be confronted by the head of the Rev. John Verschoyle bowed over a set of proofs. By special dispensation Verschoyle combined the roles of sub-editor and representative of God. Young, blond, and good-looking, there were times, at eleven in the morning, when Verschoyle concentrated middle class virtues to the point where Harris suddenly gave a deep exclamation of disgust, brushed past the surprised Verschoyle and buried himself, muttering, in his post. Even in the office he was never free from a sense of constriction.

Small scale repressions steadily built up explosive forces. His wife's jealousy grew worse. Sexually she was quite inadequate. Soon the sense that his acceptance into her group was only made on sufferance, drove him to bouts of drinking, and then, when Parnell's affair with Kitty O'Shea burst upon the embalmed correctness of the Victorian scene, Conservative politicians were suitably shocked and Harris did a remarkable thing. He was now almost certain to enter the House of Commons and many rich prizes were within his grasp, but suddenly, in two spectacular explosions he deliberately smashed the career which he had so carefully planned. The first occurred at Mrs. Shenstone's, a friend of his wife's. She was accustomed to entertain, in her huge dining-room, not less than twenty guests to food of the rarest kind, provided that they observed every social nicety which mimicry of Queen Victoria, court etiquette and snobbishness ordained. Harris went to one of these dinners. As the meal reached the sixth course, with more to follow, Harris began prematurely on the brandy. Ten minutes later he heard someone say: '. . . that dreadful woman Kitty O'Shea.' In half whispers, references to Parnell's mistress became steadily more scathing. Harris' clenched fist—notorious for its iron strength—came down with a crash on the table, several glasses spilled over, a decanter jumped, and in the

81

shocked silence his voice grated out: 'What's the matter with Kitty O'Shea?—she's a woman, she wears petticoats and she has a lover. . . .'

The silence petrified. Eyes were fixed on plates, eating stopped and the hostess went very white. Harris pushed back his chair. 'Like a lot of other women I know,' he added, emptied his glass with a flourish, wiped his mouth with his napkin, turned and drawing himself to his full 5' 5", walked out.

Later he went down to his constituency at Hackney. Before the Conservative office could stop him, he went down with an iron determination to defend the right of a man to a mistress even though his professional life was lived in the hallowed precincts of the House of Commons. Months of repression and hatred had suddenly concentrated and burst. He was bored by his wife, sick of her respectable friends, utterly impatient with behavior which seemed to him a bloodless pretence for the passionate ways he desired to follow.

His speech was short, vibrant and shocking. Gladstone was hopelessly out of touch with the times he said; Kitty O'Shea was a woman after his own heart; Parnell a remarkable man not to be lost through adolescent prudery. 'I am not,' he roared, 'fighting under the flag of Kitty O'Shea's petticoats. I am fighting under the flag of adult common sense.' Mrs. O'Shea later wrote a book underlining what she and Harris regarded as Gladstone's hypocrisy: 'For ten years Gladstone had known of the relations between Parnell and myself and had taken full advantage of the facility this intimacy offered him in keeping in touch with the Irish leader . . . But this was private knowledge. Now it was public knowledge and an English statesman must always appear on the side of the angels.' Later, Harris told friends that if a political career required puritanical deceptions of this kind, then it was not for him. He also knew that in the long run there would be no choice. He might enter the House of Commons and reach minor office, but sooner or later his nature would drive him into social or sexual offence of one kind or another. As rebellion against Mrs. Clayton and his political friends grew, Harris' love life multiplied. Within a few months, H. G. Wells claimed that his sexual vanity became overpowering. Simultaneously the last shred of the restraints he had imposed on himself for the sake of his wife were swept away with an effect which at first startled and later irritated people. Oscar Wilde wrote of him: 'You are a man of dominant personality. Your intellect is exigent, more so than of any man I ever knew; your demands on life are enormous; you require response or you annihilate; the pleasure of being with you is in the clash of personality, the intellectual battle, the war of ideas. To survive you, one must have a strong brain, an assertive ego, a dynamic character. In your luncheon parties . . . the remains of the guests were taken away with the debris of the feast. I have often lunched with you in Park Lane and found myself the only survivor.'

As his quarrels with his wife and the directors of the *Fortnightly* grew, Harris drank more heavily. As the penalties of brassy self-assertion closed in on him, he seemed anxious to do even more outrageous things. The evening came at one of Mrs. Lynton's receptions when Harris, drunk and full of eloquence, went from group to group, deliberately breaking in with appalling words. To a beautiful young girl he talked of prostitution as if that were the kind of conversation which would be natural to her; to a friend of Sir Harry Johnston he repeated in a booming voice which shocked the whole group, a quotation from Ovid not normally translated. And then at last he caught sight of a gaitered dean standing head and shoulders above a group of decorous women who were hanging on his words, and broke in with a voice like thunder, 'Tell me—Dean—did Jesus Christ wear gaiters!' A moment later his wife left the room in tears.

The results were not unexpected. Harris and his wife had both had enough. They decided to separate. Almost simultaneously the publication of an article in the *Fortnightly* sympathetic to certain anarchists brought the courage of the directors to the sticking point. Suddenly one day they decided to sack Harris.

A minor collapse followed. Whether Harris had deliberately weighed the evidence and rejected a life of ease and luxury to follow his own leading, or had simply lost control and run amok, is difficult to determine. The effect of being sacked—a second time—on a man thought to be brassily insensitive, was

CHAPTER EIGHT

The news spread through London. Frank Harris was not only back, but in a bigger and better position to do justice to his extraordinary talents. For some it meant alarm and despondency, for others the beginning of a new life in literary London. Fully recovered now, he had bullied his way back among writers and publishers, and somehow contrived to buy up no less a periodical than the *Saturday Review*. The ten per cent down payment required by the then proprietors was apparently met by borrowing the money from friends who acquired in exchange a number of shares. Repeated strokes of luck by which periodicals required either a new editor or proprietor at moments highly convenient to Harris, were matched by his ability to conjure money, and sometimes big money, out of the air at forty-eight hours' notice. He had left the *Fortnightly* comparatively penniless. Now he had bought the *Saturday Review*.

The old contributors to the *Saturday* were thrown into consternation. Edmund Gosse met Professor Saintsbury outside the Savile Club one day and warned him that Harris would not hesitate to throw the staff of the *Saturday* into the street. Whereupon Saintsbury—the essence of correct nineteenth-century criticism—hurried into the Savile Club and in his flawless script wrote to Harris explaining why it was that he found it necessary to resign from the paper. Harris did throw the old contributors into the street quite spectacularly. H. G. Wells made his way to the offices in Southampton Street, off the Strand, one day, and found fascinating things toward.

People were ascending and descending the stairs, some politely standing aside, others in a bull-rush of rage and the 'roar of a remembered voice told me that Harris was on the higher level. I found Blanchamp in a large room on the drawing-room floor amidst a great confusion of books and papers and greatly amused. Harris was having a glorious time of it above. He had summoned most of the former staff to his presence in order to read out scraps from their contributions . . . and to demand, in the presence of his Dear Gahd and his faithful henchman Silk, why the hell they wrote like that? It was a Revolution—the twilight of the Academic. . . .

'Clergymen, Oxford dons, respectable but strictly anonymous men of learning . . . came hustling downstairs in various phases of indignation and protest, while odd newcomers in strange garments, as redolent of individuality as their signatures, waited their turn to ascend. I came late on the list and by that time Harris was ready for lunch and took Blanchamp, Low and myself as his guests and audience to the Café Royal . . . I don't think we talked much about any prospective contributions. But I gathered that our fortunes were made, that Oxford and the Stuffy and the Genteel and Mr. Gladstone were to be destroyed. . . .'[1]

Presently Harris summoned Bernard Shaw—the most promising of the younger dramatic critics—to his presence, and offered him £6 a week to become drama editor; H. G. Wells was instructed to review novels, Cunninghame Graham to write travel sketches, Max Beerbohm to satirize whatever took his fancy and Thomas Hardy and Rudyard Kipling to write stories and poems.

The new *Saturday Review* which burst on its old reading public sent a wave of interest through literary London. In it Shaw was busy explaining the virtues of Ibsen and the vices of Shakespeare; D. S. McColl introduced Cézanne, Monet and Manet to an audience devoted to Frith and the 'photographic' school; Arthur Symons explained very advanced literary movements, and H. G. Wells wrote about a new novelist, Joseph Conrad, whose book, *Almayer's Folly*, he considered an important literary event.

[1] H. G. Wells, *Experiment in Autobiography*, pp. 520–1 (Gollancz and Cresset Press, 1934).

Everything went with a considerable swing but Harris was not satisfied. Determined to shake the Victorians out of their complacent assumption that England, in the late nineteenth century, was living through a serene golden age, he attacked Free Trade, the Boer War, America and presently referred to England's traditional friend Germany, as 'the first immediate enemy'. Since a periodical like the *Saturday Review* depended for no small part of its revenue on publishers' advertisements, it seemed suicidal that Harris should next single out some of his best customers for personal attack. A long article from Professor Churton Collins enlarged on 290 errors of sheer fact in books published by one of the University presses and the Press promptly stopped advertising in the *Saturday Review*. Undismayed, Harris widened his attacks, and as one scurrilous review followed another, the circulation of the *Saturday Review* rose, and its income fell. Friends tried to stem Harris' attacks only to be brushed aside with an iron rumble of laughter: 'To hell with publishers. I want no truck with people who can't see their own sins. Out with them! Out!'

The trouble was, it almost snuffed out the *Saturday*, but as his enemies multiplied, and at every hand staff and contributors stumbled on hidden plots to damage the *Saturday*, Harris' ingenuity grew. He quickly found a means of replacing the missing advertisements. If one can believe the Autobiography, this took the form of a trenchant defence of the Boer farmers against official British propaganda, which led rich mining companies in South Africa to place advertisements for their prospectuses with the paper. As the columns of the *Saturday Review* show, he sustained a masterly tight rope performance which looked occasionally as though he must crash down completely on the side of the Boers only to have him regain his balance at the crucial moment. Within the national hue and cry against the Boers, his liberal voice was enough to encourage South African financiers to maintain their advertising, and presently the *Saturday* was once more solvent.

The impossible addition of another degree of arrogance to the vibrant personality of its editor could not be denied. Yet Harris remained a deeply divided personality. He had carried over into his editorship of the *Evening News* the man of action who had ridden the American prairies; journalism was an attempt to reconcile the man of action and the man of letters, but the person who had once identified himself with Bismarck could not stop there. Harris hated sitting in an office, writing, and his restlessness soon expressed itself dramatically. He came into the *Saturday Review* office one morning, threw down his hat, boomed for Runciman his assistant, and said that he was leaving within twenty-four hours for South Africa. Runciman must take over. There was no time to waste. To get to the bottom of this appalling Jameson raid, news of which had recently shocked England, he must go personally to South Africa. Alarmed at the thought of inheriting the feuds and outrages whirling around the *Saturday Review*, Runciman asked for time, but Harris simply said—if you have any trouble consult my old friend John Verschoyle. It was extraordinary that he still seemed to regard a member of the British clergy as his chief consultant. Still more extraordinary that he was prepared to leave the *Saturday Review* in the hands of two men, temperamentally so different from himself.

As good as his word he had gone in twenty-four hours. According to the Autobiography, in South Africa, Harris proceeded to uncover one official deception after another. At the very outset he made startling allegations against a man whose character was then unimpeachable—the great Cecil Rhodes. On the day he arrived—some time in January 1896—Harris lunched with Sir James Sivewright, and at once spoke of the Jameson raid and Cecil Rhodes. As everyone knows the raid was said to have been made because the women of Johannesburg sent a telegram asking for help, and it was argued that no humane person could resist such an appeal. That afternoon, in South Africa, according to Harris, Sir James Sivewright bluntly stated: 'That telegram was written in Rhodes' office in Cape Town and sent from there to *The* [London] *Times*.' [1]

Adept at inventing the sensational story it would be completely in character for Harris to send back to the *Saturday* a scoop more lurid and damaging than anything within the range of the normal newspaper correspondent, but whatever the rights and wrongs of the Jameson raid, there was one piece

[1] Frank Harris, *My Life and Loves*, Vol. 4, pp. 51–6.

of evidence which gave credence to some of the reports he wrote. He met, in Pretoria, the genial Chief Justice Kotze, something sparked between the two men and Kotze talked very freely. Later he took Harris to meet President Kruger. When Tobin and Gertz came to prepare their biography of Harris they wrote to Chief Justice Kotze but were unable to publish his reply. As Gertz much later wrote to me: 'In the third volume of his Autobiography, Harris has a long account of what he did and said in connexion with the South African situation including conversations with Chief Justice Kotze . . . I wrote to him [Kotze] and received a long reply in which he substantiated virtually everything that Harris had said . . . on the subject of South Africa . . . almost at once I received a second letter from Chief Justice Kotze—this one frantic in tone. Since writing to me he had learnt for the first time of Harris' *My Life and Loves* and was afraid to have his name mentioned in connection with Harris. He asked me to return his letter to him. . . . It is a curious thing, in view of Harris' many twistings of the truth that he managed to be accurate in . . . the South African situation. . . .' [1]

Harris returned from South Africa to find the *Saturday* embroiled in half a dozen fresh battles, but London, by now, deeply appreciated the remarkable collection of talent he had brought together. There was no questioning the avidity with which people read Bernard Shaw, H. G. Wells, Max Beerbohm and Cunninghame Graham. Harris' sensational despatches from South Africa had added fresh color to the journal and it was freely said that nothing so alive had possessed British periodical journalism for half a century.

Many years later the *New Statesman* wrote of Harris: 'He had no sense of politics and no affiliation with the peculiar brand of Toryism for which the old *Saturday* stood. In foreign and imperial affairs the paper, under Frank Harris, took an independent line. It was, for example, dead against the then fashionable policy of aggression on the Indian frontier. It was unorthodox from the Conservative point of view, in regard to South Africa. It was Protectionist nearly a decade before Chamberlain's conversion. Yet the *Saturday Review* was beyond

[1] Letter, January 3rd, 1957.

all challenge the most vital and stimulating journal in the English speaking world.'

In the 1890s Frank Harris already behaved as if this were an acknowledged truth. Sprawling in his office chair he received a whole galaxy of writers and artists, later to become household words, and behaved as if the name Frank Harris would certainly survive theirs. Yet Wells, Shaw, Beerbohm and Oscar Wilde all agreed that Harris was a great editor. They could excuse the man who put his feet on the table and slowly read to death a poem which had cost the listening poet weeks of anguished work; they could overlook the man who sometimes tried to play the part of the editor of *The Times*; they could ignore the torrents of abuse which poured away when someone dared to say that an issue was dull; because he was, in their view, a great editor.

*   *   *   *   *

Another reputation developed hand-in-hand with editing. Between the years 1891 and 1894 Harris had written a number of short stories which received an acclaim only to be understood within the literary convention of the day. It was a convention combining near melodrama and sentimentality. When *The Elder Conklin and Other Stories* appeared from Heinemann in 1894, Coventry Patmore was moved to write: 'The manner or technical element in Mr. Harris' stories seems to me beyond criticism . . . Kipling never did anything better than the two short stories *Eatin' Crow* and *The Best Man in Garrott*. . . .Whatever it may have meant, Professor Dowden also announced that they were 'demonstrations in spiritual anatomy', and the *Athenaeum* compared the stories to those of Balzac. Later, in 1900, came another collection called *Montes the Matador*, and here can be seen the beginnings of that talent which was, in the end, destined to make him a man capable of writing short stories of a most distinguished kind. Once again, *Montes the Matador* did not deserve the extravagant praise it immediately won, but it is worth brief examination as the best known of Harris' short stories.

It was a vivid enough evocation of a bull-fighter driven by the woman he loved from one spectacular feat to another, until seriously injured, he discovers Clemencia's unfaithfulness. He then plots her lover's death and achieves a double triumph; the lover is killed by a bull and Clemencia dies in premature child-birth. Told in the first person by Montes alias Harris, the method creaked occasionally, but there were, undoubtedly, touches of originality in the story which became most marked towards the end. Questioning himself about remorse Montes says—yes! yes! he had felt remorse—remorse that he let the bull kill his rival. He should have torn his throat out with his own hands.

That was genuine Harris at the time. He had seized life by the throat and was now preparing to tear out just what he wanted at any cost. Written in 1891, it may also have released the jealousy which tormented him when he discovered Laura's unfaithfulness, and it recalled the moment when he had to hurry away to prevent himself from injuring her.

Meredith was quite carried away by *Montes the Matador*: 'Never before was there such an actual bull-ring for me. Mérimée dismisses the bulls with the somber French agglo-merate—brute, but Harris gives the animals individuality. If there is any hand in England that can do better than *Montes*, I don't know it.'

What can one say after that? *Montes the Matador* was melo-dramatic. Set beside Hemingway or Lawrence it reveals a superficial knowledge of bull-fighting. A certain passion in the pace with which it unfolded unmistakably identified its author, but the words of Ferdinand Brunetière, editor of the famous *Revue des Deux Mondes*, seem no less extravagant than Mere-dith's. Harris sent him two stories, *Montes the Matador* and *A Modern Idyll* and Brunetière quickly wrote back: 'It is the first time I have received two masterpieces in one letter.'

Precisely the kind of short story which delighted Harris, the second story, *A Modern Idyll*, dealt with a holy man who had received an offer twice as large as his present salary to preach at another church, and found himself torn between mammon and God with an equally powerful pull in the direction of a certain Mrs. Hopper. The note of piety, the restraint, the deeply religious undertones running through the story were well done. The simplicity of a West American community came alive vividly, and the clergyman's self-conscious awareness of his own nobility was subtly conveyed. The irony of Deacon Hooper raising money to keep Mr. Letgood at their local church unaware that Letgood had become his wife's lover, was also effective. And yet Brunetière's praise remained extreme. *A Modern Idyll* had no very new insight or depths of awareness to the modern eye.

'Sonia,' the last story in the collection, *Montes the Matador*, once more returned to the melodramatic. Sonia was a woman who threw bombs at the Czar and revealed herself as a desperate revolutionary, but the sympathetic study of feminine tenderness in the story flatly denied the outer Harris and reminded one of the little boy who felt, in his loneliness, that he was more a girl than a boy. Could it be that within the thickening black husk, subtle undercurrents of the sensitive person highly susceptible to injury, still ran deep, and the tough exterior was only becoming extravagant in proportion to what it had to protect? Certainly the picture of Harris drawn by Hugh Kingsmill and others can be seriously qualified. It was remarkable that nowhere in these stories appeared the harsh, cynical opportunist who should have written with the disillusion of a Maupassant. Perhaps, after all, there was some element of truth in what Shaw later wrote with such perception: '. . . Like everyone else I took you to be much more of a man of the world. . . . As I told you, it was Julia Frankau who first opened my eyes to the fact that the buccaneer of Monte Carlo, the pal of Lord Randolph, the impressive editor of the *Fortnightly* . . . the financier who gave tips to Hooley . . . was a romantic boy and even a sensitive child without the ghost of a notion of the sort of society he was living in and the people he was up against.'

*   *   *   *   *

Now a great editor and considerable short story writer, Harris' self-importance grew. Before very long there was no holding him. A cartoon by Art Young in 1896 crystallized Harris' public view of himself. It showed an elegant, straw-hatted gentleman, with a butterfly collar and bow tie, resting one hand on a cane and gesturing with the other, while he explained to Christ, Shakespeare, Oscar Wilde, and Bernard

Shaw, their shortcomings which, if only they would listen to the Great Frank might, with careful attention, be remedied. It was this person, full of flourish and arrogance, who now came upon a young woman destined to play a steadily more important part in his life. What precisely Helen O'Hara, the beautiful girl in her twenties, first saw in this ugly, thrusting little man, was never recorded, but both met by chance at a tea party, and a relationship which was to last for thirty years began. As Tobin and Gertz wrote in their biography: 'She was . . . twenty years his junior, of average height, slight of figure and with an exceedingly clear white skin. Her eyes, soft, brown and large, sparkled like clear water in sunlight and were fringed with long caressing lashes. Her oval face, with its pointed chin and tilted nose, was topped by a crown of rich auburn hair. She was Helen O'Hara from Dublin, and to Harris she was a girl to rival any beauty. . . . When W. L. George . . . first saw her he said it was impossible for him to keep his eyes off her. . . .'[1]

Harris put forth all his powers to win Helen O'Hara. Talking far into the night, lunching at the Café Royal, introducing one distinguished friend after another, he displayed his power and wealth and finally, one afternoon, bought her a diamond ring. There were great parties summoned at twenty-four hours' notice; Oscar Wilde was elaborately invited to meet the 'most beautiful woman in the world'; Bernard Shaw told Helen that he thought any woman from Dublin worth three from London and the Café Royal re-echoed to Frank's voice toasting—'the greatest race in the world, the O'Hara's from Dublin'. Days went by when he no longer appeared in the *Saturday Review* office.

The romantic conclusion was almost unbelievable. The tough, brandy-bitten Harris, who had come to regard women as so many concubines made for his delectation, eloped. One hot summer day in 1898 he rushed away with Helen O'Hara on an express train, and the place he chose to consummate the most remarkable relationship of his whole life was—Glasgow.

What precisely overtook him no one knows, but that he did experience an emotional stirring which presently grew into a

[1] A. I. Tobin and E. Gertz, *Frank Harris*, p. 139 (Madelaine Mendelsohn, 1931),

CHAPTER NINE

WHEN Harris first set eyes on Oscar Wilde, he saw a big, overdressed man with a feminine face and flabby hands. His first reaction was one of distaste, but Wilde's charm and wit, his ability to talk the night, and if necessary the following day, away, quickly changed Harris' mind. Harris, in turn, seemed, at first sight to Wilde, a rather ugly little man but he, too, was quickly carried away by the sheer power of Harris' story telling. Within a few months Wilde claimed that Harris could tell a story better than Kipling himself, 'with far higher themes, illumined by sudden flashes of poetry and humour.'[1] Over the next few years Wilde and Harris met, dined and talked, and two brilliant conversationalists extended their powers to the delight of the great houses they visited.

In the early days, it continually galled Harris that having worked his way up the social scale and made himself acceptable by sheer force of personality, time and again he strode into beautiful drawing-rooms only to find Oscar Wilde already ensconced on the hearth-rug with all the ease and charm which Harris lacked. All his life, Harris coveted and never achieved the skill he saw displayed evening after evening when Wilde effortlessly established himself in a new group by the sheer grace of his presence. As Shaw wrote: '. . . the trouble with Frank was not his dramatization and imaginary conversations, which were all in the classic literary tradition, but his appalling and ruthless candor delivered in a voice which filled the largest theatres and dominated the noisiest dinner parties. It

[1] Hugh Kingsmill, *Frank Harris*, p. 98 (Jonathan Cape, 1932).

was part of his unsuspected naïveté that he never knew and never learnt how much dissimulation is needed to make good society work smoothly; and it was this that finally made him impossible in any but the most Bohemian circles of London, though the best people had been quite ready to lionize him. . . .

'It was a rule at that time that you must not say anything to a young unmarried lady that could bring a blush to her cheek; yet Harris assumed, in perfect good faith, that every young woman over fifteen knew the tales of Maupassant by heart; was as open to the discussion of sex in all its aspects as Mr. Havelock Ellis; and had a portfolio of the etchings of Felicien Rops on her bedroom bookshelf. . . .'

What precisely sparked between Harris and Wilde it is difficult to determine, but walking away at night from big houses, they must have made the oddest pair; Wilde towering over Harris with his fur-collared coat reaching almost to his ankles, his cane held forward in his hand, and his big head inclined down towards Harris who always refused to look up. It is said that, on one occasion walking thus, they talked simultaneously for five minutes, oblivious of what the other said, and parted with mutual compliments on the dazzling effect of their respective performances. In their different ways they not merely saw through one another, but gloried in each fresh insight which provided vivid raw material for talk. Harris discovered and touched the softness at the core of Wilde, a softness which he knew could easily become rotten, and Wilde regarded Harris as a man without feeling to be treated as such. But they sparked on one another and a whole torrent of talk poured away.

It was some time after they had become intimate, that Wilde made his fatal mistake of taking proceedings against the Marquis of Queensbury and Harris immediately warned him of the disaster he invited. Far better, he said, to ignore the Marquis or pack his bags and leave the country to stew in its own puritanical juice. Harris exerted all his powers to get Wilde to leave the country and although, as Wilde said, no one could be more persuasive than the amoral Harris, it did not work.

As everyone knows, Wilde was tried for homosexual offences.

He made heroic gestures in court and languidly dispensed witticisms which did not please the judge. After the second day's proceedings Harris talked to him in a quiet corner of Queen's Gate, and dramatically revealed that he had a steam yacht ready waiting down the Thames, to smuggle him out of the country. Wilde, very pale, with great shadows under his eyes, was for a moment speechless; then, according to Harris, he said: 'How wonderful; but how impossible!' [1] Was it because he saw himself now as a necessary martyr to a cause which would lose whatever luster it had if he fled away to France? Was it, as Harris suggested, because plainly and simply, events had paralyzed his will power and he had lost his nerve? Or was it that this most dramatic scheme of Harris' invited even worse dangers than those he now faced?

Shaw treated the story with considerable scepticism and wrote: 'The whole episode leaves such a strong impression of Wilde's immovable despair during the ordeal . . . that even as fiction it would justify itself artistically. . . .'

He added: 'The truth is that Harris lost his head over the affair much more completely than Wilde, who did not lose his head at all. Harris raged at the cruelty of the law, the savagery of the sexually excited mob, the Press hue and cry against "the man Wilde" now that the journalists whom he had snubbed had got him down and could kick him with impunity. . . . In transports . . . he fills page after page with denunciations of judge and jury, of the entire British nation, and finally of pseudo-Christian civilization. He was amazed because Wilde would not rise up and echo his thunders; so abject an extremity of impugnacity he could not understand. All this was buccaneering faith. Wilde was right: he knew he was doomed and must go through with it, or else break his bail and run away, a course, as his silly brother put it, not open to an Irish gentleman. . . .' [2]

The day came when Mr. Justice Wills addressed the prisoners in the dock. 'Oscar Wilde and Alfred Taylor, the crime of which you have been convicted is so bad that one has to put

[1] Frank Harris, *Oscar Wilde, His Life and Confessions*, p. 202 (The Author, 1916).
[2] Frank Harris, *Oscar Wilde, His Life and Confessions*, Preface by G. B. Shaw, pp. xxiii–xxiv (The Author, 1918).

stern restraint upon oneself. . . . People who can do these things must be dead to all sense of shame. . . . It is the worst case I have ever tried. . . . That you Wilde have been the center of a circle of extensive corruption of the most hideous kind among young men it is impossible to doubt.

'I shall, under such circumstances, be expected to pass the severest sentence that the law allows. In my judgment it is totally inadequate for such a case as this. . . . The sentence of this Court is that each of you be imprisoned and kept to hard labor for two years. . . .'

Harris never forgot Wilde rising up to cry out: 'Can I say anything, my Lord?' and Mr. Justice Wills waving him aside as hisses and boos came down from the public gallery.

Prison dealt harshly with Wilde and his descriptions of its effect upon a man accustomed to the subtlest pleasures, were moving. Harris tried to organize a petition for his release, but the response from well-known writers of the day was small and after a time he went, instead, to see the head of the Prison Commission, Sir Evelyn Ruggles-Brise. Astonishingly, Ruggles-Brise was sympathetic and permitted Harris to visit Wilde in prison. He brought back such an appalling account of Wilde's condition and hardships that Ruggles-Brise had the prison governor changed and the remainder of the sentence was served in more enlightened circumstances.

Harris went a second time to visit Wilde, towards the end of his sentence. According to Wilde, at one point in the interview, Harris produced his cheque book, said that he had made a lot of money—£23,000—in South Africa, and promised Wilde a cheque for £500. Wilde was very deeply moved by such generosity and loyalty, but two days later a message came from Harris saying that unfortunately he could not, after all, send the cheque. Wilde wrote from Reading Gaol on April 12th, 1897, to More Adey: 'Would you kindly write to him [Harris] that you gave me his message and that I was a good deal distressed as I had unfortunately received similar messages. I loathe the promise-makers. I could be humble and grateful to a beggar who gave me half of the crust out of his wallet, but the rich, the ostentatious, the false rich ask one to a rich banquet and then when one is hungry and in want shut the door of

98

house and heart against one and tell one to go elsewhere—I have nothing but contempt for them, the Frank Harrises of life are a dreadful type. I hope to see no more of them.'

The wish was doomed to contradiction. An editorial note in the *Saturday Review* of November 26th, 1898, said: 'Our readers will hear with regret that Mr. Frank Harris has been compelled, owing to ill-health, to sever his connection with the *Saturday Review* and to resign the editorship. The *Saturday Review* has had many brilliant pens at its disposal but seldom one as brilliant as that of our retiring editor. We hope that a better climate will restore him to health and that he will then write some of those stories which we have long expected from the author of *Elder Conklin*. . . .'

'Ill-health' was a costly affair to the new proprietors of the *Saturday*. According to Tobin and Gertz, Harris sold the *Saturday* for £40,000 to Lord Hardwicke, and even if the sum is divided by two it still left him wealthy on a scale he had never known before. The sale did not escape that element of manipulation now becoming characteristic of Harris' financial dealings. When Hardwicke thought he had completed the transaction, he suddenly discovered that Harris still held 500 deferred shares which 'gave him control of the editorship and staff of the paper'. Harris then demanded a sum—said to be £10,000—for the remaining shares, and all Hardwicke's bluster and threats of exposure, completely failed to move him; there was no alternative but to pay. Free from the *Saturday*, rich in a new way and uncertain of the next step in his already richly complicated career, Harris had far greater leisure to attend to Wilde.

* * * * *

H. G. Wells remarked that England, in his time, was subject to adventurous outsiders like Bottomley, Birkenhead, Ramsay MacDonald and Loewenstein, Shaw and Zaharoff '. . . men with no legitimate and predetermined roles, men who . . . behaved at all levels of behaviour but whose common characteristic [was] to fly across the social confusion quite unaccountably, scattering a train of interrogations in their wake. . . . Whatever else they are they are not dull or formal. They quicken, if it is only quickening to destroy. Harris was certainly a superlative example of the outside adventurer. He was altogether meteoric. . . .' [1]

It was the belief of several people who knew them well that Harris, in defending Wilde, merely represented one outsider defending another. Harris was not homosexual, but affairs, like that of Lisette, had carried him into a world of sexual abandon where he, too, came within reach of the law.

It was in Paris that he met Lisette, the twelve-year-old adopted daughter of a Frenchwoman, who became his mistress. Brought up within her step-mother's milieu, she seems to have broadened her view of men with remarkable rapidity. A lovely, lissom young girl, she was blossoming into womanhood in a way which inspired a descriptive delicacy in Harris, alongside insane passion. One set his pen flowing to compare her with the slender perfection of a Tanagra statuette, the other parched his mouth and set the pulses beating in his temples. What followed cannot be recorded in detail. Suffice it to say that he came to the girl's room one day and she did not repulse his caresses. A combination of reverence in the presence of her beautiful and unrealized body and unbridled passion, drove him into the act of *cunilingus* which, if Harris's words mean anything—and in matters of passion he tended to be much more reliable—met with considerable response.

Psychologically, it is commonplace that some grown men should be sexually attracted by girls scarcely out of puberty, but few go beyond attraction. Harris was in the habit of arguing that if fear restrained them, he did not regard fear as a very inspiring motive in conduct. Fear of disgrace, of social retaliation, of what other people thought, merely revealed a weak personality incapable of formulating its own principles. If this could be seen as a clear piece of rationalization, there were, in his illicit liaison with Lisette, elements of aesthetic joy which removed it from common lust.

Just precisely when Lisette came into his life it is difficult to establish, but within a few weeks she had gone again; Harris temporarily forgot her and a steady accumulation of fresh and adult mistresses took him deeper and deeper into that palace

[1] H. G. Wells, *Experiment in Autobiography*, p. 522 (Gollancz and Cresset Press, 1934).

of sensuality where erotic skills were brought to their highest pitch. Very aware of himself flaunting the conventions, if not the law, it was not unexpected that Harris should defend Wilde.

None the less, when Wilde came out of jail and left England for France, at first his hatred of Harris persisted. 'Frank Harris has sent me nothing,' he wrote to Robert Ross in May of 1898. One month later Harris arrived in Paris from London, and became a punctilious host to Wilde, who presently addressed Ross in quite different terms: 'Frank has been most kind and nice, and, of course, we have dined and lunched every day at Durano's. . . . Frank insists on my being always at high intellectual pressure. It is most exhausting. But when we arrive at Napoule I am going to break the news to him, now an open secret, that I have softening of the brain, and cannot always be a genius.' It was to Harris that Wilde dedicated his play *The Ideal Husband* with the words: 'A slight tribute to his power and distinction as an artist, his chivalry and nobility as a friend.'

Clearly Harris, at this period, behaved very well towards Wilde. Confronted by a man whose name carried the most terrible stigma, an impoverished man, abandoned by most of his friends and without any power to benefit Harris, he spent liberally of time, money and talk in a supreme effort to lift Wilde back on the rails again. Early in 1899 Harris repeatedly encouraged him to write. They would go together to the Riviera, he said, and Wilde would be free, in the midst of café life, to write at leisure. His least word would be swallowed greedily by the waiting world, now that notoriety had reached that point where salacious tales circulated in the clubs of London, Paris, Berlin and New York.

It was useless. Idling beside the Mediterranean, Wilde presently combined real and imaginary decay, and the memory of the black hell which had been his life for so many intolerable months, made him snatch at every immediate pleasure. Sustained writing offered long-term rewards; but he could not wait. He had to drink deeply, to smoke, to talk, to idle as intensely as it was possible to idle, because at any moment the black curtain might descend again and this rich, warm reality vanish.

From Paris, Wilde wrote to Robert Ross: '. . . Frank Harris is very wonderful and really very good and sympathetic. He always comes two hours late for meals but in spite of that is delightful.'

There followed the extraordinary story of the play *Mr. and Mrs. Daventry*. The idea for the plot of *Mr. and Mrs. Daventry* was an old one to Wilde. He had conceived it some years before while working on the script of *The Importance of Being Earnest*, but catastrophe overwhelmed him before he could begin the actual writing. His prison sentence did something irreparable to him and after the completion of the *Ballad of Reading Gaol* he wrote to Robert Ross: 'I don't think I shall ever really write again. Something is killed in me. I feel no desire to write—I am unconscious of power. Of course my first year in prison destroyed me body and soul. It could not be otherwise.' [1]

So it happened that every attempt to write the play *Mr. and Mrs. Daventry* broke down. When Harris came into the picture, Wilde had already 'received an advance from George Alexander' for the plot. 'He was similarly able to raise money . . . from the American actress Mrs. Cora Brown Potter and several others, including Leonard Smithers who published the *Ballad of Reading Gaol* for Wilde.' [2] Presently the list of people who appeared to think that they had exclusive rights in the plot of of *Mr. and Mrs. Daventry* included a theatrical agent, Horace Sedgar, who suddenly announced that a new play would shortly be coming from Mr. Wilde. Infuriated, Wilde wrote: 'There is no truth in it . . . it is quite monstrous. My only chance is a play produced anonymously . . . otherwise that First Night would be a horror and people would find meanings in every phrase.' [3]

Unaware that anyone had paid Wilde a penny for *Mr. and Mrs. Daventry*, Harris now pressed him, over innumerable apéritifs, to make a fresh attempt at writing the play, damn the consequences and take whatever money he could from it. Wilde

[1] Wilde to Ross, August 16th, 1898, Clark MSS.

[2] Introduction by Montgomery Hyde to the first published edition of *Mr. and Mrs. Daventry* (Richards Press, 1957) from which some details of this account are taken.

[3] Wilde to Ross, February, 1899, Clark MSS.

repeated what he had told Robert Ross: he would never write again. He simply could not face his thoughts. After a long pause, Wilde then gently suggested to Harris that he might purchase the plot and try to write the play himself. [1]

First dismissing it with scorn—Harris never saw himself as a playwright—he quickly changed his mind and within a short time he proposed paying Wilde £50 down for the plot and £50 when Wilde had written the first act. Harris himself would then write the remaining three acts. Whether he thought he could imitate Wilde's style and wit, given the first act as a model, or whether he simply intended using it as a bait to lure people into the theatre remains obscure. Whatever the truth, the play came at an awkward time for Harris. He was already at work on a book which he intended should revolutionize Shakespearian criticism, and Wilde presently wrote to Ross: 'Frank Harris is upstairs, thinking about Shakespeare at the top of his voice—I am earnestly idling.'

Convinced that he had bought the rights in the plot, Harris decided to abandon Shakespeare in favour of *Mr. and Mrs. Daventry*. He returned to London and with no attempt to master the technicalities of the theatre, plunged into a white-hot burst of writing which produced, in remarkably short time, a second, third and fourth act.

Lord Alfred Douglas gives a very different picture of the beginning of this collaboration. 'One day, in Paris, at lunch at Durand's,' he wrote, 'when I was present, Harris said to him [Wilde] "Look here, Oscar, you will never write this play; you say yourself that you will never be able to do it. Why not let me write the play and get it produced in London and we will go fifty-fifty in the profits?"'

'After a great deal of discussion Oscar agreed, the real deciding consideration being that Harris gave him fifty pounds as "advance royalties" on the play. In those days poor Oscar would do anything for fifty pounds.' [2]

Whatever the truth of the matter, when none other than Mrs. Patrick Campbell was persuaded to read the three acts

[1] The plot was, anyway, derivative from a scene in Sheridan's *School for Scandal*.

[2] Lord Alfred Douglas, *Without Apology*, pp. 64–74 (Martin Secker, 1929).

which Harris had written, she said that she liked them and urged Harris to complete the play himself, without any further attempt at collaboration. According to Harris, when Wilde in turn had read the draft of the three acts, he was furious and informed him that he had not only stolen his play but wrecked it. Harris quietly wrote the first act himself and sent the completed play to Mrs. Patrick Campbell.

Mr. and Mrs. Daventry went into production. Inevitably Mrs. Campbell played Mrs. Daventry, Frederick Kerr was cast for Mr. Daventry, a young and quite unknown actor, Gerald Du Maurier, became Ashurst, and another person, whose name was to become a household word, George Arliss, the Irish servant. Trouble began when the play was publicly announced. Letters came flocking in from all those people indisputably the sole copyright owners of *Mr. and Mrs. Daventry*, and within a very few posts the list had developed to farcical lengths. Words flew between Mrs. Patrick Campbell and Harris. This was a stunning shock. What were they to do? One by one they met the claimants and a riotous extravaganza of bargaining, quarrels, and the piecemeal payment of compensation began.

Wittily in character, when Harris wrote protesting to Wilde and refused to pay the remaining £150 (?) Wilde said that Harris had put him in an impossible situation. Without his interference Wilde could have continued selling the play at regular intervals to managers in every European country which had any pretence to a serious interest in the theatre. He wrote to Robert Ross: 'Frank has deprived me of my only source of income by taking a play on which I could have always raised £100.'

A letter from Lord Alfred Douglas to Wilde's biographer, Robert Sherard, dated many years after this affair, [1] said: 'Unfortunately I know it is true that poor Oscar did sell the scenario of *Mr. and Mrs. Daventry* to several different people, among them Smithers and Roberts. I was in the Café Royal with Harris when he met these two there by appointment, and they produced the scenarios with a letter from Oscar saying

[1] March 8th, 1937. Letters in possession of Montgomery Hyde, M.P. See his introduction to the first published version of the play.

he had sold it to them. Harris did actually pay them something (I think it was £50) before he put it on as his own piece. Oscar also sold it to others . . . Oscar would no doubt have paid back all the money he got from various people. . . .'

The first night of *Mr. and Mrs. Daventry*, October 25th, 1900, at last arrived. Huge bills outside the Royalty Theatre, Dean Street, London, announced, 'A New and Original Play in Four Acts by Frank Harris.' The first act clearly did not grip the audience as it should have done, but as the plot unfolded a full house settled down and a mixed reception greeted the final curtain. As the lights went up, Mrs. Patrick Campbell moved towards the footlights in a welter of sounds capable of several interpretations. The author, she said, was suffering from an attack of bronchitis but she would 'convey to him the favourable reception' they had given the play. Ribald interruptions, loud enough to dismay anyone but Mrs. Campbell, came from the back of the theatre. She repeated her words 'favourable reception' and added, bridling superbly, 'to Mr. Harris' clever play.' [1]

Seen through modern eyes *Mr. and Mrs. Daventry* was another mannered and melodramatic play, unmistakable the product of Wilde's imagination, but lacking his wit. A man of rank and fashion, Mr. Daventry has married a country girl, and then, in a moment of boredom, permits his house to be invaded by a group of fashionable, *fin de siècle* men and women. That evening, after dinner, a love scene develops between Lady X and Mr. Daventry. They agree to meet in the drawing-room when everyone has gone to bed but there, unknown to them, the innocent wife, Mrs. Daventry, has fallen asleep on the sofa. With the lamp low she remains unseen and witnesses their preliminary love-making. When the husband of Lady X comes hammering on the door hellbent for vengeance, Mrs. Daventry discloses her presence, opens the door and says: 'I'm afraid I have kept Lady X up too late.'

Gerald Lancing, once the injured wife's admirer, and now disclosed as still deeply in love with her, presently appears. Act III in Gerald's rooms, brings Mrs. Daventry to consult him about her husband's behavior and it is clear that she,

[1] *The Era*, October 27th, 1900.

too, loves him. With an alacrity somewhat alarming in an innocent wife, she agrees to go away with Gerald Lancing at precisely the moment when her own husband—well-schooled in creating dramatic tension—comes knocking on the door. She retires to another room while the remorseful Mr. Daventry pleads with Lancing to intervene with his wife on his behalf. Later, Lancing tries to persuade Mrs. Daventry to rejoin her husband, but she bluntly refuses and proclaims that 'all this self-sacrifice is wrong—We were meant to live,' a comment neatly crystallizing the way of life to which Harris had long committed himself.

Three months later, as Gerald Lancing and the ex-Mrs. Daventry sit reading *Frou-Frou*, it becomes clear that the time-less method of resolving quarrels between gentlemen has forced itself on Lancing and Daventry. A duel of the most honorable kind is imminent. As Mrs. Daventry's lover leaves, her husband enters and pleads with his wife to return to him. Nothing will induce her to do that, she says, and of the two men, she would prefer him to die. When he asks, in passion-ate anguish and on bended knees, why, his wife says: 'Because the father of my child must live!'

Only one denouement was permissible within the lofty code prescribed by Victorian ethics for erring but love-lorn hus-bands and without wasting more than a minute, the husband goes outside—delicately removing the horror from the eyes of his wife—and shoots himself.

In this welter of well-intentioned nonsense, Wilde laid it down that the passion of love must dominate everything, but whether Mrs. Patrick Campbell achieved this interpretation, is not clear. Twenty-five years later, when the play was broadcast as a radio drama, its contrived plot and stilted dialogue did not survive very well. Yet here was the extraordinary thing; approaching the subtle business of play-writing with a distaste for the theatre, and without training of any kind, Harris had written dialogue which might have come from the pen of a skilled playwright.

Most of the critics did not then think so. Clement Scott led the attack describing it as 'a drama of the dustbin' and W. L. Courtney expended a whole column in the *Daily Telegraph* on its destruction. 'Relieved of its talkiness and boiled down to its actual elements, *Mr. and Mrs. Daventry* is always thin, never forcible and frequently vulgar . . . what Mr. Harris has to tell us is vulgar in its very essence. . . . Why not call his play *The Adulterers* and hang the conventions?' *The Times* went further. Referring to the sofa scene it said, 'it goes as near to indecency as anything we remember on the contemporary stage.' *The Times* could not get over Harris' best witticism in the play: 'One touch of passion makes the whole world sin.'

Max Beerbohm saw the play very differently. He had taken over from Bernard Shaw as dramatic critic of the *Saturday Review* and now wrote on November 3rd, 1900: 'The character of Mr. Daventry is admirably drawn. It sets Mr. Harris very far above the level of ordinary dramatists and does much to atone for his faults of technique. . . . Mr. Harris is to be congratulated on a perfect essay in psychology. There are many other good things in the play. But the character of Mr. Daventry is the dominating feature of it, putting all others into the shade. . . .'

Characteristically indifferent to the explosions of the more august weeklies the public was not greatly bothered by the thunderings of its dramatic critics. Recovered, in twenty-four hours from what he described as bronchitis, Harris hurried round to see Mrs. Campbell and found her in despair. Not given to facile despairs himself and quite incapable of believing that his play had failed, Harris offered to defray the expenses she had incurred, whereupon Mrs. Campbell brightened visibly. The next night she threw herself into her part with new inspiration, and a play which should have withered under so much scorn, quickly showed signs of surviving.

Drawn by the very 'vice' which high-minded critics thought should damn the play, people continued to flock to the theatre night after night, some firmly under the impression that Harris had lent his name to a play by Oscar Wilde. If any suspicion remains about authorship, Shaw trenchantly declared his own opinion in the preface to the English edition of Harris' Life of Wilde. Some people, he said, appeared to be under the impression that Harris had not merely 'lifted' the plot of the play but a great deal of dialogue too: 'either [they] do not know chalk from cheese, which seems improbable, or else [they had] never read a single line of Daventry or seen it acted. If Oscar had written it, it would now be a classic.' [1]

The play became a success. The twentieth performance developed into the thirtieth. Soon the second month was entered and still the theatre remained crowded. News of the play's success reached Oscar Wilde in France and he sent a number of what can only be described as 'begging letters', full of pathos. Impoverishment, pressing creditors and developing ill-health, had driven him into depths of depression. According to Harris, it was in the autumn of that year that he went to Paris and tried to get Wilde to see reason. A fresh sum was agreed between them—said to be £175—but when Harris met with nothing but studied abuse from Wilde, he paid £25, regretted that he had left his cheque book in England, and did not settle the remainder. Later a *Daily Chronicle* reporter succeeded in tracing Wilde to a small hotel on the Left Bank where he was living, to avoid enemies of all sorts, under the name of Sebastian Melmoth, and he talked freely of Frank Harris.

'The first part of the conversation on his side was a mixture of defiance and bitterness. . . . I did my best to console him and he suddenly burst into tears. I felt deeply moved as he told me the sad tale of blight and misery through which he had passed.' Wilde was a very sick man. He had fainted once in Wandsworth Gaol and falling to the ground, had damaged his ear. Pain in the ear had now become an agony and a strange purple rash had broken out to irritate him night and day. The doctors recommended a serious operation, and at last he 'decided to succumb to them'. Some weeks later, he wrote in November 1900, from the Hotel d'Alsace to Harris again: '. . . had you really forgotten your cheque book in London? It is difficult to imagine you living in Paris—in the style and luxury that you like and are accustomed to—without a cheque book! I don't suppose that you are like President Kruger and travel with bullion.'

'I have survived the operation and terrible five weeks of physical pain aggravated by mental anxiety . . . I owe about £180, the cost of my dreadful illness. It is due to doctors,

[1] Frank Harris, *Oscar Wilde, His Life and Confessions*, p.25 (The Author, 1916).

surgeons, chemists [and] the Hotel itself, whose bill will be enormous.'

Lord Alfred Douglas commented that Wilde, 'had nothing in writing from Harris, he was an ex-convict, an exile from England, utterly discredited and almost universally ostracized. He had no money except three pounds a week from his wife's estate and what I gave him . . . and he was thus at the mercy of Harris, who, being the vainest of men, was furious because Wilde said he had spoilt the play. Harris' answer to Wilde's protest was, in effect, 'the play is mine. *I* wrote it. You admit that you could not do it yourself. I changed and enormously improved it; it was I that got Mrs. Campbell to put it on, and you now say yourself that it is not *your* play and that I have ruined it. Well, if that is the line you take, I see no reason why I should give you any further share of the profits.' [1]

Presently Harris received a wire from Wilde's friend Reginald Turner. Wilde, it said, was seriously ill and in great need. Harris appears to have genuinely believed that this was so much bluff to blackmail him into sending more money. For the moment he dispatched his secretary Tom Bell to Paris to investigate the actual situation, and gave him money which was to be paid to Wilde and no one else on the understanding that Wilde had not become a hopeless alcoholic.

In Paris, before Bell arrived, Wilde had indeed reached a sorry state. The operation on his ear had not relieved the pain, the terrible purple rash had returned to trouble him and three doctors disagreed violently about the source of his troubles. [2] As the ravages of what was later discovered to be meningitis advanced, his wit did not desert him, and a moment after anguished expression of his suffering, he would drink a glass of champagne, provided by his sister-in-law, and say: 'I am dying, as I have lived, beyond my means.'

Soon they were giving injections of morphia to ease the pain, phases of delirium came and went, and sometimes he gripped his sweating face in his hands and tried to stop the pain in his head by sheer brute pressure.

When Bell at last arrived, on November 30th, he carried out

[1] Lord Alfred Douglas, *Without Apology*, pp. 67–68 (Martin Secker, 1929).

[2] Frank Harris, *Oscar Wilde, His Life and Confessions*, p. 365 (The Author, 1916).

Harris' instructions to enter the Hotel d'Alsace by a side door, met a chambermaid carrying a bundle of washing, and asked to be directed to Wilde's room.[1] She gaped at him for a moment and then muttered and pointed. Bell climbed the gloomy stairs, came to the room, saw the door open, and at once concluded that the bird had either flown again, driven off by his creditors, or was sufficiently well to be out drinking.

He looked into the room. It smelt vaguely, the light was very dim and he started suddenly as he saw a white coifed nun sitting beside the bed. His eye travelled to the wax tapers burning steadily in the heavy air and he knew then that the nun had been summoned to watch over the dead.[2] Wilde had died a few hours before his arrival.

[1] Introduction by Montgomery Hyde, M.P., to the first published edition of *Mr. and Mrs. Daventry* (Richards Press, 1957).
[2] Ibid.

CHAPTER TEN

Harris was now 45. Much plumper, the lines of his face had deepened and the mouth tightened. Still vigorous, thrusting, upright, a hint of duplicity was evident on the swarthy face. He would come striding into the office of some city business man, his great moustaches bristling, his emerald tie-stud a-glitter, his buckskin shoes flawlessly polished, his straw hat set at a rakish angle, and plough his way through any outer defences, scattering lesser staff in confusion. Tapping his stick on whatever object offered itself he then announced that he had AN APPOINTMENT. No exaggeration of print could convey the mighty assurance he put into that single sentence. Sometimes it was pure invention. Sometimes he simply burst his way into the presence of influential men who had failed to respond to more conventional advances, and proceeded to talk so forcefully and brilliantly that they were enthralled. But bursting his way in was not often necessary. He had perfected by the year 1900, an underground system of intelligence which kept him informed of financial movements ranging from the shady to the Napoleonic. Financial editors, stock-brokers, promoters, all the big and small fry crowding round the mysterious pools of the City, were now his cronies, but few of them came to their schemes with such magnificence as Harris. Time and again he sat, pensively listening, in some rich stock-broker's office, to schemes of great daring and originality, with the air of a lord.

In 1899 one of these schemes took the form of buying an hotel. Overtaken with the vainglory of the fortune for which he was said to have sold the *Saturday Review*, he simultaneously bought an art gallery and an hotel. For the art gallery, in London, he commissioned none other than Rodin to produce original sculptures, and sent the famous hotelier Cesari to Monte Carlo to establish the hotel. There was a grandiosity in everything he now did. He knew greatness when he met it, he could convey the Olympian moods of the world's most distinguished writers, and there were times when he stepped, himself, into another dimension where the services of great men were automatically at his disposal.

His hotel in the South of France offered a poor view and a not very distinguished address and the famous hotelier Cesari did some wild things to remedy these shortcomings. Intoxicated by grand gestures, Harris did not wait for success but plunged into yet another hotel venture. This time a company was formed to conduct a Rich Man's Reserve, a place where the rich could relax in the South of France. A number of distinguished men invested money in the enterprise. Once more Cesari was sent to put things in order and strode about like a Roman emperor ordering the most lavish furnishings. When inspired he was quite capable of knocking down whole walls to carry out reconstructions, and presently his activities alarmed even Harris who decided to send his secretary Bell off on another mission to discover exactly what was happening to the two hotel ventures. Breaking through a smoke-screen of evasions Bell at last discovered enormous bills waiting to be paid and telegraphed Harris, warning him of threatened disaster. Suddenly the temptation of the underworld proved too much for Harris and in a wild effort to retrieve a fortune which threatened to disappear in the illimitable sands of the South of France, he took the first decided plunge.

Lord Alfred Douglas was his first victim. He invited Douglas to invest £2,000 in the Cesari Reserve which was certain, he said, to yield rich profits once completed. Eloquent, forceful, with his slender scruples fast diminishing, Harris either found the game easily learnt or came to it with natural skill. He persuaded Douglas that he was buying £2,000 of surplus Reserve stock when he had in fact simply transferred certificates of that value from holdings of his own in the land on which the Reserve was built. In effect, he 'unloaded the stock', and legally the £2,000 became Harris' own money and not part of the company's capital.

Worse followed. It was one thing, by sleight of hand to bamboozle a lord into accepting 'false' stock, and quite another to visit the brother of Lord Alfred Douglas at his country home, get him slightly drunk and sell him, ostensibly, two thousand more shares in the same company. When these shares, in turn, were shown to belong to the doomed 'Palace' at Monte Carlo and not to the Rich Man's Reserve, the last pretence to decency had vanished. A combination of fear, audacity and skill in swindling had at last driven Harris over the edge.

A man who did nothing by halves, simultaneously he indulged some broad sexual tastes whenever he visited his property in the South of France as if he sought to forget his financial troubles in sexual abandon. Many stories were told of the 'orgies' which were said to have taken place: some are unprintable; some open to serious doubt. One example will illustrate the type of story which quickly came to circulate around his name. According to this, one hot summer evening the half-finished and very beautiful drawing-rooms of the Palace Hotel became the meeting place for a number of girls still in their teens, attracted by Harris' obvious wealth and power. One large room, lit by four crimson lamps placed on its floor, was carpetless, and a young girl, wearing the flimsiest clothing, turned the handle of the gramophone (for a fee of £10). A special drink, mixed at Harris' direction, was repeatedly served, and within an hour, whatever pretence to inhibition the company might have had, vanished. Four or five couples, including Harris, danced to the gramophone, but whenever the young woman in charge chose to stop, it was the signal for both men and girls to take off one item of clothing and to change partners. At twelve o'clock there was little left to remove and all permutation of partners had been exhausted. The party was said to have continued until three next morning.

Over the next year, as his taste in depravity developed, he chose younger and younger 'guests' until, once more, he almost came within reach of the law. The accounts of parties organized by his Italian gardener in the big villa which he next rented on the Italian Riviera, began with mild examples of young virgins still in their teens lured into beauty competitions which entailed undressing in separate bedrooms to be judged by Harris and his confederate. According to Harris, the number of young girls who were prepared to behave in a highly unconventional manner when they understood him to be a wealthy and influential man, multiplied. Soon, they were not merely disrobing, but responding to his caresses and quickly reaching that stage of emancipation where they indignantly proclaimed themselves the possessors of organs more suited to love than their rivals.

It is worth noting, among the riot of sexual adventures to which Harris confessed in his Autobiography, that he scrupulously avoids the smallest deviation from the normal, which would, in itself be abnormal; yet the long recital of girls and women seduced, the details of *fellatio* and *cunilingus*, the statistical examination of orgiastic performance and the minute description of the response of male and female, are not in themselves remarkable. If the multiplication of mistresses and a surrender to straightforward lust characterized many years of Harris' life, it is not unknown in the lives of others.

By 1900 the increasing threat of financial disaster seriously interfered with his pleasures. As Harris' bank balance dwindled, no amount of manipulation could presently prevent the white elephants in the South of France from trampling him down. A change came over him. His arrogance and bluster began to falter and he was overtaken with new fears. All his life he never quite mastered the fear that one day he would be hungry, penniless and unwanted as he had been ugly, isolated and abused as a child. Early conditioning still dominated his life, and exaggerated fears played no small part in pushing him over the edge into the first petty swindles. As he struggled now with creditors, wrote innumerable letters, and devised wilder and wilder schemes to save himself from disaster, there were nights when he did not sleep from sheer anxiety.

His wife could not escape the stresses and strains. The beautiful Nellie O'Hara had long ago discovered the real nature of the man she had married. So far as I can trace she knew nothing of the early swindling, but when she heard, one day, that he had written a cheque for the last £8 in the bank it came as a terrible shock. Yet, near despair, with long streams of unintelligible complaints from France, and bankruptcy staring him in the face, Harris would suddenly rear up again and say to her with a dash of the old *braggadocio*, 'I have something—I have something tremendous. Don't look so anxious, Nellie old girl. This is going to make them sit up. A corporation with two million pounds capital—that's what I'm after.'[1]

Instead he became involved in a tainted little property called the *Candid Friend*. He suddenly decided that if only he could recover his journalistic power and glory he could retrieve his fortune, even if it meant demeaning himself for the moment to edit a weekly with the most inappropriate title. He came to the *Candid Friend* a tired, worried man, and revealed the first beginnings of that mixture of cunning and fear, which years later, so often looked out of his eyes. Mysteriously, he claimed that the *Candid Friend* was started to oppose the Boer War, but it seemed as much concerned with promoting the stock of dubious companies, and his close association with Catton, a notorious company promoter, produced some odd advertisements.

It could not last. Expediency of this kind contained the seeds of its own destruction. And now began a run of small and doubtful papers, each one part of a desperate plan to regain power and influence. It was at this time that 'one in a position to know' wrote: 'The vilest thing in connection with Harris is not the fact that he robs his friends. It is that after having robbed them, he makes it a part of his policy to attack them directly or indirectly so as to cover up his rascality. The attacked one's cry then, about having been swindled, seems like an angry man's retaliation.'[2] Sometimes the attack was launched in the *Candid Friend* or another of the many small papers he consecutively edited. Even contributors were not safe from abuse. Harris would offer £12 for an article, allow months to go by without payment and when reminded of the debt, at once begin an elaborate haggle to settle for a third of the sum. Horace Wyndham one day asked Harris for 'something on account' for various articles and Harris snapped back, 'I print your stuff, don't I? What more do you want?'

[1] Verbal evidence from Hesketh Pearson.
[2] A. I. Tobin and E. Gertz, *Frank Harris*, p. 198 (Madelaine Mendelsohn, 1931).

Despite his bluff and self-deception, Harris was not happy to be lost among these small magazines and continued to play for bigger fish. He was not really interested in editing gossip sheets quite without influence, and his attempts to recover the glories of the *Fortnightly* presently included some correspondence with Winston Churchill. There are, in existence, eight letters from Churchill to Harris dated between July 22nd and November 27th, 1905, two written, three signed and three dictated. The first headed 'Private' begins, 'I must be in the H. of Commons on Tuesday; for the unexpected appears with its usual regularity. . . .' Sending Harris proofs of his biography, *Lord Randolph Churchill*, Winston Churchill says, 'Pray forgive me trespassing upon your leisure. I do so because I know your interest in my father's life has always been real and warm. . . . Please pencil whatever comments occur to you.' In the third letter dated September 22nd, 1905, it is apparent that he has been trying to help Harris to recover his lost prestige. He says that he has seen Harmsworth, the proprietor of the *Tribune*, 'and talked about your powers and gifts.' Astonishingly, the fourth letter (October 1st, 1905) authorizes Harris to negotiate with various publishers for the sale of Churchill's life of his father. It has since become clear that Harris not only met Churchill several times and impressed him, but sold the book to Macmillan for 'a higher price than I had expected'.

Churchill failed to re-establish him as the editor of a reputable weekly, but there was a brief excursion into *John Bull*. Inevitably the element of rascality in Frank Harris and Horatio Bottomley made them mutually attractive to one another, and when Bottomley launched *John Bull* he invited Harris to join the staff. Harris got to know Bottomley well, played a considerable part in planning the make-up and contents of the first issue of *John Bull*, and briefly even became its literary and dramatic critic; but this in turn could not last. Two such spirits were bound to quarrel, and presently they did.

Later, Harris was said to have blackmailed Bottomley as successfully as Bottomley blackmailed others. Passing Bottomley's house one day he observed a certain famous man leaving it and recalled that Bottomley had been attacking him in *John Bull*. Harris at once called on Bottomley, and told him that he required £500 of the hush money which the celebrity had just paid him, or he would make the whole thing public. Bottomley went to his safe, counted out the money and said as he paid it over: 'How did you know?'

Taking the money, Harris did not reply until he had reached the door. 'I didn't,' he said and closed it behind him.

If he had deliberately chosen to burlesque his own nature in the titles of the magazines he next edited he could not have done better. From the *Candid Friend* (1901–1902) Harris moved to *Vanity Fair* (1907–10) and from *Vanity Fair* to *Hearth and Home* (1911–1912). Bernard Shaw was ribald about *Hearth and Home*. He simply could not visualize Harris editing such a paper, and even Harris did not dare to tamper with some of its regular features. Under his editorship the Health and Beauty page still had 'Dame Deborah Primrose' assuring 'Moorland Nymph' that too prominent a bust was not quite in the best taste; the Jabberwocky Guild still welcomed new members with the qualification that they must be ladies; 'Miss Dowdy' was told by 'Betty Modish' that skirts were long and drab in circles which she had little chance of frequenting; and a mysterious letter from a reader called Delia was answered with the reassurance that a man could never truly love but once. The scattered correspondents in remote homes who conducted these columns and circles would sometimes converge on the offices of *Hearth and Home* to discover an ogre sitting in the editorial chair, quite liable to roar out, 'there's only one use for a woman—get out of here before I show you.'

From *Hearth and Home*, Harris went to another small paper called *Modern Society*. Enid Bagnold worked with Harris on *Modern Society* and she has given me a vivid picture of what life was like on the paper. 'Its offices were an upstairs and down-stairs room in King Street, Covent Garden. From here [Harris] spun his schemes and crossing to the Savoy for lunch talked in his tremendous voice heard over seven tables . . . to Bottomley, Dan Rider, Katherine Mansfield, Hugh Lunn and sometimes to me. Hugh Lunn, who later became Hugh Kingsmill, and I, were the bulk of the staff of the paper. But there was also a slim girl who did the advertisements and strange men came in and out.

'We had a great *schwärmerei* for Frank Harris which would come like measles and go as completely . . . He was an extraordinary man. He had an appetite for great things and could transmit the sense of them. He was more like an actor than a man of heart. He could simulate everything. While he felt admiration he acted it and while he acted it he felt it, and "greatness" being his big part he hunted the centuries for it, spotting it in literature, poetry, passion and acting. . . .' [1]

Office life brimmed with drama. One day the bailiffs arrived and clattered upstairs while Frank Harris' cherished possessions were romantically lowered away to safety by rope. 'I was there but I can't remember whether into the street . . . or whether there was a window opening out at the back.' [2]

Returned to normal, within a few days a man called Lemoine would appear in the office, wander about suspiciously, waiting for Frank, and suddenly reveal to the astonishment of the entire staff that his pockets were full of diamonds. Some mysterious lottery was conducted by Harris in the teeth of the police, under the guise of *Modern Society*, and one evening Enid Bagnold challenged a seedy looking individual hovering about the office who said that he was the man who spent his nights posting letters in different pillar boxes. 'It seems the police spot it,' he said, 'when too many letters go into one box.'

Methods of filling the paper with copy varied from blunt lifting to subtler forms of plagiarism. At Harris' suggestion Enid Bagnold 'wrote' the weekly story by the simple method of 'translating a Maupassant and incompletely disguising it. . . . I also did the cookery article lifted from a French magazine. . . . When it came to tracing the legs from *La Vie Parisienne* and attaching them to bodies from a different page, my father ordered me home, but it was then that Frank Harris went to prison and my father . . . was too generous a man to force an issue at a moment of disaster. . . .' [3]

[1] Herman Ould (Editor). *The Book of the P.E.N.*, p. 14. 'The Poster Episode', Enid Bagnold.

[2] Ibid.

[3] Ibid, p. 15.

118

Prison, a humiliation he never forgot, overtook Frank Harris in this way. A Mr. Leslie-Melville had launched a divorce suit against his wife naming two co-respondents, one of them Lord Fitzwilliam. Harris commented on the case in *Modern Society*, and Lord Fitzwilliam at once took action claiming that the article was liable to prejudice his case in the eyes of the law and public. Two versions of what followed revealed Harris bringing his powers of invention to an even riper pitch.

'One day,' Harris told Tobin and Gertz, his American biographers, 'I got a letter from the office asking me to come back to London at once, as someone had brought a suit of libel against me . . . I was served with a summons to appear before Mr. Justice Horridge.' With that brassy *savoire-faire* which served him well on such occasions, Harris explained to Mr. Justice Horridge that he had been away when the article was published and could hardly be held responsible for it. 'The mere fact that you were away at the time doesn't relieve you from responsibility . . .' Mr. Justice Horridge said. 'Well,' commented Harris, 'not entirely. I was still responsible for its finances.' Mr. Justice Horridge looked at him sharply. 'I hope you are not trying to teach this Court a question of law,' he said. Harris shrugged his shoulders and Mr. Justice Horridge continued: 'It seems to me that you have a certain disdain for this Court.' Harris promptly agreed that he had. There was a long pause and then the Judge quietly asked for an apology ' . . . but this I refused to give and was sent to prison.'

So much for Harris' story. The facts are these. When Harris consulted his counsel Cecil Hayes, he was warned not to abuse the courtesies of the Court. He then filed an affidavit which did not include an apology. In court, Harris offered to apologize, but the offer was rejected, and Harris thereupon went to prison.

It came as a terrible shock. He just could not believe that any-one would dare to attempt to restrain the person of the Great Frank in a place of confinement, but once the prison door was locked behind him, it dawned on him that this would go on, and suddenly he was overtaken with an appalling fit of rage. He raved, he beat the door of his cell and threatened to bring down such vengeance on the heads of his persecutors that one of the jailers confessed to having his blood curdled; but it was all useless.

It is easy to understand how Mrs. Nellie Harris, infected by her husband's lying, and anxious to defend him, romantically recalled what happened next. 'Yes,' she told Gertz, 'I used to visit Frank every day and so managed to feed him. Through some friends I know I got him transferred to the infirmary. That's where Frank spent most of his stay in prison. As you can imagine, I tried to see everyone of importance to help Frank out. Max Beerbohm visited Frank in prison and then drew his famous cartoon, "The Best Talker in London—with one of his best listeners." It showed Frank at one side of a table talking, and Max on the other side, listening intently —with a bottle of wine between them. Max gave it to me on the promise that I wouldn't show it to anyone. But Frank's freedom meant more to me than my promise to Beerbohm, so I had prints made . . . and had them posted all over London with the heading, "This is the man that was sent to prison." That cartoon and my seeing some people of influence got Frank out of prison.' [1]

Enid Bagnold's testimony reads very differently When Frank was taken off to prison she had been left with full responsibility for *Modern Society*. In near despair she combed the pigeon holes marked 'We want to know', 'Stories' and 'Little Bird Larder' where spicy bits hung waiting on various hooks. A handful of copy promised quick exhaustion and simultaneously came a message from Frank saying that the magazine must be kept on the bookstalls or it would lose its licence. In a burst of inspiration, Enid Bagnold wrote off to Bernard Shaw, Max Beerbohm, Haldane McFall and others, explaining the emergency and asking if they would please help to fill the next issue of the paper. Given a generous response from everyone, she still reckoned that blank pages would remain, but she decided that they would 'just have to remain blank'. Shaw said something handsome about Harris in his reply, regretted his inability to supply any copy and added, 'you can't put an elephant to hatch hen's eggs.' (Harris hurriedly carried off this postcard as soon as he was in a position to worry about such matters again.) Max Beerbohm rallied magnificently and produced the

[1] A. I. Tobin and E. Gertz, *Frank Harris*, pp. 184-5. (Madelaine Mendelsohn, 1931).

120

drawing which Nellie said became her property. In fact it was sent to Enid Bagnold 'on the solemn promise' that it should never be used either as a cover or poster, and by special arrangement with Brixton Goal, Enid Bagnold carried off this drawing, her 'personal triumph', to her editor. A subdued and somewhat shabby Frank Harris 'was brought at a smart pace across the prison yard' to a glass room where, over a wooden table, he plunged into questions about the paper, the outside world and the Max Beerbohm drawing. When he heard Beerbohm's stipulation, he did not 'seem pleased with either Max or me', but promised that the restriction would be faithfully observed. Within twenty-four hours the young girl who represented the 'Advertising Department' of *Modern Society*, visited the prison and received instructions to 'go it strong on publicity' with Beerbohm's drawing, and damnation take these fancy promises.

Two days later, Enid Bagnold hurried towards the office to discover a single horse-cart drawn up outside and a man delivering many rolls of posters, each one plastered with Beerbohm's cartoon. A young woman of integrity, not long since plunged into the iniquities of Frank Harris' world, she shuddered to think what Max would say when he idled one day from his discreet door and noticed on a hoarding this considerable sample of his own work.

As Enid Bagnold picked up the telephone directory her hand shook with rage. Presently she drove furiously in a cab to his house, rang the doorbell and sent up an urgent message via the maid. Still not dressed, the gracious figure with the porcelain forehead, came down 'in a wonderful dressing gown,' and listened, his 'two very blue eyes . . . serious with anger.' Seeing how genuinely distressed she was, he dressed quickly and hurried out beside her, carrying a beautiful cane with a loop at the handle. They drove back to the office, examined the poster, dragged the roll into a cab and hurried round to the printers. There, with some difficulty, they managed to commandeer the block. Twenty minutes later, they walked down the Savoy steps to the river, threw plate and posters wholesale into the black water, watched the block disappear and saw the posters unroll and begin to submerge. As a gracious gesture

Max finally presented Enid Bagnold with the original drawing, and there, in her dining-room, it hangs to this day, to the confusion of Nellie's story.

Meanwhile, strange things happened to Frank Harris in prison. It was almost as if the failure to challenge and over-whelm the law drove him beyond even his exaggerated re-actions. 'Years ago,' he kept repeating to himself, 'they would never have dared send me to prison.' [1] In his cold cell in the grey world of Brixton Prison, a man cut off from the company and conviviality which was his life blood, the blunt, down to earth Harris dissolved, and he began to have delusions that he was a prophet who had a message to deliver. It all happened with alarming rapidity, reason so quickly merging into bouts of delusion. Within a few weeks . . . 'He drew parallels between himself and the Divine One, who was crucified at Calvary. "I am being punished that I may teach more efficaciously," he said. It was then that the words of Jesus began to take on a personal note. They became his words too, and constantly they flowed from his lips, infecting him with what were vir-tually Messianic illusions . . . "Father, forgive them for they know not what they do!" he sometimes cried.' [2] Presently there were times when his jailers wondered whether he was quite right in the head.

It was an extraordinary interlude. It pointed to a state of paranoia, brought about in part by early conditioning, in part by his failure to become the great man he believed himself to be. If he could not win proper recognition in the real world, he would win it in the world of fantasy.

Not unexpectedl,, the return to the harsh realities of the outer world, where his reputation had suffered even in the eyes of his more iniquitous confederates, did not sustain the grey, unshaven Frank Harris on the heights which imagination had granted him, and in the first few hours of freedom the shock reduced a man, whose spirit was nourished on thundering cascades of words, to near silence.

[1] A. I. Tobin and E. Gertz, *Frank Harris* (Madelaine Mendelsohn, 1931).
[2] Ibid p. 187.

CHAPTER ELEVEN

I<small>N</small> these mature years there were two writers who came to know Frank Harris very well indeed—Hugh Kingsmill and Middleton Murry.[1] Hugh Kingsmill had arranged to meet Harris in the vestibule of the Café Royal one day in the summer of 1909. Arriving late, he observed a man of less than middle height pacing up and down, but his bowler hat, braided overcoat and general bearing were 'so unlike my idea of a bitter, impoverished genius and so near the conventional notion of a Jew financier that I walked past him'. Later Harris took Kingsmill to the Savoy and they had not been seated more than a few minutes when Harris rumbled in a deep whisper, 'Would you change places with me? There's a South African millionaire behind you whom I whipped once in one of my papers. I can't enjoy my lunch if I have to look at him.' [2]

Harris was then living at Roehampton. Kingsmill drove out one evening and Richard Middleton, the poet, joined them to walk across Wimbledon Common. Harris had helped Middleton and genuinely liked him, perhaps because they shared the same sensuality. In a melancholy sing-song voice Middleton said that the Common was a wonderful hunting ground for girls. 'I passed two the other day . . . They could not have been more than twelve . . . I heard one say to the other, "that's Mr. Richard Middleton the poet. 'E ain't 'alf 'ot".'[3]

A few minutes later they approached two girls still in their

[1] I was fortunate enough to receive considerable help from Middleton Murry only a few months before Murry's death.

[2] Hugh Kingsmill, *Frank Harris*, p. 105 (Jonathan Cape, 1932).

[3] Ibid, p. 106.

teens. Harris raised his hat, half bowed and said, with considerably dignity, that he hoped they would be passing at the same time the following afternoon because he proposed bringing his motor-car and taking them for a drive. Tittering at first, his earnestness presently impressed them and they both agreed to the rendezvous.

Middleton Murry's first meeting with Harris was very different from Kingsmill's. In those pre-war years Dan Rider's bookshop, off St. Martin's Lane, London, was a meeting place for journalists, writers and painters and one day, 'to my mingled joy and alarm,' wrote Murry, '[Harris] came striding in and deigned to notice me, deferential and apprehensive . . . He referred with affable condescension to my "little magazine" which was sold in Dan's bookshop, and even hinted that he might not be unwilling to write something for it. Straightway I was hooked. The very next day I was taken off to lunch at the Café Royal, to be a rapt listener to his talk and his stories, and an admiring witness of his imperial manner with waiters and managers. When at the end he paid his bill by asking for a sheet of notepaper and writing on it something which (he explained to me) *made* a cheque for £20 and received £5 notes in his change, I was overawed.' [1]

Later, one afternoon in June 1912, Middleton Murry, Hugh Kingsmill and Harold Weston were waiting, once more in Dan Rider's bookshop, to introduce Harris to Katherine Mansfield. Suddenly there was 'a stir in the outer room of the shop, a movement of the air such as precedes an avalanche, and Frank Harris was with us.' [2]

He brandished in his hand the June number of Murry's paper *Rhythm* and burst out at once in his vibrating voice, 'Good God, Murry—what have you done!'

Murry, going pale, came to his feet, 'What is it, Frank—what . . .' Harris boomed across at him, 'Listen to this—listen all of you—"James Stephens is the greatest poet of our day . . . henceforward James Stephens stands with Sappho, Catullus, Shakespeare. . . ." Pah!'

'But, Frank . . .'

[1] Middleton Murry, *Between Two Worlds*, pp. 176–7 (Jonathan Cape, 1935).
[2] Hugh Kingsmill, *Frank Harris*, p. 10 (Jonathan Cape, 1932).

'You wrote this, eh?'

'Yes—but . . .'

Harris read out another quotation which, according to the article, was better than Milton. 'God's great fist!' he roared. 'And you call this better than Milton. You, Murry, wrote this drivel about *Paradise Lost*?'

Harris threw down the magazine and picked up the contents bill for the July issue. His great voice rumbled out the three titles:

'Who is the Man?

'Drawing.

'The Shirt.'

He threw down the bill with a laugh. 'Drawing of a man in a shirt, eh? By God, Murry, this paper of yours is going to make a stir.' [1]

Rabelaisian inspiration drove him to improvize on the man in the shirt until Murry suddenly burst into tears and fled from the shop. Harris swung round in amazement. Such sensitivity displayed publicly was outside his comprehension. Katherine Mansfield dashed after Murry crying, 'He'll kill himself.' Hugh Kingsmill explained to Harris that the lady who had set out in pursuit of Murry was Katherine Mansfield, and Harris at once exclaimed, 'Great God, why didn't you tell me?'

Harris then pressed two coins into Kingsmill's hand and told him to go and fetch them back at once because he was infinitely sorry, and wanted to make his apologies. 'Take a taxi both ways,' he said, 'both ways,' he repeated dropping his voice to its deepest note. Discovering the two coins in his hand to be pennies did not prevent Kingsmill from taking a taxi. Half an hour later a great reconciliation was carried out in that red plush, Victorian shrine, with its long marble tables and Bohemian company, where those still undeceived by Harris continued to worship him—the Café Royal.

Harris' skill as a talker was now phenomenal and his favorite haunt for the display of his powers was the Café Royal. Austin Harrison, editor of the *English Review*, told Gerald Cumberland in the Café Royal one day: 'Frank Harris is the most astounding creature! He will tell you a story and tell it so marvellously that, when he has finished you say to yourself, "That is the most wonderful thing I have ever heard," and you say to him,

[1] Hugh Kingsmill, *Frank Harris*, p. 12 (Jonathan Cape, 1932).

"Why in God's name don't you write that?" Well, he does write it, and when you read it you see that, after all, it is by no means so wonderful a thing as you had thought. . . .'

Cumberland himself wrote: 'In telling a story Harris is elliptical; a faint gesture serves for a sentence; a momentary silence, innuendo; a lifting of the eyebrows, a look, a dropping of the voice, a slowness in his speech—all these take the place of words. He is an exquisite actor and he is at his best when he is sinister and menacing.'

An exquisite actor. There it was again. What a wonderful life Harris might have led and how differently his character might have developed if he had not refused to compromise with that profession which seemed to him so distasteful. Perhaps it was his acting powers which made such a profound impression on so many people in the early 1900s. Whenever he chose, Harris could step into whichever role he thought would best please his listener. Shaw found the racy language, the great oaths, the explosive eloquence and the ability to quote from several European literatures in a voice like thunder, as refreshing and entertaining as a day at the sea; Harris' mistresses were overwhelmed by his low voice full of passion quoting Catullus or Rimbaud like the perfect lover; business men were quickly impressed by his drive, ruthlessness and power to argue any opponent under the table; and he could convert the philosophizing Harris, pouring out sonorous periods from the Bible with the air of a major prophet, into the sparkling journalist brimming with novel ideas and witty asides, in a trice. It was all a splendid one-man conjuring trick with the certainty that the next character emerging from the magic box would have the power to win Frank Harris another concession, privilege or mistress.

It could be said that this was one explanation of the lack of any principle in Harris' character. There was no core holding his different selves together. He was simply and supremely the very thing he did not want to be, an actor mesmerized by his own powers into an inescapable chain of highly successful masquerades. For the moment, among the many young writers who became his disciples, one other very simple explanation of his attraction remained—Frank Harris could, unquestionably, write. Middleton Murry found himself driven to comment in his paper, *Rhythm*, 'I knew and loved the work of Frank Harris long before I knew and loved the man. To me, two years ago, the name Frank Harris meant a prince of artists too great for the people among which he wrote . . . But now the name means a prince among men, a prince of talkers and critics, a prince of the lovers of life as well. It means a man whose word of praise can change the whole of life for me for months, and a word of condemnation makes me cry till I think my heart would break . . . Frank Harris is one of those great spirits whom I can but accept wholly, it may be even blindly, but with the security of knowledge that if I am mistaken, then life and art have no more meaning for me. . . .' [1]

Murry quickly regretted this outburst. His god was shattered one day in dramatic circumstances. Harris had written a short story, *An English Saint*, and sold it to the *English Review*. Murry, browsing through Stendhal, a wrapt disciple, gripped, if anything, more deeply by Stendhal than Harris, suddenly saw on the printed page certain details which carried a familiar ring. Familiarity became certainty in the next few minutes and with an appalling sense of shock, Murry suddenly knew the origin of Harris' story. 'I kept my discovery to myself but my attitude to Harris was changed in a moment.'

Another strand in the complicated web of duplicity which Harris was to spin, flashed for a moment to the surface and disappeared again. But Murry never entirely lost faith in Harris. Where others came to regard him as poison incarnate, Middleton Murry, Shaw, and, to a lesser extent Wells, never entirely abandoned him. Frankie, as Murry called him, might revile Murry's work in *Rhythm* and reveal himself as a not very subtle plagiarist, but thirty-five years later Murry could still write: 'I have it at heart to say candidly that Harris never treated me badly. On the contrary, he was generous to me; he once gave me, without my asking for it, ten pounds, which was a lot of money to me, and more to him in those his later days—I came afterwards to suspect—than the mere flea-bite he pretended it to be. And if I am told that this was done simply to impress me, I must answer that I do not altogether believe it. Harris

[1] Middleton Murry, *Between Two Worlds*, pp. 179–80 (Jonathan Cape, 1935).

could have impressed me at a cheaper rate. My finding is that there was a genuine streak of kindliness in Harris' nature.'

Murry's impression remained radically different from that of Hugh Kingsmill, but he believed Kingsmill's view to be the result of Harris' attempt to exploit Kingsmill's wealthy father. ('All wealthy fathers were legitimate prey to Harris.') Certainly, as Harris himself often put it, he was prepared to soak the rich bourgeois to help the poor artist, but all too frequently the poor artist seemed to stop short at Frank Harris. None of it destroyed Murry's belief in him. 'If I called him always to myself "the old ruffian" as I did, it was a term of affection. . . . Maybe it was because there was a bond of instinctive and unconscious sympathy between one social outcast and another; and, indeed I was always impressed by his bravery. It takes a man of courage to stand up to the social order as he did, with a gulf always yawning before his feet; and so far as I know he always stood alone. Therefore I respected him and I respected his aloof and beautiful wife for the way in which she kept her end up, and I respected Bernard Shaw for the way in which he stood by Harris. I think too that Mr. Kingsmill's clever book about Harris would have been a better one if it had been warmed with a little more sympathy. It exhibits Harris, but does not understand him. . . .' [1]

Does not understand him. Understanding Harris now plunged one into contradictory thickets as he zig-zagged away and left a steadily more confusing trail. Understanding him involved every complexity of insight, and it was possible to distil two or three classic patterns from his highly original behavior; but which came first? Did economic pressures drive him to outrage the conventions and finally the law in order to survive, or was it a deliberate choice springing from the deeper wellsprings of evil conviction? Did greed and the craving for power and wealth lead him to exploit every other situation which confronted him, or was it an attempt to satisfy Nellie's love of luxury? Deeper still, were the psychological demons of childhood still driving him into even more daring compulsions as though they constantly urged him—you can do it— you can live just as you please and escape with impunity? It was still early to know the answers.

[1] Middleton Murry, *Between Two Worlds*, p. 178 (Jonathan Cape, 1935).

CHAPTER TWELVE

I N the year 1908 Harris read the details of an outrage in America which inspired him to consider writing a novel to be called, very simply, *The Bomb*. A bomb had been thrown at a meeting which took place in Chicago in 1886, a meeting intended to protest against the brutality of the strike-breaking police. Excited by the whole episode and the idea of a book which would recapture the events leading up to it, Harris decided that he could only measure the true possibilities of the story if he went to the scene of the outrage himself. He thereupon rushed off to America to touch and see the raw material for his novel, and to talk to the people involved, for whom he had conceived a grim admiration. Arriving in New York, he claimed that he went from person to person piecing together the story, but there is some evidence to show that much of the material was gathered by agents. When he turned to the newspaper files he was appalled to find the trial a judicial farce. The anarchists claimed that the police had engineered the whole incident and had themselves thrown the bomb, killing seven policemen by mistake; the police claimed that the bomb came from the direction of a group of anarchists, and recalled the Pittsburgh Manifesto which demanded the 'destruction of the existing class rule *by all means* . . .' and the resolution 'Death to foes of the human race'. According to the newspaper reports, two anarchists had been hanged on November 11th, 1887, two received life sentences, one a sentence of fifteen years and one committed suicide in prison. Six years afterwards Governor Altgeldt publicly denounced the whole trial as a scandal and pardoned the surviving prisoners.

This was the story: superb material; Harris plunged into writing the book with all the gusto his enormously vital person could command. It did not in the least trouble him that as editor of the *Evening News* he had passed for publication a report which testified to 'the horrible character of these desperate fanatics'; they were now men who had carried his own revulsion against society to its ultimate conclusion and they exercised a powerful fascination on him. In the novel Harris gave his hero a love-life which proved too much for the printers, but even when, under pressure, he removed certain passages, Birmingham Library still banned the book. The love scenes were, in fact, sadly artificial and the real trouble with *The Bomb* had nothing to do with indecency. This was a first novel and as such a considerable feat. It brought New York alive, it revealed the terrible sufferings of foreign workers, it drew pictures of the exploited poor which were harrowing, and the tension of throwing the bomb arose from something more than the compulsions of the plot. One felt that the anarchists had every right to throw the bomb—and the book was alive enough to make the reader approach the climax with growing horror. The trouble, again, was not the bomb, the plot or the chief anarchist, who seemed convincing enough; it was the remaining characters. They were puppets jerking on the strings of a preconceived story, and the splendor of men prepared to go to their own death in one explosive gesture of total defiance, collapsed, so far as they were concerned, in dramatic tinsel.

In alliance with Birmingham Library the *New York Times* said '. . . chapters upon chapters of mere love-making reduced to its primal elements become ridiculous when not offensive.' [1] But the *Saturday Review* believed that Harris was 'a born writer of fiction. Mr. Harris has been so grudging to his mastery. . . . The book is a thoroughly fine piece of work, worthy of the creator of *Conklin*. We hope it is the precursor of many other books from Mr. Harris.' [2]

Harris sent a copy of *The Bomb* to Arnold Bennett in the hope of a review. Bennett wrote a complimentary reply: 'You know

[1] *New York Times*, February 27th, 1909.

[2] *Saturday Review*, November 28th, 1908.

as well as anyone what your work is, and you must be sure that anyone who can distinguish between literature and the other thing cannot fail to appreciate it very highly indeed.' Why didn't Harris run down to Fontainebleau to see him when next he visited France? he asked. 'There is no author in England whom I would more like to meet.' [1]

Bennett assumed that *Vanity Fair*—which Harris was then editing—had received a copy of *The Old Wives Tale*. 'It is extremely long. But I really should like to know what you think of it, and of its chances for 1958.' Harris duly replied on November 27th, 1908, with some prolonged comments on *The Old Wives Tale*. Having praised the book highly, he burst into a penetrating piece of criticism about Sophia.

Bennett wrote another letter on November 30th, 1908: 'My dear Harris, I am not at the opposite pole to you because I am at both poles. I quite agree with your fundamental criticism of *The Old Wives Tale*. That is to say I quite agree with it in certain moods. I am capable of regretting that Sophia developed as she did. My original intention was to make her a magnificent courtesan. But I altered this after due thought. At bottom I regard your attitude as flavoured with a youthful sentimentality. At bottom I am proudly content with the *Pentonville Omnibus*. Why not? If I cannot take a Pentonville omnibus and show it to be fine, then I am not a fully equipped artist. (And I am.) . . . What you wanted in reading *The Old Wives Tale* was another book but not a better one. To me the difference between one form of human life and another is insignificant. *It is all almost equally exciting.* . . . I shall be very much indebted to you if you will say in *Vanity Fair* exactly what you think of the novel. Go for it with all your fervour. If the article is as good as your letter it will be very good. But shove the article in at once or it will be commercially useless. . . . P.S. I need not say that I am relying on you to write, *soon*, another of those "dozen novels" which you have in you. A.B.' Harris replied on December 3rd. It was another example of his sycophantic skill in holding the interest of the great literary men of his day, and of his moments of critical insight; the first evident from his eulogistic description of Bennett's letter and the second from

[1] Reginald Pound, *Arnold Bennett*, p. 198 (Heinemann, 1952).

his wish—expressed with blasphemous vigor—that Bennett should have stuck to his first interpretation of Sophia as a splendid courtesan.

By December 13th, Bennett was writing: 'My dear Harris, . . . Every novelist (and dramatic poet) has his favourite characters which he draws over and over again. You know how often Wells has drawn his Kipps. My character is Critchlow in *The Old Wives Tale* . . . Yours is Shakespeare! Have you noticed this? . . .

'Your review of me is a most gorgeous affair and gave great joy. But I don't know anybody else that could have successfully carried it off at that pitch. What pleases me, of course, is that the writer of it was a man who knew what he was talking about. Nearly all the praise one gets is so infernally wrong and out of shape. As though the critic had arranged a nice little piece of praise and then dropped it in the street and let a motorcar run over it. Your choice of extracts did my heart good . . . I hope you will go on with the stories, and that we shall meet in March next. I want to have a whole series of yarns with you. I wish I had met you about fifteen years ago. Yours ever, Arnold Bennett.'

*   *   *   *   *

The Man Shakespeare appeared one year after *The Bomb*, in 1910, and was commonly said to be the biggest book that Harris ever wrote. Certainly it was alive, in a very unacademic way, savaged a number of dons and spoke grudgingly of one of their number who had undoubtedly inspired him. Two years before Harris wrote his first article on Shakespeare, Dr. Brandes had produced a study which set out to challenge the 'idea of Shakespeare's impersonality . . . to . . . prove that Shakespeare is not thirty-six plays and a few poems . . . but a man who felt and thought, rejoiced and suffered, brooded, dreamed and created.'

The Romantic Movement and the Victorians had, between them, depersonalized the author of the plays, one removing Shakespeare to remote marble halls, and the other denying any identity between the more passionate of his characters and Shakespeare himself. As Hugh Kingsmill pointed out in his very acute comment: 'Flaubert and Maupassant had familiarized France and Europe with the analysis of individual character, and in due course the method was applied to Shakespeare. . . .' [1] Harris came along to re-echo and develop the work of Brandes but he never seriously acknowledged his debt. His references to the eccentric Thomas Tyler were more generous and at least acknowledged Tyler to be the first person to identify Pembroke as the 'man right fair', but Harris never intended his Shakespeare to be a scholarly book.

There were two views of the possible nature of the greatest poet Britain had ever known. The first, represented in the work of Fripp, had seen him as the Perfect Husband faithfully matched with a good wife, a man of wisdom, balance and a divine gift of words; the second interpretation saw him as a wayward, melancholy fellow forced into an unsuitable marriage, running away to London, refusing to meet his wife's debts and eventually reducing her to the 'second-best bed'. [2] This was the view which Harris took, and indeed, to some extent pioneered, playing a considerable part in its development and popularization.

It was still a novelty in Shakespearean criticism in his day to find any detailed comparison between Shakespeare's own moods of melancholy and despair, and equivalent states in Macbeth, Richard II and Brutus, but if Shakespeare had continually represented himself in one character after another, Harris thought the portraits were idealized. He proposed to reconcile 'imperial intellect' and 'small snobberies', virtues and self-deceptions. [3]

He proceeded to show Shakespeare drawing his own portrait from the wayward young man to the mature poet, from the romantic to the sensualist, from the unhappy husband to the ageing person grown into wisdom. He took Thomas Tyler's work on the sonnets—which identified Mary Fitton as a Maid of Honor to Queen Elizabeth—and carried it over into the plays. The pale-skinned, black-haired beauty disclosed in the sonnets, Harris claimed to have traced under the name of

[1] Hugh Kingsmill, *Frank Harris*, p. 116 (Jonathan Cape, 1932).
[2] Ivor Brown, Shakespeare, pp. 61–2 (Collins, 1949).
[3] Frank Harris, *The Man Shakespeare and His Tragic Life Story*, p. xvii. (Frank Palmer, 1909).

Rosaline in *Romeo and Juliet*. Suddenly transferred from Verona to Navarre he next 'found' her under the same name in *Love's Labour Lost*. He showed Shakespeare allowing the artistic balance of *Love's Labour Lost* to be upset by 'strong personal feeling'. [1] Berowne in the play he believed to be Shakespeare himself and Rosaline the woman Berowne [Shakespeare] loved. This established what he thought to be a trustworthy rule. Whenever Shakespeare forced one of his characters into unconvincing behavior or gave him or her an emphasis false to the play itself, he was allowing personal experience to overwhelm art. This happened, he argued, with Rosaline. Shakespeare described her as 'a wanton to the detriment of the play'. [2] At root she was clearly Mary Fitton, Maid of Honor to Queen Elizabeth and the woman he loved.

Inevitably there were other implications in the book of a highly personal kind. There were moments when it was almost as if Harris managed to see himself in the Shakespeare accepted on sufferance by the aristocracy; to see, in the upstart without college training, the Harris first buffeted by hostile London; to find, in the man who made Mary Fitton his mistress, an abandoned passion like his own, and to claim that passion as a great forcing house for genius. He was incapable of not confusing himself, in some degree, with any great man about whom he now wrote. He also got some facts wrong.

The portrait that emerged of the young Shakespeare—hot, impatient and sensual—was not unconvincing, the fluctuations between admiration and envy did not entirely undermine the criticism in the book, and even today it remains stimulating reading.

In his day Harris' book on Shakespeare caused a considerable stir and the *New York Times* wrote: 'This is the book for which we have waited a life time. We know this now it is come and we mark the day of its publication as a red letter day in the history of literature.'

C. H. Herford saw the book very differently. *The Man Shakespeare*, he said, in the *Manchester Guardian*, was 'a disgrace

[1] Frank Harris, *The Man Shakespeare and His Tragic Life Story*, p. 225 (Frank Palmer, 1909).

[2] Ibid., p. 225.

to British scholarship'. Unable to let his critics get away with anything, Harris took the occasion of a lecture in Manchester, which had nothing whatever to do with Shakespeare, to launch a blistering attack on Mr. Herford. Gerald Cumberland has left a very interesting account of this lecture and its preliminaries. '. . . from the very first moment he [Harris] intoxicated me. While he changed from his travelling clothes to evening dress he talked and ejaculated, beseeching me to remain with him, as he had had "a rotten journey from London and felt unutterably bored".'

The assembly to which he presently spoke consisted mainly of pale, earnest men and spectacled women who were horrified beyond their highest hopes when Harris threw out one daring theory after another. He pulverized respectability, condemned the human race 'and particularly that portion of it seated before him. Ladies rustled, men stirred . . . he paused. A clock ticked. He looked defiantly at us and still paused. A fat lady in the front row, palpably embarrassed by the long silence and, no doubt, feeling that she had reached one of the most dramatic moments of her existence, banged her plump hands together and ejaculated: "Bravo!" A few other ladies of both sexes [*sic*] joined her, but Harris was not to be placated.'

Described by Cumberland as a semi-invalid, asthmatic and bloodless, Professor Herford now received the full blast of Harris' invective. 'Each sentence he spoke appeared to be the last word in bitterness, but each succeeding sentence leaped above and beyond its predecessor until at length the speaker had lashed himself into a state of feeling to express which words were useless. He stopped magnificently and this time the room rang with applause. It is probable that not half a dozen people present believed his attack on Professor Herford was justified . . . Nevertheless, they applauded him with enthusiasm and they did so because they had been deeply stirred by eloquence that can only be described as superb and by anger that was lava hot in its sincerity. . . .'

*   *   *   *   *

Between 1908 and 1910 Harris wrote fifty-eight letters to Arnold Bennett which have not been taken into account in any previous biography. Several times Harris tried to engineer a review of *The Man Shakespeare* in the *North American Review* for which it seems, Richard Rawlinton would pay at the rate of £10 or £15. This had all the appearance of trying to 'plant' a review for which Bennett would be paid twice over, once by Rawlinton, an American publisher, and once by the *North American Review*. If the warm relations between Harris and Bennett were destined to collapse into mutual abuse, there was no sign of it in these early letters.

Bennett wrote at length about *The Man Shakespeare*: 'I cannot expertly criticize the . . . book because I don't know enough. To me as a piece of constructive criticism it seems not the best piece of work of its kind that I have ever read, but rather the *only* piece. It is merely and simply amazing. What of Coleridge I have ever had the patience to read is not to be compared to it. More damned nonsense has been talked about Shakespeare than on any subject on earth except metaphysics, and reading your book is like walking out of a lunatic asylum for Dowdems into an open field. What I should say of your portrait of Shakespeare is, in very modified form, what Hume said of Berkeley's philosophy: "It admitted of no answer but produced no conviction!" The epigram is as false as epigrams usually are. What I mean is that you have to fight against a popular conception of Shakespeare which has been gradually growing up for over a century. To me, for example, your portrait was at first most disconcerting. I had an image of Shakespeare as a successful, hustling, jolly playwright of immense artistic power, but somewhat disdaining that power, and keen on material needs; always thinking of an easy old age at Stratford. Of course I knew some of Hamlet was in him, but I thought it was quite lost for practical purposes in practical qualities. . . . You smash my image to atoms, but it keeps reconstructing itself again in spite of you—from mere habit. I shall have to get used to it. . . . For the general public your book is at least thirty years before its time. And in thirty years (or so) people will be beginning to admit that in the way of constructive criticism it marked an era. . . .

Yours ever,
Arnold Bennett.'

One year after the publication of *The Man Shakespeare*, Harris produced a second, companion book, *The Women of Shakespeare*. It, too, deeply impressed Bennett. *The Women of Shakespeare* developed the theme of Mary Fitton set out so boldly in *The Man Shakespeare*. Harris dealt with Shakespeare's mother, wife, mistress and daughter, and his words carried the certainty of a man privy to their thoughts, which excited, all over again, the scorn of the scholars. Shakespeare's wife he saw as a 'scolding shrew' many years older than Shakespeare and destined to leave a mark on all his younger work; his daughter Judith, he saw as a pure young woman who consoled him like 'an angel' when the sensual Mary Fitton, his mistress, and the Dark Lady of the Sonnets, finally deserted him. Mary Fitton's story itself seemed to him simple. Shakespeare had fallen in love with her and she dominated his life for twelve years. In his book Harris suggested that Shakespeare asked his young friend Lord Herbert to commend him to Mary Fitton, differences of birth rendering this means of communication desirable. A highly susceptible lady, who bore two illegitimate daughters to Sir Richard Leveson, not unexpectedly Mary Fitton fell in love with Lord Herbert, a high-born person like herself, and Shakespeare was left to reconcile his grief in noble verse. Words which Spalding and other critics had attributed to Shakespeare's regret for his acting, Harris now saw as applicable to the love he shared with Lord Herbert:

> Let me confess that we two must be twain,
> Although our individual loves are one,
> So shall those blots that do with me remain,
> Without thy help, by me be borne alone.

According to Harris, for reasons not convincingly explained, Shakespeare finally chose to attack Mary Fitton's behavior in the words of none other than Ulysses:

> 'Fie, fie upon her!
> There's language in her eye, her cheek, her lips,
> Nay, her foot speaks; her wanton spirit looks out
> At every joint and motive of her body.

O, these encounters, so glib of tongue
That gives accosting welcome ere it comes,
And wide unclasp the tables of their thoughts
To every ticklish reader! Set them down
For sluttish spoils of opportunity
And daughters of the game. . . .'

'Sluttish spoils of opportunity' appealed to Harris and he thought the phrase admirably described Mary Fitton's less reputable activities. He believed her to be a thoroughly ubiquitous woman, seeing her likeness, or part of it, in Rosaline, Cressid, Cleopatra and Portia, but he claimed that Shakespeare's knowledge of women was overrated. One woman, and one woman only, Shakespeare ever knew thoroughly: Mary Fitton. Once more there were logical inconsistencies in the book which entranced the academics. They were even more delighted when he wrote: 'His intimacy with Mary Fitton lasted, *I feel sure*, up to his breakdown in 1608 or thereabouts, and was probably the chief cause of his infirmity and untimely death.' 'I feel sure' was a phrase scholars tended to avoid like the plague. But here, once more, was the remarkable thing about the book. Crisply written, with all the dash which came naturally to Harris at his best, it gave a vivid impression of being in touch with long dead spirits, bringing them to life as no book of scholarship dared to do.

Close on the heels of these two books came a much shorter piece of writing which caused far more trouble. Early in 1911 Harris wrote an article for the *English Review* called *Thoughts on Morals* which suggested that since love and passion were so much more natural to woman, her failings in these matters should be treated with greater leniency. Conversely, Harris believed that puritanical restraints imposed on sexuality in England tended to do far more harm than those excesses which might occur in the first rush of passion. The Japanese knew this, Harris said, and their moral code was directly opposed to the old Hebraic interpretations which we had inherited. Similarly, the Italians had a proverb *peccato di carne non e peccato* (the sins of the flesh are not sins) which found application in cultures untroubled by sacred books and outdated taboos.

Harris' article did no more than re-affirm what Havelock Ellis and H. G. Wells had already stated, but reprisals against him were rapid and vicious. That masterly hypocrite W. T. Stead, and St. Loe Strachey, editor of the *Spectator*, both threw up their hands in horror. Strachey refused to include a notice of the *English Review* in the *Spectator* because of Harris' article, and G. W. E. Russell very forcibly agreed with him. Austin Harrison proclaimed in reply that the *English Review* was the Great Adult Review: 'Our standard is NOT that of the young person, either the callow lad or raw schoolgirl. . . . We oppose Mrs. Grundy and all self-righteous societies. . . .' Arnold Bennett plunged in to attack the *Spectator*'s attitude, Ford Maddox Hueffer ranged himself alongside Bennett and soon the *Spectator*'s columns were loud with thrust and counter-thrust.

Harris' rejoinder, when it came, was magnificent. No one reading it could have doubted that he was the lofty crusader moved by a desire to liberalize the conventions without under-mining them. He bitterly complained of dishonesty in the *Spectator*'s omission of that part of his article which dealt with self-denial. Certainly the *Spectator* had conveniently overlooked his statement that abstinence renewed energy and was, accord-ing to Harris, in part responsible for the mighty world which Balzac had brought to life.

The *Spectator* was determined to hound him down, Harris said. Week after week the paper found new ways of adding savage footnotes to letters for and against him. Its editors were not concerned, he believed, to examine his case, but to apply a kind of lynch law based on hot-headed prejudice. They con-sidered any law to be immutable no matter what false assump-tions it might be based upon; they believed that adultery by the wife was ground enough for divorce, but that precisely the same offence in a husband should escape scot free. Mr. Lloyd George had spoken of St. Loe Strachey, editor of the *Spectator* as 'a pompous pretentious and futile sort of person', but when one looked at Piccadilly Circus on a dark night and saw the degradation to which the savagery of moral repressions drove men and women, the words did not seem strong enough . . .

'there is a pit fouler than any imagined by Dante, a cesspool bubbling and steaming with corruption and all shining with putrid iridescence of hypocrisy . . . and one of the foul bubbles on it is the *Spectator*.'

It was Harris at his contemptuous best. H. G. Wells rubbed his hands with glee when he read the letter, Bernard Shaw let out a great Irish oath and proclaimed, 'magnificent idiot, I must support him at any cost.' Thomas Hardy, John Galsworthy, W. B. Yeats and D. H. Lawrence all joined forces to sign a petition of protest against the *Spectator* and Harris, carried away by their joint eloquence, suddenly saw himself once more as a martyr who might yet, given sufficient persistence, emerge as a prophet.

Against the advice of Arnold Bennett, Harris continued to scribble away for dear life in a number of papers far cheaper than the *English Review*, driven to earn a living by popular journalism. No one took much notice of this froth, but when, in February 1911, he published his 'Talks with Carlyle,' another storm broke. As we know he suggested in the article that Carlyle had never consummated his marriage with Jane, and stated, in cold print, that this was a confession personally entrusted to him by Carlyle.

Carlyle's nephew, Alexander Carlyle, launched a ferocious attack on Harris which seriously doubted whether he had ever met Carlyle at all. Alexander Carlyle continued: 'The view and sentiments attributed to Carlyle are so utterly unlike him, and so palpably culled at secondhand from mere gossip spoken or written, that they cannot fail of being discredited by all people, except perhaps those who are totally ignorant of Carlyle and those who are predisposed to welcome everything that may be said in his disparagement.'

Harris replied in the *English Review*. Alexander Carlyle's case seemed to turn on the date. Harris claimed that he had known Carlyle in 1878–79 and Alexander Carlyle had disinterred a letter written by Harris to Carlyle which established the date as 1877. Alexander Carlyle also claimed that Harris had seen him for half an hour only, and that all the four long meetings to which Harris referred, were a myth. Harris admitted the mistaken date: the rest he stood by. Moreover, he did not know why Carlyle's nephew was in such a state of indignation, Harris continued, and once more revealed that he could write with a colloquial vividness beyond the powers of most of his detractors: 'I said nothing disagreeable about Carlyle. My article was written with reverence and pity—love even. And yet Mr. Carlyle rages, and calls me a liar, a defamer, a libeller, a vile calumnator, basely ungrateful, cynically brutal and goodness knows what besides.' The implication of impotence was clearly a light matter to someone like Harris who had never come within hailing distance of such a condition.

David Wilson presently launched a one hundred page analysis of the battle under the title *The Truth about Carlyle*. Mr. Wilson was a man steeped in the puritanical tradition: 'Nobody can deny that the discussion of sexual topics in a biography is detestable. . . .' Repercussions reached France and Masson wrote his *Boutades Carlyliennes* which did not advance matters very much.

Harris still had not forgotten the trouble which this article caused when he came to write his *Life and Loves* many years later, claiming in Volume I that none other than Sir Richard Quain, doctor to Carlyle, had recalled Mrs. Carlyle's 'crushing disappointment' on her bridal night. Today there is some evidence to show that if half of Harris' interview was an invention, his shot in the dark about impotence need not have been false. As Julian Symons remarked in *Thomas Carlyle*, 'The attempted rebuttal of the charge is as vague as the evidence . . . if Carlyle was not impotent, he was a highly unsatisfactory lover. . . .' [1]

The Carlyle interview became the big set-piece in yet another book by Harris, the first of the series to be known as *Contemporary Portraits*. Re-read today, the early interviews which make up the first volume of these portraits, have, in many details, a doubtful ring. It was one of Harris' more entertaining shortcomings that he never troubled to polish his lying, and stories which might have carried authority, given carefully built up detail, were left hopelessly unsupported. Yet time and again elements of truth broke through, even if it sometimes turned out to be an accident.

[1] Julian Symons, *Thomas Carlyle*, p. 104 (Gollancz, 1952).

Indisputably Harris knew and talked to scores of the most distinguished men of his day and now in the First Volume, he drew vivid word pictures of men like Carlyle, Whistler, Guy de Maupassant, George Meredith and Oscar Wilde using, as was customary in some literary circles of the day, the painter's vocabulary and calling them portraits. But once launched into a portrait he could not stop. He had to embroider, to imagine privileges and insights of a kind which rendered him privy to the innermost workings of many remarkable minds. What happened in the case of John Galsworthy we shall presently see. For the moment the first volume of *Contemporary Portraits* was received with the wildest contradiction, some critics recoiling in near apoplexy, others regarding it in almost the same light as Aubrey's *Brief Lives*.

*   *   *   *   *

Between the years 1913 and 1916 Harris published two volumes of short stories, another novel and the first volume of *Contemporary Portraits*. However scattered the actual writing, it destroyed the widely circulated myth that he was idling from one burst of sensuality or blackmail to another. The second novel was not of great consequence. A highly romantic affair opening in the French Revolution, *Great Days*, published in 1913, gave him an opportunity to indulge, at one remove, his love of old fashioned sea battles. Well written in parts, it was too long drawn out and even close friends found the book boring before the end. Its sales were negligible; its critical reception poor.

In the same year the Bodley Head published *Unpath'd Waters* which developed Harris' powers as a short story writer. The opening story, *The Miracle of the Stigmata*, was original, ironic and written with a spare beauty which sometimes became moving. 'It was after the troubles in Jerusalem,' the story began, 'that a man called Joshua, a carpenter and smith, came to Caesara . . .' An everyday Jew, to all appearances, he yet had that stamp of suffering which gave his countenance special distinction. To his grasping compatriots he seemed 'a rather poor creature', because he never bargained over money, and yet there were moments when something about his bearing made them uneasy. Simon, who modelled wax figures of the Phoenician gods, liked the newcomer Joshua, and presently, Simon's wife Tabitha, became interested in this strange man in whose face she saw the soft, affectionate nature of a girl. She sent for 'her sister's daughter Judith', a young woman of 25 and told her of Joshua a man she regarded as in some mysterious way disappointed with life.

But when it seemed likely that Judith and Joshua would marry, Joshua said to her, 'I am old and broken and my house is empty of hope.' They did at last marry and for some time the marriage suffered from only one shortcoming; there were no children. And then, one day, came talk of a new Messiah with remarkable powers who drew to his meetings scores of fervent disciples. Presently, Paul appeared in person to overwhelm Judith, and one day she returned from hearing him preach, with flushed cheeks and glowing eyes.

The description given in the story of Paul might easily have fitted Harris; 'not big, nor handsome; small indeed and ordinary looking, but as soon as he begins to speak he seems to grow before your eyes. I never heard anyone talk as he talks! You cannot help believing him; he is like one inspired.' At last Judith, in deep distress, confesses that she is about to be baptized a Christian 'for I believe in Paul', but Joshua, who has listened to Paul, finds his teachings different from those of Jesus and is deeply and strangely disturbed.

Because of their conflict over Paul, Judith at last leaves Joshua and goes to live with her mother, while Joshua falls into the old life of the gentle recluse. Soon people notice that Joshua is spending more and more time indoors, until at last, there comes a day, when he does not emerge at all. Forcing open the door, they find him dead at his bench. Then, suddenly, someone notices the strange marks on the palms of his hands the 'puckered white cicatrix', and in wonder they listen to Judith's explanation that these were the result of an accident in Jerusalem; but when they come to bind his feet they find similar scars, and turn swiftly in awe to his side, to see another deeper scar. In near terror they run to tell Paul who at once misunderstands magnificently. To him it is a miracle, but not a miracle like the one which threw divine light across his path on the road to Damascus. Joshua was an unbeliever. He had failed to follow Paul 'and for a sign to the whole world, the Stigmata of Jesus the crucified had been put upon him . . . And all the inhabitants of Caesara . . . were converted and turned to the Lord through the . . . miracle of the Stigmata that had been wrought on the body of its last unbeliever in Caesara. . . .'

The last unbeliever. In one sense Harris regarded himself as that. He had rebelled against all conventional faiths and been crucified. He had been cast down and no one any longer had much faith in him. Whatever psychological compulsions went into the story they served only to intensify its power, and being himself stirred, he seemed to reach and evoke those depths of awareness which sometimes came echoing out of sonorous biblical periods. There were several levels in the story—straightforward narrative, insights into character, spiritual awareness—and a continuous irony reaching the supreme climax when Jesus himself is acclaimed as the last unbeliever to be saved. It was a pity that, later in life, George Moore claimed the plot of the story to be his own. Such complications were becoming too familiar to be overlooked. But the *Observer* described Harris on the appearance of *Unpath'd Waters* as, 'one of the best writers of the short story in English.'

CHAPTER THIRTEEN

In 1915 Frank Harris left England for France. There were many reasons why he had to leave. All his writing, his attempts at financial manipulation and his small scale papers had failed. Slowly, relentlessly, he had been reduced to the humiliating condition of an undischarged bankrupt. Everything combined to make him hate England. He had given an interview to Carl Stelling of the *Daily Sketch*, after his prison sentence, in which he raged against England and all things English. Beside himself with fury he had said that if some great author in France had suffered equivalent humiliation, France would have risen in her wrath to defend him, but England . . .

England, he now concluded, was effete, puritanical, poisonous. It was W. H. Smith's in England who refused to sell the *English Review* because it contained Harris' story *An English Saint*; England which made sordid his attempts to liberalize its morals; England which had financially ruined him and reduced him to the state of an undischarged bankrupt. England had become his arch-enemy and he decided to get away to France.

The First World War had developed on all fronts, and Harris simultaneously found it convenient to do something for which even Arnold Bennett could not forgive him. He gave every appearance of shifting his allegiance from England to Germany. The result was that when he arrived in France, the French, a logical people, did not at all care for his views on the war, and trouble quickly threatened. As German troops closed in on Paris, Harris went off down South and there he tried to forget the French authorities, his own troubles and the war by concentrating on a MS. about Oscar Wilde which he had begun writing four years before.

Augustus John went to visit him one day in the South and later wrote: 'I arrived at Nice with little baggage but my paints and panels. Harris awaited me on the platform in evening clothes. He viewed my corduroys with evident distaste before carrying me off to the Opera House where he occupied a box lent him, he said, by the Princesse de Monaco. . . .' [1]

Nellie, Harris' wife, stood waiting in the foyer dressed 'in somewhat faded and secondhand splendour'. When the opera was over, the composer, Isidor de Lara, joined them, and Harris and de Lara showered compliments upon one another until it became apparent to John that he was assisting at a meeting between 'the modern Wagner' and the 'greatest intellectual in Europe'. This uproar continued for some while and then Nellie, in her dowdy finery, was packed off home, while Harris hurried John away to an expensive hotel where they sat up very late drinking champagne.

Back at last at the villa—'typically suburban in character'—where Harris was staying, a remarkable ritual became apparent. Harris conducted John to his room, explained, with a smile, that Nellie's room was next door, and carefully indicated that his own room lay remotely round the corner. With these words, a flourish and a twist of the moustache, Harris himself disappeared down the corridor.

The following morning Harris and Augustus John went to Nice together. The method of transport was highly original. 'There were always a few private cars waiting in the high road, and Harris found no difficulty in persuading one of the chauffeurs to run us down to the Promenade des Anglais where we alighted in style. This maneuver not only saved us a walk, but tended to reassure Frank's tradesmen. Frank was always reminding them that his Rolls Royce was still *en panne*, and under repair somewhere in the center of France. I guessed that this vehicle, like Elijah's chariot, was purely mythical.' But Frank's talent for mimicking the famous and playing the clown delighted John, if it marked the limits of their single and quickly exhausted affinity.

[1] Augustus John, *Chiaroscuro*, p. 128 (Jonathan Cape, 1952).

From John's point of view, the behavior of Nellie and Harris' secretary became, over forty-eight hours, steadily more extraordinary. 'These two, possessed, as it seemed, by a mixture of fright and merriment, clung together at my approach, while giggling hysterically as if some desperate mischief was afoot.' [1] Presently Harris showed John the manuscript which, he said, was to become a 'Life' of his 'old friend Oscar Wilde'. Reading the manuscript John found it alive with references to 'Our Saviour' and continually interlarded with pious references. 'I asked him what the devil he meant by dragging in Jesus Christ on every other page. He looked black at this but in the end did largely purge the book of such allusions.' [2]

By the third day, what with the giggling secretary, the slightly hysterical Nellie and Harris' interminable monologues, John came to the conclusion that if he himself was not mad then he must be living in a mad-house. 'On the evening of the third day, my relations with Frank Harris, always precarious, broke down altogether. He was looking his ugliest; neither of us now attempted to conceal our mutual antipathy. At dawn next morning I arose, gathered my belongings and silently departed: this time I descended to the harbour on foot and, entering a seaman's bar, breathed with what relief, a purer air.' [3]

Later, John received a letter from Harris. It said that Shakespeare had possessed him for a score of years before he had been forced to write a book to get him out of his system; Oscar Wilde had become part of him for many years and this too meant another literary purgation; once he had similarly ejected Rhodes and Churchill, he would be able to write a great novel or two.

Not only Augustus John but the French authorities were unimpressed. French inquisitiveness about the beliefs and habits of Frank Harris had steadily increased until suddenly one day the police became altogether too pressing and Harris decided that the time had come to leave. Rumor and counter-rumor surrounded what seemed to be a humiliating return to England. H. G. Wells took up the story in his *Experiment in Autobiography*.

[1] Augustus John, *Chiaroscuro*, p. 129 (Jonathan Cape, 1952).
[2] Ibid., p. 130.   [3] Ibid.

'One morning in wartime, somewhere in 1915, my neighbour Lady Warwick came sailing down from Easton Lodge to Easton Glebe. It is not her way to beat about the bush. "Why does Frank Harris say I am not to tell you he is here?" she asked. . . . He had found some reason for bolting from Paris and he had thrown himself upon her never failing generosity . . . He had been boasting too much in Paris about his German sympathies and his influence with the Indian Princes, and the French who are a logical people and take things said far too seriously, made themselves disagreeable and inquisitive . . . He gave way to panic. He fled to England with Mrs. Harris and a couple of valises. He still saw denunciation in every tree and the rustle of the summer leaves outside the windows at Brook End seemed the prelude to arrest. . . .' [1]

Presently they all met and Wells wrote: 'Harris, a very subdued Harris, brightened up and we did what we could to make his stay in Essex pleasant until he could get a passage to America. He sat at my table and talked of Shakespeare, Dryden, Carlyle, Jesus Christ, Confucius, me and other great figures. . . .'

Shortly afterwards Harris decided to leave Easton Lodge, Lady Warwick and Wells for America. Nellie was to follow him when he had succeeded in finding a place to live and presumably, some work. In due course his ship sailed and a bombshell followed. Lady Warwick called once more on Wells, and as they walked together in his rose garden, she disclosed that she had shown Harris a number of highly confidential letters from a certain royal person. Alarmed, Wells said: 'You did not *give* them to him?'

'Oh, no! But he asked to look through them. He thought he might advise me about them. One doesn't *care* to destroy things like that. They have historical importance.'

'And they are now in his valise on their way to America?'

'. . . How did you know that?'

Wells commented: 'Even if the ship is torpedoed . . . Harris will stick to those letters.' [2]

[1] H. G. Wells, *Experiment in Autobiography*, p. 526 (Gollancz and Cresset Press, 1934).

[2] Ibid, p. 527.

148

There were two alerts on the ship and once a torpedo attack seemed imminent but Harris arrived safely in New York with the letters, and promptly wrote, as Wells expected, to Lady Warwick. What precise sum exchanged hands before the letters were recovered and deposited once more in discreet hands, Wells did not disclose; but Harris' career as a skilled black-mailer had taken another step forward.

On November 2nd, 1915, Hugh Kingsmill wrote, in an un-published letter to Enid Bagnold, '. . . Frank Harris is to my mind sentimental, i.e. his ideals and actions don't react on each other. His ideals please his fancy and flatter his vanity, while his actions suit his convenience.' That convenience was steadily becoming more ruthless and demanding. As he wrote, with one hand, the equivalent of a blackmailing letter to Lady Warwick, with the other he turned the pages of the Bible looking for an appropriate quotation. While he professed Utopian ideals, he indulged petty swindles. His protestations of love to a beautiful young girl were delivered in a voice rumbling out of what seemed to be the most profound con-viction but was in fact lust. And yet . . . It is easy to oppose black and white in any character. There were in Harris many more subtle shades. Men like Bernard Shaw saw them and refused to join the chorus of total condemnation.

It was Shaw who said that Frank Harris believed America to have been discovered the day he landed there, but his arrival now, in New York, passed almost unnoticed by the American press. Harris bitterly reflected that notoriety in England was respectability in New York. He had written half a dozen books but New York literary circles seemed not to have heard of them; he had become the greatest literary editor of his day but New York had forgotten it; he had practically committed treason to sympathize with the Germans but no one was interested. His bitterness was understandable when one remem-bered the expectations of a man whose last entry into New York had been in the guise of a boot-black.

Within forty-eight hours he called on the editor of an important daily newspaper who tilted back his chair and said, 'Glad to meet you, Mr. Harris. I seem to remember that name. You have written a book, haven't you?' Harris agreed that he had. He then asked whether he could go aboard incoming boats in order to interview celebrities for the paper. 'Why,' said the editor, 'that's what we give our cub reporters to do. You wouldn't like that.'

'I wouldn't,' Harris said, 'but the celebrities would.'

'Why?'

'They would all know me,' Harris said, picked up his hat and walked out. [1]

Within a few weeks his prospects improved. According to Gertz, the *New York Sun* arranged to take a weekly article from him at $500 a week. The price was no less extravant than the opinions which Harris proceeded to express. Five thousand miles away from the seat of war, he whipped up his attacks on England and his first article—by the Famous English Writer Frank Harris—was called 'The Real Reason for the English Censorship.' It caused a considerable stir. The second article, 'Who Will Win the War,' was by the Well Known English Writer, and the third article dropped the superlatives and carried the bare description—By the English Writer. When the editorial staff of the *New York Sun* attempted to curb his German sympathies they met with explosive abuse and the only concession Harris made in his writings, was to shift the scene of his attacks. He personally chose and insisted upon the title of his next article—'American False Estimates of Greatness,' and the editor of the *Sun* began to wonder whether the famous ex-editor of the *Saturday Review* wasn't perhaps too outspoken a person even for the American press. It is impossible not to admire Harris' courage. He had broken into journalism again and made a fresh start on the American continent, but he was not prepared to compromise in the interests of his own survival. He believed he had something to say and he wanted to say it in his own way.

Inevitably the day came when friction between himself and the editorial staff of the *Sun* broke into open quarrelling. One glorious afternoon, Harris walked into the office, took out his contract, tore it into small pieces under the eyes of the editor, and threw it into the wastepaper basket. Of course it was false

[1] A. I. Tobin and E. Gertz, *Frank Harris*, p. 217 (Madelaine Mendelsohn, 1931).

The original drawing of 'The Best Talker in London, with one of his best listeners', which was given to Enid Bagnold by Max Beerbohm

The poster of the caricature

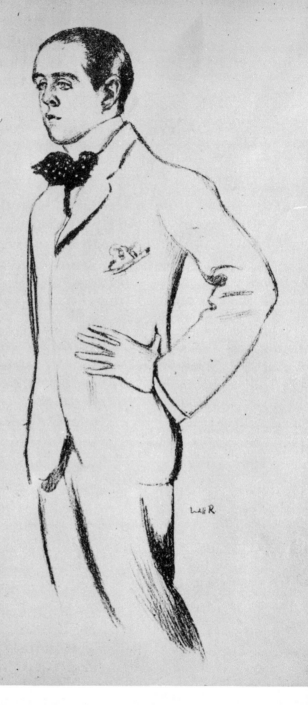

Max Beerbohm in 1893, a drawing by Sir William Rothenstein

bravado. Of course he could not resist the temptation to make one splendid gesture even at the cost of his own destruction; but the number of people capable of gestures in the grand manner which left them destitute, was not great.

From journalism he turned swiftly to lecturing and once again would brook no compromise. He travelled about the States talking his pro-German extravagancies; he did not hesitate to abuse American culture and spoke, with unabated gusto, on whatever subject took his fancy. Every variety of hostile reaction did not check the flow of invective until he reached once more the city of Lawrence, that city where his university days really began, and memories of Byron Smith caught at his heart.

For a man of blood and iron dedicated to the ruthless realization of his own satisfactions, it is remarkable how easily Harris could burst into tears. He walked the streets of Lawrence alone one night, felt the past stirring to life again, and was moved. He went over the university once more and his arrogance softened out of all recognition. A subdued Harris moved through the corridors and lecture rooms and remembered the comparatively innocent young man who had struggled to make himself felt all those years ago. He knew now that he made himself felt too much, but there was no turning back. Presently, a picture of Professor Byron Smith caught his eye, he stopped in front of it, tears came into his eyes and suddenly he muttered to himself the mysterious phrase, '. . . the ultimate.' [1] That he was genuinely moved by his return to the shrine where his ideals had first taken root is clear enough; perhaps more moved because they were now rotting away and hopelessly defiled.

When he heard that Kate Stephens was still alive, he at once wrote asking to see her. The meeting took place in the South Hall of the New York Public Library and Kate Stephens has described it in her own flowery prose: 'In the gallery we sat on a bench and, in laughter . . . recalled men and women grouped . . . about the University. During this visit this man . . . proved a pattern of ingenious innocence. Now and then

[1] A. I. Tobin and E. Gertz, *Frank Harris*, p. 220 (Madelaine Mendelsohn, 1931).

only, a disappointed cynical man without a country flashed from his poise of a joyous minded child.'

When she pleaded an appointment with her publishers in order to get away from him, 'to my amazement he went with me—a confiding child, seemingly loath to leave, clinging in . . . pathetic, wordless appeal. . . . It was an afternoon of soft airs. The sun shone through gold-red haze . . . the beauty of the scene struck me and pointing to the tide of people trending uptown, I turned to him and said, "Good folks hurrying home to rest and dinner."

' "Swine," Frank shot back with a sneer. "Not a new idea in this country for more than a hundred years".'

Correspondence developed between Kate Stephens and himself. Presently there was some discussion about Harris editing the letters of Professor Byron Smith, and on June 6th, 1915, Kate Stephens wrote: 'In a late letter you spoke of reading Professor Smith's letters—of coming here to do so. I am writing to say that yesterday the typist brought her fresh copy. Any time you find it convenient to come. . . .'

Soon, Harris was addressing her as Dear Diotima and signing himself Yours ever, Frankie, and she broke into what was for her the surprising colloquialism, 'My dear Jimmie Harris.' They met again one hot June day. 'Laughing, flushed in face, his breath heavy with wine—"been lunching with Mexican friends at the Claremont"—he rang my bell at twenty minutes past four on the day his letter named,' Kate Stephens wrote.

She placed Byron Smith's letters close to a window overlooking a garden, wheeled an easy chair into position and left pencil and paper ready for him to make any extracts he wished. Shown into the room, Harris appeared to settle down to work. Half an hour later she rejoined him and with one brief reference to the letters he plunged into reminiscence which seemed to have no other purpose than the 'arousal of her passions'. He explained how Lord Randolph Churchill came by the disease from which he died; how he, Harris, had married a woman much older than himself, had several illegitimate children and visited a brothel with two 'Hebrews'. Probably because Miss Stephens showed signs of becoming steadily more frigid as his stories mounted, Harris suddenly changed his tactics. But it was of no avail. In the end they agreed to go on corresponding and parted.

Some of the letters which followed this meeting showed considerable warmth of feeling. On Saturday, October 7th, 1916, she wrote: 'Dear Jimmie Harris, Thank you for the letter and the copies of *Pearsons* . . . too bad you find our climate so hateful or hostile . . . I fear, dear boy, you are not with the right sort of Americans and so are getting distorted notions. . . .

'As a sort of quasi mother of yours, who thinks a child needs a good deal of spanking and a little petting (or is it, perhaps, the other way?) I do hope you are physically well and happier than your letter would show. . . .'

By October 18th she was writing: 'I had a rather extraordinary letter from you tonight. Don't send me another like it, dear boy . . . Now be the beautiful, lovable laddie you can be—drop all hyperbole and exaggeration and hatred as this letter of yours sets forth. . . .'

Gradually the tone of Harris' letters changed. Slowly his words and behavior upset her all over again. In the end, things went hopelessly wrong once more. By November 25th, 1919, she was writing:

'. . . Sometime in those months you spoke in [a] letter . . . of "doing" (as you called it) Professor Smith—and me.

'From what I have learnt of your activities since then, I know very clearly that you can have no real comprehension of Professor Smith and that what you would write would be a terrible travesty of him and his spirit. . . . I am therefore writing this to ask you very kindly never at any time, in any way, to write of Professor Smith or to make any reference to him—or me. . . . I am, very faithfully, Kate Stephens.'

Harris replied that she need not worry. He only undertook pen pictures of people with genius. In the end, Kate Stephens not merely decided that Harris was no man to edit the letters or even to write about Byron Smith; she prepared part of the damning book *Lies and Libels of Frank Harris* which exposed his true relations with her dead fiancé, and accused him of a whole calendar of crimes.

In the years 1914–19, while he was in America,

Hesketh Pearson became Frank Harris' chief correspondent from England and Pearson's memories of those days remain vivid. Life in America was tough for Harris. He quickly came to feel himself doomed to be an exile in whatever land he lived, and a neglected and victimized exile. Presently he was forced to become an advertising agent to the Chesapeake and Ohio Railway, in order to earn a living, and there were periods of near despair. Journalistic work was scarce, New York society did not seem anxious to know him and his attempts to edit another paper of his own were frustrated in circumstances approaching the humiliating. But an advertising agent—the great ex-editor of the *Saturday Review* an advertising agent! It was too much even for his hard-bitten ego.

Hesketh Pearson's relations with Harris had begun in 1912, when Harris lived in Lexham Gardens, South Kensington, and lectured at an underground club called the Petit Cabaret in Heddon Street. They had also met, one gymnastic evening, in the studio of Davidson the sculptor. Davidson had just completed a bust of Harris. The bust was carefully baptized in whisky and prolonged repetitions of the ritual eventually found them rolling across the street to a pub where Harris was introduced to the barman as Shakespeare, Davidson as Michael Angelo and Pearson himself by the portmanteau name Shells, derived from Shaw and Wells. Everything went agreeably 'until someone decided that someone else had insulted him. Then the glass-breaking phase commenced . . . Finally the police arrived. . . .[1]

Now, from America, Harris wrote continuously to Pearson and his letters were very revealing. Meanwhile, Harris' anti-British views broke his friendship with Arnold Bennett, and verbal brawls developed across the Atlantic with Bennett turning ferociously on Harris, Harris replying in the *New York Times*, Hesketh Pearson keeping Harris informed of the varying temperatures in England, and continuously helping him in one way or another. It was something of a shock to Harris to have his erstwhile admirer Arnold Bennett suddenly become a bitter enemy.

The immediate flash-point was the publication of Harris'

[1] Hesketh Pearson, *Modern Men and Mummers*, p. 106 (Allen and Unwin, 1921).

book *England or Germany*, a book which could hardly be said to be tactful, at that stage of the war. In it Harris claimed that England had attacked Germany and in such a manner as to make it clear that she envied German superiority. Endless newspapers, Harris said, had turned from admiration of Germany before the war, to envy and from envy to hatred. There was one great source of the poison which had infected the army, the judiciary, the legislature and the Church in England, and that source continued to pour its venom into all British veins—the aristocracy. Once sympathetic to its autocratic habits, social life, manners and tastes, Harris had achieved a complete volte-face and now saw, beneath its surfaces, two preoccupations which he described with journalistic succinctness as—bed and board. As a result of these preoccupations he claimed that half the artistic life of England had been vitiated. Artists were treated like public entertainers, ideals had been tarnished and snobbery enthroned as a god. The book ran on for several pages in this vein. Then came the statement that the Kaiser now had a remarkable opportunity. The sinking of half a dozen food ships would probably bring about a threat of revolution in England upon which the Government would be forced to accept defeat and England, after a suitable interval with Germany dominating the high seas, would settle down into the position of a third rate power. There was no doubt about it, the book—for those impeccably correct gentlemen who thought patriotism an inevitable part of the British bloodstream—was practically treason.

The *New Statesman* attacked the book *England or Germany* on June 15th, 1915. Its opening sentences set the tone of the whole review: 'Frank Harris, since last autumn a resident (or refugee) in America, with an address in Fifth Avenue, New York, contributed a number of articles on the war to the Sunday edition of the *New York Sun*. They were anti-British in a decidedly mischievious fashion. . . .' The review continued, 'As editor of the *Saturday Review* in the . . . nineties, he was the first journalist in England holding any post of importance to preach war upon Germany. . . . As he now informs us, Frank Harris was even then an American citizen . . . But . . . there was little to choose between the *Saturday*'s tone towards the two great rival nations.

Mr. Arnold Bennett told us that he never "knew hatred of America quite so fierce as Frank Harris". . . . In the years 1897–8 the attacks upon American policy and the American character were as offensive as anything appearing in the English press; and as a matter of fact Frank Harris gave the note which sometime afterwards led an important newspaper to assert that the *Saturday Review* would never be content until it had embroiled England and the United States in war. Today Frank Harris, a fugitive from England, is an advocate in America of German civilization and German aims. The directors of the German Press Bureau take pains to circulate . . . Frank Harris' recent articles from the *New York Sun* in order to prove by the word of an English publicist how abominable England is. . . .'

Shaw quickly came in to defend Harris, but it was almost as if he was searching for small justifications and Harris might have been better off without his aid. The one phrase worth repeating was Shaw's statement that he saw in Harris' book 'a wounded concern for England—a high if bitterly disappointed ideal for England.'

Harris himself plunged in on July 31st, to reply to the *New Statesman*. He recapitulated the arguments against him, he said that consistency went with mediocrity, he quoted Shaw's view of his concern for England and tried 'to lift this controversy out of the gutter'; but the facts deduced to prove his case were not very convincing. With one of those extravagant leaps into the empyrean which characterized several of his pronouncements at this time, he ended his reply with the statement that life was still good, that some great spirits were still alive to cheer him on—and the final contradiction—his soul still found profound delight in God. One day he would write his autobiography he said. It would be called *How I Fell among Thieves*.

Within a year of the publication of this book, events brought a revolutionary change in Frank Harris' life. He had written to Hesketh Pearson early in 1916 that the world of advertising no longer interfered with his high calling in quite the same degree, because he had at last managed to find a small interest in an organization concerned with unpuncturable tires. He hoped very soon, he said, to free himself or his real lifework. By July he had abandoned, in turn, unpuncturable tires, and

leapt suddenly into the editorship of a magazine called *Pearsons*.
How he did this remains obscure, but Shaw quickly wrote to
Hesketh Pearson: '. . . Frank is going to be very irritating for
a while. He has become editor of the American *Pearsons Magazine*; and he has already started personal reminiscences in it,
which he will keep up for three numbers at least—the usual
period of his attention to any rag he professes to edit. It is
even possible that he may be kept to his work by his circumstances and by American slave-driving. I have read the first
instalment; and it is clear that he is going to tell how he
discovered and rescued from poverty and obscurity not only
Wells, Kipling and myself, but probably Henry James,
Thackeray, Dickens, Goldsmith, Shakespeare and Chaucer. He
is quite welcome as far as I am concerned but the others may
be touchy. . . .'[1]

Gertz and Tobin believed that Harris himself largely wrote
the first few issues of *Pearsons*. Certainly there is every reason
to accept the splash he made as he plunged back into journalism
as highly personal, but from the day Harris took over *Pearsons*,
the circulation began to fluctuate wildly. Some say that the
circulation rose, some that it fell. Whatever overtook the paper
statistically, it drew attention out of all proportion to its circulation, a situation which had become common to any paper
which Harris now edited. Presently people as diverse as H. G.
Wells, Bernard Shaw and the Postmaster-General of the United
States were reading every page of *Pearsons*, but their motives
differed widely. Shaw roared with laughter at Harris' more
abandoned statements, Wells read it with fascinated disgust,
and the Postmaster-General was hopeful of finding reasons for
the paper's suppression.

If only he had known. Behind the scenes, Ricker, the business
manager of *Pearsons*, was running a stock promotion scheme
the proportions of which left even Harris a little breathless
when he discovered it. Invited to join what was plainly an
unscrupulous racket, Harris resisted for two reasons: the oil
wells in which people were expected to invest their money
were highly temperamental and the capital, put at a million
shares, consisted of no more than $650.

[1] Hesketh Pearson, *Bernard Shaw*, p. 344 (Collins, 1942).

What happened next should be emphasized. For the black-mailing ruffian Harris, not only refused to join Mr. Ricker's enterprise; with the aid of Hackenberg, a person known as a lawyer-adjuster, he secured an injunction against his own magazine and had an official receiver appointed. When, at last, *Pearsons* came under the exclusive control of Harris, it was in a sad state, and a long struggle began to stop it collapsing into the void. Creditors frequently called at the office and threatened to have Harris turned into the street; twice the police came nosing around and once the printer struck; but *Pearsons* continued to appear. It needed formidable courage, energy and toughness to keep the paper alive under such conditions because there was one enemy more hostile and persistent than any other.

The Postmaster-General, a man called Burleson, took an almost sadistic delight in holding up the paper on one ground or another, in the hope of uncovering seditious material. Time and again it was bluntly confiscated and held off the market for as long as three weeks. 'In desperation Harris wrote offering to supply an advance copy of the magazine regularly, but Burleson refused to accept the offer.' [1] Sales were thrown into confusion, nobody quite knew when the paper would appear, advertising fell away, and what were optimistically described by Nellie on one occasion as 'mounting difficulties', sometimes drove Harris to despair. There were also occasions when tremendous fits of rage seized him, he pounded his desk, his body shook and the great voice thundered out unprintable words, all concentrated around the person of the Postmaster-General Burleson. It was of no avail.

As his enemies multiplied and his sudden accession to the glory of editing *Pearsons* did not yield the results which he expected, Harris began to speak of getting away from what had once more become a philistine land. His hatred for America mounted. It was, he suddenly discovered, part of the cultural prescription in America that a man must amass material wealth in one form or another, to the exclusion of all the finer shades of personality. It was no place for an artist; or even an editor.

[1] A. I. Tobin and E. Gertz, *Frank Harris*, p. 233 (Madelaine Mendelsohn, 1931).

Matters reached a climax when the landlords of his office premises strongly objected to having advertisements for *The Bomb* plastered all over the building and Harris was forced to move to 57 Fifth Avenue. There he promptly replaced *The Bomb* advertising by huge notices which read PEARSONS MAGAZINE, FRANK HARRIS. Meanwhile his hatred of America grew.

CHAPTER FOURTEEN

WITHIN all these troubles Harris somehow completed, privately printed and himself published his biography of Oscar Wilde, a book which he had begun writing as far back as 1910. Quickly, it began to sell, but for reasons which will presently appear, it was not published in England. Harris sent copies to Hesketh Pearson asking him to arrange to have the book reviewed in the English press, which Pearson did with not very great success. Shaw writing to Pearson commented: 'McCarthy was delighted when I told him that you were furious with the papers because they dismissed Frank's book in a brief paragraph while devoting whole pages to *Mr. Britling* [by H. G. Wells] and an insignificant little item like the war. . . . The notice in the *Manchester Guardian* is very generous for an old man of seventy. Did you expect him to write three columns proclaiming Frank as the Messiah?'

The reception in America was very different. A number of American critics described Harris' biography in such glowing terms that the sorely pressed editor of a struggling magazine was suddenly approached by a film company and promised to recover overnight the fame which had once been his in England. 'The best biography ever written by an American—an astonishingly frank, searching and vivid reconstruction of character —a piece of criticism that makes all ordinary criticism seem professional and lifeless,' wrote H. L. Mencken. Upton Sinclair and Middleton Murry were equally impressed, and Bernard Shaw himself wrote to Harris: 'You have written the best life of Oscar Wilde. Wilde's memory will have to stand or fall by it.'

Presently the film company made a fresh proposition to Harris. If he could persuade Shaw to co-operate with him to produce a screen version of his book, a spectacular sum of money would be made available. Frantic letters passed to and fro across the Atlantic and Harris decided that the occasion was big enough to send the most beautiful and persuasive emissary at his command. Mrs. Harris set sail from New York, and Harris duly warned Hesketh Pearson that she was coming to persuade Shaw to permit certain parts of his correspondence about Wilde, to be shown on the screen while the film was in progress.

Hesketh Pearson remarked, in his excellent biography of Shaw, that 'certain of Harris's qualities appealed so strongly to [Shaw] that he could not be antagonized by the qualities which repelled other men.' Writing once to Sutro Shaw said, 'all the literary blokes loathe me, and I should spoil the dinner.' All the literary blokes also loathed Harris which gave them at least one common standpoint. Shaw loved the incredible adventures of Harris, the shocking stories, the blasphemies, and delighted to mimic the *basso profundo* voice delivering a particularly appalling example of amorality. 'Harris,' wrote Hesketh Pearson, 'was a holiday for him; an hour of his company was more invigorating than a day in the country. But an hour was quite enough. . . .' [1]

In some extraordinary way Shaw maintained that Harris' blackguardism sprang from pure innocence. Highly skilled himself in the delivery of great oaths invoking Jesus or any convenient saint, Harris' outbursts struck a sympathetic note and Shaw simply regretted that so many examples of his blasphemy were unprintable.

Mrs. Harris duly arrived and called upon Shaw. Hesketh Pearson wrote this account of the interview: '. . . After expressing his amazement that she had not divorced Frank years before and married a millionaire, [Shaw] pointed out that the [book] could not be screened, as too many of the characters were still alive and powerful, notably Edward Carson. . . .' [2]

All Mrs. Harris' attempts to persuade him failed, and

[1] Hesketh Pearson, *Bernard Shaw*, p. 342 (Collins, 1942).
[2] Ibid., p. 346.

she thereupon appealed to Hesketh Pearson to intercede on her behalf. Pearson went, in turn, to see Shaw. Asked why he would not help Harris, Shaw said: 'Frank's a baby, Mrs. Frank's a baby, and you're the biggest baby of the three.'

Pearson continued to press the point. 'Are you really such a thundering lunatic as you make yourself out to be?' Shaw said. 'Do you honestly believe that the only thing these American people want is my letter on the screen . . . Can't you see that what they want to do is to advertise the fact that the scenario is by Bernard Shaw (in capital letters) and Frank Harris (in small letters).'

'Oh, but Frank told me . . .'

'Humbug. Frank knows nothing about these film people. I do. They have approached me hundreds of times. They have offered me a quarter of a million pounds to release half a dozen of my plays for the screen. I have refused and I shall continue to refuse. . . .'

They were trying, Shaw continued, 'to bamboozle Frank— and me. Well let them try! If my name is even breathed as having written a syllable of their wretched scenario I'll have the law on them.' [1] Nellie's stay was brief. In the end she was forced to return to America empty-handed, to face an infuriated Frank, and there is no record of what passed between them.

All this was long before Mr. Robert Harborough Sherard wrote his book *Bernard Shaw, Frank Harris and Oscar Wilde* which the publishers introduced as an exposure of THE GREATEST LITERARY IMPOSTURE OF ALL TIME IN THE HISTORY OF ENGLISH LETTERS. Sherard stated that Harris, in his life of Wilde had plundered, in the most ungentlemanly manner, one of his own earlier books; that a professional liar like Harris could not escape spinning a tissue of misrepresentation around Oscar Wilde; that Harris had deliberately exploited his late 'friend's' misfortune to make money for himself and that 'Oscar Wilde was a man of spotless and almost angelic domestic character. . . .' Since Wilde, he continued, was as innocent as a lamb of the charges brought against him, it was impossible

[1] Hesketh Pearson, *Bernard Shaw*, p. 347 (Collins, 1942).

162

for him to have told Harris that the facts of the case for the prosecution were largely accurate.

The gulf between Shaw's view of Harris' book and Mr. Sherard's, was filled, over the years, by brawls, arguments and quarrels which even now, over forty years after publication, still re-echo. Certainly there were many abominable things in Harris' book. It misrepresented and libelled Lord Alfred Douglas. It said that he was Wilde's accomplice in what were referred to as his 'worst excesses'. It pictured Wilde travelling with Harris to La Napoule in France and unburdening himself on the relative merits of boy and girl love, when Wilde's letters to Ross indicate that such a journey never took place. It showed Wilde bursting in one day on Harris to say that George Alexander had cut him dead in the street when Harris did not arrive in the South of France until a week after the Alexander incident. Many quotations from conversations with Wilde, far from carrying an authentic ring, bore signs of that imaginative extension in which Harris specialized, but the vivid writing brought Wilde alive as a person, the refusal to overlook blemishes gave him flesh and blood reality, and if Harris himself came bursting into the narrative on the slightest provocation, no one in his senses would have expected a book written by Harris to develop in any other way. *Oscar Wilde* does not fall into any known category in the field of biography. Strictly it is not biography. It is dual-biography in which Wilde with a struggle dominates Harris, but it is still immensely readable.

It was inevitable that Lord Alfred Douglas should, in due course, challenge this book and challenge it more forcibly than Robert Sherard. Harris had first met Douglas in 1894, and in those days Lord Alfred 'admired [him] because he was, as I believed, "a hell of a man" one who was capable of knocking out a prize-fighter in a street "scrap".'[1]

Admiration quickly gave place to hatred. Within a few years it reached a point where Harris tried to blackmail Lord Alfred Douglas and Douglas in turn threatened to go straight to Bow Street Police Station to expose Harris. Now, many years later, Harris had his revenge in *The Life and Confessions*

[1] Lord Alfred Douglas, *Without Apology*, p. 69 (Martin Secker, 1929).

of Oscar Wilde. In his book, Lord Alfred became the man who deserted Wilde at a crucial moment, introduced him to abominable practices and refused him money when he desperately needed it. Douglas commented: 'I knew Wilde much better than Harris did . . . and I can truthfully say that Harris' account of Wilde is quite as false, misleading and perfidious as his account of me in the same book. . . . Moreover, Harris omits to mention . . . that two or three months before Wilde's death they had a violent quarrel over Harris' appropriation and spoiling of what should have been another of Wilde's inimitable comedies, *Mr. and Mrs. Daventry.* . . .' [1]

To Frank Harris, revenge was one thing; limiting a wealthy market turned out to be quite another. The scurrilous account of Lord Alfred Douglas made it impossible to publish The Life of Oscar Wilde in England as it stood, but presently letters passed between Douglas and Harris, as he sought some means of correcting the biography and reaching an English audience. It was at last agreed that a new preface should be written, a preface explaining that Ross had misled Harris about the part played by Lord Alfred Douglas. According to the new interpretation Ross, not Douglas was the villain of the piece, and all these accusations which Harris had so carelessly levelled at Douglas in the biography, should have been directed at Ross.

Prepared to admit his mistakes in a new preface, Harris conceded, with that mixture of cunning and generosity which marked out his more penitent moments, 'that I should have misjudged the foremost poet of [my] time is my keenest regret, that I could have believed such noble gifts could go with corrupt meanness of character shows the malignant cleverness of his detractors.'

This first revised preface was to be a joint venture. Later, Harris wanted to write the whole preface himself, whereupon Douglas insisted that footnotes should qualify every passage in the book which he regarded as defamatory. Harris, when it came to adding the footnotes, suddenly changed his mind once more. And then, ignoring Harris, 'Douglas . . . issued the New Preface in its original form "omitting only a few words which

[1] Alfred Douglas, *Without Apology*, p. 65 (Martin Secker, 1929).

might be held to reflect unfairly on a well-known barrister who is still living".' [1]

This preface was dated September 1925, and within five months Harris had hit back vigorously. He wrote an introduction for a new edition of *De Profundis* and explained what had happened to Tobin and Gertz. 'This new preface to my *Oscar Wilde* was published by the traitor Alfred Douglas. He . . . persuaded me among other things that he had paid for the whole of Wilde's trial, and I wrote the new preface. . . . I soon found out from Wilde's son and others that Alfred Douglas had lied to me again and again. I wrote him at once withdrawing the preface and sending a truthful one in its place, but the dirty skunk published the first preface though he knew it was founded on his own lies. . . .'

This could be read in the old Harris tradition. Accuse your enemy of the very crime of which he complains and everyone will imagine that he is merely indulging a piece of spite whenever he attacks you. Yet another preface appeared from Harris in 1928, entitled 'The Final Preface to the Life of Oscar Wilde'. It said that *Oscar Wilde, His Life and Confessions* was, after all, the true story and that Douglas had 'introduced Wilde to the male prostitution of London'.[2]

Many years later Lord Alfred Douglas wrote to Gertz, one of Harris' biographers: 'I suppose you can hardly expect me to deal seriously with such an accusation. No one but a lunatic or a congenital idiot would believe, or pretend to believe it. . . . Anyone therefore who tries to make out or pretends to believe I introduced Wilde to vice in any form is obviously not in good faith to put it mildly.' There followed further evidence from him which clearly showed that nothing of the kind had ever occurred.

In 1929, Vyvyan Holland, the son of Oscar Wilde, was asked what he thought of the *Life and Confessions of Oscar Wilde*, and wrote: 'I replied that I knew nothing whatever about the matter but that I had heard Robert Ross say that, although it

[1] A. I. Tobin and E. Gertz, *Frank Harris*, p. 287 (Madelaine Mendelsohn, 1931).

[2] Ibid, p. 294.

was a thoroughly bad book, written with the sole object of glorifying Harris himself, it did, on the whole, contain some elements of truth. I think Robert Ross meant that Harris had put Alfred Douglas into his proper perspective. . . .' [1]

Within a few months Holland himself received an infuriated letter from Douglas: 'You are quoted as saying (1) that Harris' book *The Life and Confessions of Oscar Wilde* contains the truth about my association with your father. . . . You were a small child when the affair took place and you can have no personal knowledge of the matter. . . . Harris himself has admitted that his story about me is untrue in almost every particular. . . .' [2]

Vyvyan Holland finally summed up a situation threatening to become hopelessly complex. 'I . . . heard so many contradictory stories about my father and . . . read so many statements and retractions and repudiations that I was seriously beginning to doubt whether any such person as Oscar Wilde ever existed?' [3]

[1] Vyvyan Holland, *Son of Oscar Wilde*, p. 193 (Rupert Hart-Davis, 1954).

[2] Ibid., Appendix D, p. 265.

[3] Ibid., p. 266.

H. G. Wells taken at the turn of the century

Bernard Shaw in 1901

CHAPTER FIFTEEN

INEVITABLY Nellie Harris stood by her husband in the struggle which developed around the Life of Oscar Wilde. By the time the book appeared in America their relationship had reached that stage where periods of cynical disillusion were inevitable. Years of bitter experience had taught Nellie many truths about her husband and the harsh reality of their long stay in America drove them home. Harris' mistresses came and went leaving different reactions on Nellie according to whether she knew of their existence, had enough money to live expensively, or was overtaken by one of those furies when she insisted that she would leave him if he did not behave.

Harris' technique as a lover had undergone many changes. There remained, with some women, unexpected elements. As one mistress who was in love with him said: 'He always talked as if he held the key to life—with a big "L". As if only with his help could one pass into the kingdom of experience. What nonsense that all was about Passion and Freedom! And how it impressed one! And one was sorry for him, too. . . . One thought of him as a rebel who had refused success in disgust at the price one has to pay for it. Yet there *was* something there —a tangled, troubled light. Disturbed, I know, betrayed, sullied, but there! . . . I still see the horizon of his eyes and talk flaming like a sunset . . . And yet it's gone—how it's gone! I suppose because it was all so unreal. I thought it real enough then—but there was too much "Love" and too little natural affection. And yet . . . There was something beautiful there once, even if it had died. . . .' [1]

[1] Hugh Kingsmill, *Frank Harris*, pp. 185-6 (Jonathan Cape, 1932).

At the opposite extremity stood the New York shop girl who sold him cigarettes one day and went out with him the next evening. He plied her with drink, took her to his room, embraced her and became very indiscreet with his hands. She protested '. . . you think you can do this to me because I am just a shop-girl. You wouldn't dare if . . .' According to Harris one single kiss silenced her for the next few minutes, but then she burst away from him and slapped his face. Whereupon such a roar came out of Harris' chest, his face suffused with such anger, his arms closed with such steely power about her body and his great voice began to boom with such vibrating force that she 'simply melted away—trembled violently and melted away. . . .' [1]

There remained the woman in Hugh Kingsmill's biography who said: 'He hasn't the least idea how to touch a woman's heart, her intellect or her passion. He is brute, but not brute enough, or not brute in the way that every woman of flesh and blood will forgive—and more than forgive.' [2]

Nellie Harris herself has remained a mystery in the studies so far written. While she was still alive no one dared to commit to paper what seemed to be the not very pleasant truth. In America, the women in Harris' life may have multiplied to the point where she was sadly abused, but there is some evidence to show that she herself first married Harris not for love, but for money and position. Younger by twenty years and with considerable beauty, in those early days there was no lack of suitors, but Harris dazzled her with wealth, rushed her off her feet in a social whirl, and she found it irresistible.

When, suddenly, it all collapsed, she might easily have left him, but Harris, adept at conceiving money-making schemes, proceeded to invent one after another with such eloquence that she lived continuously in expectation of renewed wealth. Hesketh Pearson believed that after the first raptures, Nellie Harris quickly became indifferent to her husband. Finding that she had married a magnificent monster she thought first of divorce, and then decided to realize his remarkable powers of re-creating the rich web at the center of which she so much

[1] As told to Bernard Shaw.
[2] Hugh Kingsmill, *Frank Harris* (Jonathan Cape, 1932).

desired to sit. She was not a literary person. She could not talk in any depth about his books, but she had a quick Irish brain, a ready tongue, and was never at a loss for an answer. In company, a sparkle of superficial conversation carried her over dangerous and deeper rapids and men, to Harris' delight, found her beauty and vitality powerful attractions.

For many years he was undoubtedly proud of her. A visitor about to meet her for the first time would be expected to witness a certain ritual, highly derivative from royalty. Harris would receive the visitor alone, and suddenly say, in the middle of the second drink: 'Listen—I think I hear my wife.' Some faint disturbance could, in fact, be detected from another part of the household and if, later, old hands came to suspect a deliberate cue, there was no questioning the warmth with which Harris at once left the room to greet her. A momentary pause; voices coming down the passage; another pause in silence; then the door slowly opened and Harris entered very calmly, his face austere, his wife—taller than he was—on his arm. Harris half turned, spread one hand in the direction of the guest and said in measured tones, 'My wife'. Frequently he remembered to mention the name of the guest, but sometimes even that was swept away in the regal tide of Nellie's appearance.

She could behave like a perfect lady or remain a silent decorative presence, but there were occasions—Hugh Lunn knew several—when she was roused to fish-wife pitch and then she screamed out words not much less vivid than Frank's. If she did not, herself, set out to compete with the rich web of her husband's affairs, the suspicion of more than one lover over the years not unexpectedly occurred.

Wild variations in the relationship of two such people were only to be expected. When Frank was behaving himself or successfully concealing his latest mistress he treated Nellie punctiliously. He would never keep her waiting a moment, he would abandon important engagements to meet her request for company on a difficult expedition, and he would sit patiently waiting while she was interviewed by music teachers. He regarded her as by far the best judge of anything he had written, and would wait days and even weeks, for her opinion. He would kiss her good night gently and if that was a night when

Nellie felt unresponsive, he did not force himself upon her.

There were long periods when he tried not to make Nellie jealous; he sometimes explained that the women in his life were passades which could never challenge her position; but she hated it when, as sometimes happened, a female admirer referred to him as Master. The messianic streak in his nature more easily imposed upon women than men, and produced in some that near slavery which went with the profound satisfactions of an autocratic past. [1] Frank would, in his best moods, cultivate people he heartily disliked for Nellie's sake and she—just as extravagant as he was—continued to run up bills with a glorious disregard for the fact that her husband was suffering from brain fever not so much in an attempt to pay bills already years overdue, as in the hope that he might qualify for fresh credit. Harris rarely complained on this score. He accepted with a growl, a sigh or a string of blasphemy, a web of debt which, while he busied himself in one corner sweeping it away, multiplied in another.

There was a child in odd circumstances. It was born 'some time after their elopement' and died within two or three years. Two accounts of the death were given: one that it died from the effects of vaccination, another that the child, left in the care of a nurse one night, while the Harrises were entertaining, was accidentally smothered. Whatever the truth of the matter, it distressed Nellie very deeply, and she determined never to have another one.

The intervals when things ran smoothly between Mr. and Mrs. Harris varied in frequency and duration, but there were certainly others. Nellie remained very strongly pro-Ally in the war for the simple reason that three of her brothers were killed in the fighting, and that led to bitter battles between herself and Frank. It was Hugh Lunn who gave a picture of the darker side of their marriage in his novel *The Will to Love*, and Hesketh Pearson, who knew all three, agreed that it was an accurate 'likeness'.

Of course, details differ, geographical facts are changed, the

[1] From an interview Gertz had with Frank Harris' niece, Gwladys Price-Williams, which he was unable to use in his own biography.

pattern forced into the mold of effective fiction, but the novel took the reader into a world torn by the kind of tension which frequently disrupted the Harris household. The picture of the seduction of Barbara in the novel closely parallels many known seductions carried out by Harris. Travelling from Paris to Boulogne, in the novel Barbara enters the restaurant car, and is surprised when a stranger ignores several empty tables to come and sit beside her. She buries herself in a copy of H. G. Wells' *New Machiavelli* and then suddenly 'an indignant roar startled her . . . she looked hastily up, dropping her eyes immediately and flushing with vexation at her lack of self-possession.

'A waiter dashed up in answer to the roar. "The service on this line is abominable," boomed the stranger in a rich deep voice. "I have been better served on a tinpot track railway in the Argentine. What have you?"

'The waiter snatched the menu, which was within a few inches of the stranger's nose and flashed it to his grasp as though a moment's delay would involve them both in instant annihilation. The menu appeared to inspire nothing but disgust and loathing, and the suggestions of the waiter were treated as the irrelevant maunderings of a half-wit. . . .' [1]

These opening scenes are powerfully familiar. Presently the stranger says to Barbara: 'You are disgusted by my treatment of that fellow,' and Barbara busies herself even more deeply in her book. When, finally, the stranger ostentatiously offers the waiter a five franc piece, she is completely outraged, but by then the ice between them has been broken, and he is looking at her with an eye 'which expressed in equal degree sympathy, compunction and esteem'.

Soon Parker (alias Harris) detects in Barbara the seeds of something which Harris could so brilliantly canalize in real life—rebellion. Throughout his most successful days, Harris represented for those young men who seemed to succumb so easily to his influence, all the forces they felt stirring within them to rebel against convention and bourgeois morals.

Something similar happens in the novel. Parker (alias Harris) sees this beautiful young virgin as 'a born revoltée'. He plays upon it, attacks just those targets which she despises, and in

[1] Hugh Lunn, *The Will to Love* (Chapman and Hall, 1919).

no time he has her saying enthusiastically, 'that's true; oh, how true!' Scrutinizing him more carefully she listens to him as he begins the well-practised compliments. '. . . Eyes as magnificent as yours should not condescend to scrutinize others.' Presently she realizes that he too has 'amazingly expressive eyes, large and varying with his emotions, from blue to black; the one feature that differentiated his face from the thousand similar faces of pleasure and power hunters, who from the art-loving statesman to the bogus company promoter constitute the shaping force of our modern civilization'.

At every turn the portrait picks upon a less emphasized characteristic of Harris and brings it into fresh focus. When he spoke of the artist and his high calling, when he quoted Shakespeare and Balzac at Barbara, Parker's 'marvellous eyes seemed suffused with an emotion too high and pure for rhetoric. . . .'—which is precisely the effect Harris' eyes had upon several young women in fact. Before they leave the train Barbara, in the novel, gives Parker her address and he promises to send her a couple of books. In the end Barbara sleeps with Parker for a reason which inspired some of Harris' mistresses in real life—she believes herself to be serving a high purpose, by satisfying the passions of such a born artist.

Since so many details about Harris fall into place in the novel with the ring of truth, it is interesting to read of Mrs. Parker (alias Nellie Harris):

'His wife noticed his moodiness at dinner and wondered venomously which of his love affairs was doing badly. Outwardly she was sweetly sympathetic as usual, the pose which in her husband's presence replaced her normal air of embittered ennui. She was the one woman who had managed to attach herself permanently to Parker; winning him twenty years earlier with her exquisite loveliness and keeping him by the extraordinary skill with which she played up to his favourite theory that the key to a man's character is supplied by the nature of the woman he really loves. . . .'[1]

Harris believed that whatever kind of woman a man loved represented an extension of his idealized self. Thus, in real life, Harris could only condemn his wife by condemning his

[1] Hugh Lunn, *The Will to Love* (Chapman and Hall, 1919).

idealized self, and that made their conflicts so much worse. Harris had projected into her all that altruism, concern for others, and love, which he himself so sadly lacked, and to attack it, or even to doubt it, was self-destruction of a most unpleasant kind. In one sense such a supremely convenient arrangement, in another it was very dangerous. Underneath, it generated a sea of hatred. Both wearing the mask the other required, occasionally they could not stop sinister scenes breaking through.

There was an occasion for instance, early in 1916. Nellie stood waiting for Harris at New York Station when he returned from an alleged interview with H. L. Mencken which she had discovered to be a week-end with a mistress who adored every word he wrote. Christine Maerling was barely 22, the daughter of a very respectable family of 'merchants', and Harris at this time approaching 60. The week-end had been highly successful, but when Harris sighted Nellie, standing very stiffly upright, her umbrella gripped fiercely by her side, he instantly knew that his alibi had succumbed.

He tried to kiss her and she brushed him aside. In the taxi, she was icy and silent. Half way home she turned and spat at him, 'Either that little bitch goes or I do.'

Suddenly Frank was roaring back at her. What precise words he used is not known, but both stung to fury they fought like hell-cats and the taximan drove at break-neck speed in fear that they might murder one another.

Nellie determined, that night, that she would leave him. But six months later she was still by his side. [1]

Verbal evidence from Dorothy Richardson.

CHAPTER SIXTEEN

Harris was now 61. America, on the verge of bursting into the war, did not like him, many of his friends had deserted him, *Pearsons* was in a confused state and every immediate situation charged with depressing possibilities. He had aged. His eyes were not so brilliant, the lines around his mouth were deeply scored, and somewhere beneath the bold exterior a hunted expression remained like a ghost waiting to materialize.

He continued to live to the hilt. He wanted and imperiously ordered life to yield up all its pleasures and never once expected to take the consequences. There were times when he ate several helpings of roast pork, gorged roast potatoes served with spiced sauce, drank a bottle or two of wine, topped off a meal of six courses with several of his own special liqueurs, turned pale green ten minutes afterwards and disappeared into the bathroom. There, with a practised hand and without haste, he took the rubber tube of his stomach pump, thrust it down his throat, pumped two pints of warm water through a funnel into his stomach and brought back all the troublesome foods with the matter-of-fact air of one performing a commonplace.

Still the huge moustaches were perfectly trimmed, the tie elegant, the clothes perfectly fitting, but his taste in waistcoats had become louder, his flourish of whatever cane he carried more ostentatious, his use of his voice more self-conscious.

A wealthy woman visited the dust-ridden offices of *Pearsons* one day, bent on replying generously to its appeals for money. She took one look at Harris decked out in white-striped trousers, Eton tie, Queensbury waistcoat and dove-grey spats and left without relinquishing a cent. Another lady, with similar intent, called at his apartment to be confronted by a beautifully dressed Japanese butler, who showed her into a room so richly furnished with expensive rugs and *objets d'art* that she, too, turned tail and left. One was never quite sure of Harris' poverty. Sometimes, in his worst moments, he seemed to live in rich surroundings, sometimes he raised big sums by dubious means and forgot about his creditors; but fear of prison now went hand in hand with every new deception, and no one could miss an occasional shiftiness in his manner, as if, eternally, he glanced over his shoulder in case one of the myriad creditors was at his heels.

Sometimes driven to leave his apartment and stay away from the office, literally in hiding, he would choose an obscure hotel and wait until another climax in the hue and cry for unpaid debts had dwindled away. More rarely, and never seen except by very close friends, there were nights when, walking between the skyscrapers of New York, a face vaguely familiar would flash past and the beginnings of fear lit Harris' eyes.

A sense of guilt, easily repressed, still was not quite over-whelmed. Playing fast and loose with the man who thought himself supremely free from the troubles of anything so bourgeois as conscience, it would suddenly look out of the eyes of a passing stranger, to Harris' intense discomfiture.

There were nights, too, when sleep evaded him, nights when he would rear up in the grip of a nightmare and Nellie had to quieten him; Nellie, who remained at his side, sometimes deeply hurt at the news of a new woman, sometimes indifferent, sometimes full of wrath.

In New York there were now new disciples, male and female. Alexander Samalman sat at Harris' feet as Harris had once sat at the feet of Byron Smith, and occasionally Harris was to be seen trooping along Fifth Avenue, surrounded by four or five young people, all hanging on his words. Samuel Roth was sometimes among them.

Roth's first meeting with Harris gives some idea of the remarkable reputation which Harris had achieved in the eyes of certain young Americans in those days. Roth ran a Poetry Bookshop in 1916–17 on West Eighth Street, and one evening

Harris wandered into the shop by chance. Roth recognized him at once, shook him by the hand and described what followed in these words: '[Roth] stood there holding his hand, stunned for a moment by the magnitude of "his" unpreparedness for such an encounter.

' ". . . have you nothing intelligent to say to the author of *The Man Shakespeare*?" [Harris] asked pleasantly, taking advantage of [Roth's] embarrassment.

' "Indeed I have," [he said], "but it's not the sort of thing I would allow the author of *The Bomb* to overhear."

'And Harris answered with a faint uncertain smile: "You are perfectly safe . . . the author of *The Bomb* hasn't heard a thing in almost a decade." '[1]

Roth asked Harris to make himself comfortable, 'and if any of these poets annoy you. . . .' He made a broad gesture to the books stacked on the shelves. Harris spread himself elegantly and indicated that he didn't think Mr. Roth had any poets capable of disturbing him. American poetry had not fared any better since Whitman than before him, he said. 'It's a serious mistake,' Roth protested, 'to make Whitman a rallying point of our national poetry.'[2]

'National fiddlesticks,' Harris cried, 'you haven't anything national here, and you certainly haven't any poetry.' [3]

In the discussion which followed Bruno's name occurred. Guido Bruno was Harris' chief assistant on the staff of *Pearsons Magazine*. A very tall man, with fat hands and an oily face, he said very little and rarely looked a stranger in the eye. It was Guido Bruno who told Buckland Plummer that Harris had made over $60,000 by a system of begging letters, artfully distributed to readers of *Pearsons*. Buckland was in a position to explain the technique from personal experience: 'In 1916 I sent to *Pearsons* for a copy of Harris' *Wilde*. After a week the books [*sic*] came and by next mail a letter from F.H. (whom I had never met or corresponded with before) asking if I would kindly give my opinion of it. This I did at some length. He replied, praising my insight, and begged

(1) Samuel Roth, *The Private Life of Frank Harris*, p. 14 (William Faro, 1931).
(2) Ibid.
3) Ibid.

176

me to read two other books of his which he was sending me. The correspondence continued for a month or two and then came a letter saying he was bringing out a set of all his books and lacked some seven thousand dollars. Could I let him have five thousand or so against his personal note—even two thousand would help greatly. He missed fire in my case, but there were plenty of others who responded.[1]

'The begging letter game reached its height during the time Bruno was working with Harris. Bruno had a rather better approach than Harris for the smaller fry. If he could only dig out a working man or woman who had saved a few hundred dollars and who showed the slightest disposition towards idealism, he could be relied upon to separate them from their savings in short order. . . . The begging letters went out on one plea or another about every two weeks, and begging appeals were published regularly in the magazine and for years brought in thousands of cheques for amounts varying from one dollar to fifty, and, in a few exceptional cases, for sums running into three or four figures. . . .'

When Guido Bruno left the magazine, Buckland Plummer was asked to take charge of the business side. 'I recall the morning of my arrival . . . when I found [Harris] propped up in . . . bed looking like a Chinese brigand, cursing his secretary, but in a very good humour withal. . . .'

'Observing the obvious prosperity in which he lived, I really began to wonder if I had not struck a gold mine after all,' Buckland Plummer commented. The illusion was shattered after luncheon, when Plummer went over to the office to meet the staff of *Pearsons*. 'The motley nature of the crew was only exceeded by the "junky" nature of the place—hundreds of old magazines strewn all over the place, dust, dirt, books, pamphlets by the thousand all mixed up together, and in the window a huge plaster group of three females, which I must confess was entirely in keeping with the surroundings. Harris insisted on having it in the center of the window. "Very effective" he called it.'

Ten days later, Buckland Plummer arrived at the office to find the book-keeper disposed between three chairs in a state

[1] Hugh Kingsmill, *Frank Harris*, p. 223 (Jonathan Cape, 1932).

which first resembled profound sleep but later turned out to be a drunken coma. It transpired that the book-keeper had consistently doctored the accounts to pay for his drinking, and when challenged by Plummer to explain the discrepancies, claimed that he had been driven to drink and deception by Frank Harris.

Whereupon Buckland Plummer sacked the man and looked for a successor. Several applicants were interviewed, amongst them, a John Burns who was seen personally by Harris. The interview which followed is worth recording.

Asked by Plummer to state his qualifications, Burns began a long recital, in a deep powerful voice, with the words 'I know double entry and trial balance, I know . . .' It ran on for ten minutes, leaving the impression of a complete virtuoso of accountancy. Stirring restlessly in his seat Harris suddenly roared at him, 'The question is, do you know book-keeping?' [1]

Burns came to his feet and pounded the table. In a roar which momentarily outdid Harris, he bellowed, 'I can take care of books even better than you can write them!'

Harris replied with an approximation to reverence: 'That is saying a great deal.'

A pause, a swift exchange of glances between Harris and Buckland Plummer and then Harris said: 'I like the colour of your eyes. You're hired.'

Harris, it seems, was intuitively drawn to people of his own temperament, because the long run of fraud and deception carried out with considerable imagination by the constantly changing staff of *Pearsons*, once more repeated itself with Burns who presently ran off with a considerable sum of money and was never seen again.

Trouble now recurred. His drunken predecessor, it seems, had deliberately stolen some letters addressed by women to Frank Harris, and among them was a telegram which indicated that F.H. might be prosecuted under the white slave laws. . . . When Harris learnt of the theft his anger boiled over in a torrent of blasphemy. 'After he had cooled down,' Buckland Plummer wrote, 'he commissioned me to get the letters, and I

[1] A. I. Tobin and E. Gertz, *Frank Harris*, p. 301 (Madelaine Mendelsohn, 1931).

sent a message to M. who turned up at my hotel with his hat cocked on one side and generally showing signs of being extremely well lit up. He greeted me thus: "I guess you're surprised I came, but I'm a gen'l'man, you're a gen'l'man too, we're both gen'l'men, but Frank Harris is a son of a bitch, by God".'

Plummer began to cross-examine M., whereupon he burst into tears and delivered a long catalogue of services rendered to Harris whose only response had been, he said, to insult him. Some hard bargaining followed. At last M. yielded up the letters in exchange for the assurance that he would not be prosecuted. Clearly the most inexperienced blackmailer, he wrote a week later saying that he was 'flat broke' and desperately needed—three dollars! Plummer duly sent the three dollars and M. vanished into the void without further word.

It is clear from all this that Harris' worries were not only those of a constantly hounded debtor. His begging appeals, the books which were never launched with innocently subscribed money, and some mysterious traffic which led to the telegram threatening prosecution for white slaving, made his periodical disappearances a matter beyond the small necessities of the bankruptcy court. Another step had been taken. Another step into the black pit where easy rewards lured him on and glittering prizes waited on the most unscrupulous.

The wife of Buckland Plummer gave a vivid picture of Harris as a lecturer at this time. His days seemed to be divided between evading his enemies, affairs with women, lecturing, writing and editing, with fresh expeditions into the jungle of fraud and vice. Amongst it all his lecturing had lost nothing of its originality.

'On the evening he was to appear, A.P. and I went to the Congress Hotel to call for him,' Mrs. Buckland Plummer wrote. 'On knocking at his door we were asked to go away as he hadn't finished dressing. Half an hour later a terrible bass voice boomed like a thunderclap "Plummer, where are you?" On our entering the room he presented me with a pin, and asked me to fix his tie on to his collar so that it wouldn't slip. He had (so he said) two gold clips for that purpose, but the maid had stolen them. I couldn't get the pin through his stiff collar and he was terribly annoyed and said: "My wife can do it." This remark proved to me that he had not lost his gold clips, neither had he any. He complained of his very sore throat and for an hour (at least) gave us a detailed account of his sufferings. . . .

'I believe he was to begin his lecture at seven, but we reached the hall at ten minutes to nine. We could easily have got there to time, but Harris fumed and delayed and fidgeted with the express purpose, I always believe, of making us late.

'The hall was in East Chicago, in a very disreputable neighbourhood and was half-filled with evil-smelling foreigners. On entering the hall, Harris, who had hitherto practically ignored me, affectionately took me by the arm, continually patting my hand, and thus he and I walked down the centre aisle like a bridal couple. Every now and again he would bend towards me and smile into my face, moving his lips as though whispering sweet nothings, but in reality saying nothing.

'When Harris eventually got on the platform he turned to A.P. and said in a distressingly audible voice: "What a disgusting crowd of people! I have never spoken before such filth in my life and how dreadfully cold the place is!".'

For three weeks, advertisements had proclaimed the arrival of Harris to lecture on Bernard Shaw, but now he turned to his audience, announced that Bernard Shaw was not of sufficient consequence for a prolonged lecture, and said that he would talk about Shakespeare instead.

'The lecture itself was wonderful—the acting superb—it lasted over an hour. He wound up by reciting "The quality of mercy is not strained". It was obvious that he had given the same lecture, in precisely the same words, a thousand times before. . . .

'It certainly was a night out for me. I laughed for a week at this poor little man, so very childish, he reminded me of a peahen wishing she had the lovely tail of her brother.' [1]

[1] Hugh Kingsmill, *Frank Harris*, p. 216 (Jonathan Cape, 1932).

CHAPTER SEVENTEEN

T HE climax had to come. It was not merely that many people in New York were now determined to hunt Harris down for debt, blackmail, libel and misrepresentation. Granted very considerable talents, he had, for many years, automatically assumed that he could succeed in any role he chose, but having failed to become Bismarck, fallen short of the House of Commons, and abandoned pretensions to editing *The Times*, he was now desperately trying to find some unexplored role which would recover his lost fortunes.

Before the climax arrived he published two more volumes of *Contemporary Portraits*. In these books he purported to draw portraits of Bernard Shaw, Rudyard Kipling, Lord Dunsany, H. G. Wells, G. K. Chesterton, Thomas Huxley, John Galsworthy and others. Once again, his sitters refused, with some consistency, to recognize themselves. In each case he claimed to have met and talked at length to the men he described and if there was no denying great dash and color in the result, his skilful extension of dialogue and incident beyond their true limits, frequently wrecked the total impression.

Hesketh Pearson has since disclosed what took place between Harris and Galsworthy, an account hilariously different from that which appears in the *Portraits*. Of course, Harris made no pretensions to detailed accuracy. What were details, he would ask with a magnificent sweep of the hand; what was accuracy? What did they expect of an artist? Scientific measurement? He had not psychoanalyzed Galsworthy, he did not know how many inches he stood in his socks or the correct number of his mistresses. But he *knew* Galsworthy. He *knew* Shaw. And they were alive and talking in his books, not dead biographical dummies made of plaster from facts and figures. There was considerable truth in this. Very often his portraits did come vividly to life.

His first meeting with Galsworthy took place one day when he arrived in New York to deliver a series of lectures. The year was 1919, with the war at last over, and America in a far more relaxed state. They met after the first lecture, and according to his own account, Harris opened the conversation by praising Galsworthy's 'insistence that democracy as a method of government must be judged by its success in producing the best men.' [1] He then strongly attacked Galsworthy's view that the true purpose of democratic selection was to affirm the spirit of aristocracy. When Harris received no more than a shrug of Galsworthy's shoulders in reply, he pressed on to explain that America had a greater sense of equality than Britain, and Britain a greater sense of freedom. Galsworthy appeared not to grasp this remark completely.

Harris now stated that it was possible to meet great men in the United States 'on an equal footing', whereas in Great Britain, they were kept at stiff distance. Harris paused long enough for Galsworthy to utter two words, 'Well perhaps,' before hurrying on to carry the conversation into a different field.

Already the pattern of the first half of the interview had become clear. Harris was telling Galsworthy precisely what he thought about every question he asked. A temporary lapse in which Galsworthy was allowed to compound his opinions on George Washington, Mesopotamia, Egypt and the Irish question was followed by another prolonged statement from Harris about the dangers of an Anglo-American alliance. This was followed by a description of the behavior which he, Harris, had mistakenly expected from President Wilson.

Galsworthy's eyes began to glaze. 'Perhaps,' he said, 'we had better agree to differ.' A desultory discussion of books reached the point where Harris asked what book Galsworthy

[1] Frank Harris, *Contemporary Portraits*, Third Series, p. 35 (The Author, 1920).

was now working on. 'Another novel,' Galsworthy said, whereupon Harris was moved to express the opinion that he always associated a new novel with a new love affair. 'Oh, no,' Galsworthy answered. 'Surely one love can furnish forth a good many books.' [1]

Although Harris did not record the closing phases of the interview in any detail there is some evidence to show that he at last achieved his object and Galsworthy was busily engaged in interviewing that distinguished author Frank Harris. The most accurate statement in this typically Harrisian farrago was the final suggestion that they 'parted almost without meeting'. Hating the upper middle classes to which Galsworthy so clearly belonged, Harris believed that Galsworthy had become a serious victim of his social advantages, and was not really worth talking to at all.

Turn now to Hesketh Pearson's account of this interview based upon evidence given him by Galsworthy himself.

'Having recovered from the shock which the mere sight of Harris commonly produced, Galsworthy found himself in the midst of a discussion on Bolshevism . . . Harris intimated that he expected great things of Russia where, fortunately, there was no Upper Middle Class in the English sense of the term.

' "This Communist state that they are building up over there"—Harris pointed in the direction of Fifth Avenue— "holds out a new hope for humanity. I am thrilled by the promise. . . ."

'Galsworthy did not feel at all confident on the point and held his peace.

' "Cannot you see the beacon-lights?" pursued Harris.

'Apparently Galsworthy could not, on the spur of the moment, spot the beacon-lights. . . .

' "We mortals crown our greatest with thorns," mused Harris.

'Galsworthy was trying hard to discern the relevance of the last remark when Harris confused the issue still further with another.

' "It will call a new ideal into life, an ideal that will not find

[1] Frank Harris, *Contemporary Portraits*, Third Series, p. 40 (The Author, 1920).

183

consummation in rich viands, vintage wines and scented cigars!"

'Galsworthy contented himself with the monosyllable—"Quite." Harris next asked him whether he liked America. "Very much," said Galsworthy. "That may mean anything," said Harris. "No—it means very much," Galsworthy replied. "Do you like it?"

' "I," said Harris with the fierceness of one whose nationality was in doubt, "am an American, and I am at home in the flesh if not in the spirit."

' "Then why not," said Galsworthy, "live where your spirit is at home?"

' "France!" cried Harris rapturously, "dear France. The heart of her is warm, the soul noble. France is my spiritual home. I shall write my autobiography there . . . I shall describe love as that Goddess divine has never been described before." There was a pause; then he finished the sentence with a shout: "Naked and unashamed!"

' "Really" was the polite but slightly diffident rejoinder of the typical Englishman.

' "I will paint the ecstasy of passion," Harris went on, "and the intoxicating bliss of love's golden-glorious hours".

'. . . Galsworthy interjected a reluctant "Oh". "In my book," Harris continued, "no puritan drapery shall hide the loveliness of limbs or the beauty of breasts. I shall paint them to the life," he searched for the right word while Galsworthy held his breath, "voluptuous—nude!" ' [1]

Upon which Galsworthy was reduced to making a single sound in his throat capable of many interpretations. There followed the conversation about the necessity of starting a new love affair with each new novel, which led to the gentle remonstrance from Galsworthy. Harris, according to Pearson, concluded with a pitying smile: 'What an Englishman you are.'

'Yes,' said Galsworthy apologetically. 'I suppose I am.'

Many of the remaining portraits were not so falsified as this one but wherever one turned among them, there was always doubt. Sometimes this was expressed by infuriated relatives. Leonard Huxley, son of Thomas Huxley wrote to Tobin and

[1] Hesketh Pearson, *Thinking it Over*, pp. 147-9. (Hamish Hamilton, 1938).

Gertz: 'I very much doubt whether the interview with my father took the precise form as set forth . . . thirty-four years after the event. Internal evidence seems to show that having had interviews in the nineties, Frank Harris wrote them up long afterwards with the Life and Letters before him; working on more or less relevant passages but often, in his eagerness to make a point, missing the express qualifications and critical balance of statement . . . The upshot is that Frank Harris is not a trustworthy witness of fact in these medicated accounts of interviews. Nor had he sufficient acquaintance with T.H.H.'s real views to make him a competent critic. . . .'

That Frank Harris knew a high proportion of the celebrated men of his day is indisputable; that he knew a small percentage well, equally true; but the view that he had been exercising considerable influence over the great ones of this earth for years, a man entrusted with confidences of the most intimate and sometimes embarrassing kind, found support in his own writings alone.

The New York papers strongly criticized the second volume of *Contemporary Portraits* when it appeared, but Harris continued to dash down his impressions of every important person met, and in due course they were collected together to extend the second volume into a third.

Meanwhile he continued to edit *Pearsons Magazine*. It would be a mistake to imagine that his work in its columns went unappreciated. Eugene Debs wrote from prison on October 14th, 1920: 'I shall not see your magazine, to my deep regret, as it may not enter here. You have fought and are now fighting a heroic battle against overwhelming odds and but for your genius and personality *Pearsons* could not have lived. You have in fullest measure my admiration, my love and best wishes. . . .'

Shaw, too, appreciated *Pearsons* in a quite different sense. He wrote on September 27th, 1919: '*Pearsons* proves my case as regards the papers you don't edit. *Pearsons* is quite obviously edited by Frank Harris. Whenever you really edit a paper, there is no mistake about it. . . .'

Unfortunately *Pearsons* continued miserably and monotonously to lose increasing sums of money and among many less respectable activities, Harris had to go on lecturing. Without putting himself to too much inconvenience, he mastered the necessary facts for four or five stock pieces and trudged to distant parts of the States, 'talking at the top of his voice.'

But things were piling up. He said to Buckland Plummer one day that his nerves would not stand much more and there were times when he felt his brain was literally on fire, so hot and strange did his head feel. Yet he had—somehow—to continue to write and lecture. He claimed that for thirty years he had gone about the world telling what he regarded as the truth, with a total disregard for the consequences. Now, in his sixties, he began to hedge, to worry about the reactions of an audience, and there were times when he said wearily to Nellie: 'To hell with it, old girl. I'm going to have a bit of quiet and compromise for a bit.'

It was not so easy as he thought. Suddenly blinded by severe headaches and finding long nights sleepless, he decided that he must have a change. Walking down Fourth Avenue with three disciples, he announced, one day: 'Boys, I must get away for a vacation, and I could get it if you would help me. . . . Why don't you pick out some good stories from old copies of the *Cornhill Magazine* and fill up *Pearsons* with them?' [1] [2]

It was all arranged overnight. Temporarily Harris went off to Savannah and left Alexander Marky to run the paper. Legend has it that it was the one remaining way of escaping his creditors. Two months later he returned to find Marky in confident control and decided to leave for a longer vacation.

Before he went, Samuel Roth called on him one day and was greeted by Nellie. 'Frank overslept a bit,' she said. 'He's upstairs dressing.' Roth went upstairs and Harris immediately stormed, 'Overslept nothing. I'm so full of a new and really grand enterprise I wasn't able to sleep at all last night.'

'He stopped in the midst of adjusting his red tie and looked at me with a terrible intentness. "I am going to write the story of my life," he said quietly.'

Roth could hardly believe that he had heard aright. Those were his words '. . . Words uttered by God knows how many

[1] Mrs. Harris to Hugh Kingsmill.

[2] A. I. Tobin and E. Gertz, *Frank Harris*, p. 302 (Madelaine Mendelsohn, 1931).

actors, actresses, seamstresses and retired generals before him. But he really meant me to believe that the heavens were about to open over my head for a rain of prophecy.' [1]

Harris was so absorbed in his new venture that he 'did not notice Nellie as she stopped to pull up his coat collar against the cold. "I'll show them," he muttered. . . .' [2]

For his second vacation he decided to visit once again his beloved Nice in the South of France. *En route* he attended the Genoa Conference of 1922, interviewed Winston Churchill, Briand and Lloyd George, and sent back vivid accounts to *Pearsons*. Nice he found as wonderful as ever and spent some weeks there, idling in the sun.

Returning once more to America, he quarrelled fiercely with Marky, and accused him of ruining the paper by publishing it late every month. They bickered and bargained for days. Finally, Marky bought Harris out for $2,500 and in a great burst of enthusiasm, Harris decided to rush off to England, settle down and write the autobiography which, he proclaimed, would shake the stars in their courses.

Out of the blue came an altogether unexpected blow. The authorities refused him a visa to England. At first he could not believe his ears. He, Harris, the Great Englishman, the Author and Editor who had found and made some of the greatest British writers, who had written at least three of the finest books in the English language, refused a visa to the land of his birth. It was iniquitous. It was—unnatural. But he must get away finally and irrevocably from an America which had once more become intolerable. In the end he decided to return to the South of France. There, in what he now claimed was his spiritual home, he would give himself up to writing his biggest book of all.

Three days before sailing, he gave a farewell dinner. Gloriously drunk he toasted his friends, reached heights of bitter eloquence and came to his last sentence with the solemnity of a judge. 'The two most typical things in America are straw hats which cannot be worn after September 15th, and cash registers . . . .'

[1] Samuel Roth, *The Private Life of Frank Harris* (William Faro, 1931).
[2] Ibid.

There was one more memory from the following night. Sober, subdued, Harris walked down Fifth Avenue with three of his disciples, Samalman, Ruth Trask and Gwladys Price-Williams. His power to arouse a curious kind of loyalty had held this trio together for some time. Now, no one said very much. Presently Harris stopped, looked slowly round at them and said: 'I wonder if I shall ever see New York again. . . .' [1]

[1] A. I. Tobin and E. Gertz, *Frank Harris*, p. 308 (Madelaine Mendelsohn 1931).

CHAPTER EIGHTEEN

H<small>E</small> arrived in Nice in September 1923, took a villa on the Boulevard Edouard Sept and lived in the style which was expected of the ex-editor of *Pearsons*. Every morning at 11 a.m., his ageing form, clad in a perfectly pressed suit, Eton tie, stiff white collar and spats, sauntered down towards the sea, nodding occasionally to complete strangers who failed to recognize Frank Harris. Sometimes he sat alone, sipping an apéritif, and lowered his eyes to watch the skirts and silk stockinged legs of any woman under 20. But the old fires did not blaze so easily. Once, in New York, before he left for France, a young woman had called asking for work and only when she had gone did he suddenly realize that her beautiful figure had failed to stir him. He described it in his Autobiography. As always on such occasions, he was moved to tears.

But now the warmth, the wine, and the carefree clothes of young women, revived the beat in his pulses and presently he was stirred to an odd enterprise. If he could not in physical fact, recover the life of the roué, he would do so at one remove. Gertz has stated that the whole of the Autobiography was not, as is commonly supposed, written in the South of France. He first thought of it years before and in July 1922, Harris had gone to Tannersville, in the American Catskills and rapidly poured down on paper the first volume of *My Life and Loves*. The remaining three volumes were written in the South of France. He worked with an inspiration drawn from George Moore who had written to him: 'You have, in yourself, a subject that will carry your name down the ages, if you write it with the necessary sincerity; that of Jean-Jacques; and it will not surprise me if you do write it.'

Volume One opened with a long preface intended to justify the frankness of the pages to follow, and made the case in such a way that many readers came sympathetically to the first chapter. In this preface Harris said that there were two traditions in English writing; one the tradition of outspokenness, represented by Chaucer and Shakespeare in which smut, lascivious asides and virile freedom of speech were not forbidden; and two, the Puritan tradition 'gelded to tamest propriety', which, under Queen Victoria, had produced a number of feeble provincial novels where sex and all its corollaries had almost disappeared. Dickens, Thackeray, and Reade were the sexless servants of the second tradition. Place them beside Balzac, Flaubert and Zola and their books appeared as passionless caricatures of reality.

Harris quoted Grant Allen on the sexual instinct: 'Its alliance is wholly with whatever is purest and most beautiful within us. To it we owe the evolution of music, of poetry, of romance, of belles-lettres, of painting, of sculpture, of decorative art, of dramatic entertainment. To it we owe the entire existence of our aesthetic sense which, in the last resort, is a secondary sex attribute. From it springs the love of beauty, around it all beautiful arts circle as their centre. Its subtle aroma pervades all literature. . . .'

Few of these lofty protestations were really borne out by the first of the four volumes of Harris' life. There was an ill-defined borderline where Zola remained within the bounds of literature proper, and Harris' description of male and female responses became pornography; but since the definition of pornography varied from person to person, in the last resort it resolved itself into a question of taste. Certainly Volume One horrified some of its readers beyond their highest hopes and taste of the most emancipated kind was outraged.

Confusing sincerity with sexual abandon, Harris quickly outdid Jean-Jacques Rousseau. In a flurry of sensuality he hurried past commonplaces like birth, family and upbringing, for early sexual adventures, and presently committed to paper those secret details which are part of many lovers' lives, but read like pornography once placed on paper. Perhaps that under-estimates the effect of Volume One.

More and more Harris wrote in a white heat of remembered lust, distilling every microscopic drop, until the fever which ran through his ageing veins conveyed itself to paper. The remembered accounts ran riot, and the occasional bursts of feeling were overwhelmed by the words of a lascivious old man stimulating his body to respond to its former glories.

Chapter One claimed that Harris took memory as his main guide but it was memory of a very obsessive kind. On the second page he threatens to blackmail a nurse because of the man he has seen in her bed, and on page three he explores the legs of the girls at school. Within a few more pages, a man called Strangways gives a graphic account of his first skirmish with a nursemaid, masturbation follows, sodomy supervenes, and the whole chapter is alive with unprintable words.

Some chapter headings made concessions to his more con-ventional readers. He frequently married his love life with ordinary down to earth fact. 'Some Study' had to combine with 'More Loves', 'Work' with 'Sophy', 'Holidays' with 'Fresh Virtue'. But the whole of the first volume was sprinkled with aphrodisiacs calculated to make the second volume com-pulsory reading to every other person who happened upon the first. There were of course non-sexual and well written chapters in Volume One—'Life in Chicago', 'Life on the Trail', 'New Experiences', 'Europe and the Carlyles'—and factual back-ground of a colorful and most interesting kind also broke through from time to time; but it all tended to be over-shadowed by steadily more fabulous sexual exploits.

Volume Two was quieter and complained bitterly of the reception given to Volume One. Some interesting facts under-went the usual exaggeration, but there was much of normal interest in Volume Two which the chapter headings revealed: 'How I Came to Know Shakespeare', 'German Student Customs', 'Goethe', 'William I', 'Bismarck', 'Wagner', 'Athens and the English Language'. Harris protested that only two men out of thousands had understood the first volume of his *Life and Loves*: Bernard Shaw who would have defended it but for the photographs of naked young girls, and H. L. Mencken, the American critic, who said that the universality of sexual impulses justified their description in minute details. The hostility of the remaining thousands did not prevent Harris from making expeditions into forbidden territory in the second volume. They occurred under painfully obvious headings— 'The Ebb and Flow of Passion', 'A French Mistress' and 'A Passionate Experience in Paris'. Even when Harris came to the last chapter and seemed to strike a deeper note—'The Foretaste of Death from 1920 Onward'—the foretaste turned out to be the threat of impotence. For Harris, impotence was a kind of death in life, and such was his respect and veneration for the sexual impulse that it could move him to tears. There were, indeed, moments when he successfully evoked the poetry of passion, sheer intensity of feeling lifted his writing to a quite different level and the loss of potency became, as it deserved to be, a profound tragedy.

None of this interested his detractors. As he said in the last chapter of Volume Two: 'Everywhere I feel the unspoken condemnation . . . the sneer or the foul sidelong grin.'[1] With a mixture of sincerity and insincerity difficult to disentangle from one another he added: 'Many men and some few women will read me when I am dust and perhaps be a little grateful to me for having burst the fetters and led the way out of the prison of puritanism into the open air and sunshine of this entrancing world.'[2]

Volume Three was dedicated to Escar Levine—who had by now gone to prison for handling the earlier volumes—and the chapter headings were less spectacular: 'Mental Self-Discipline', 'Heine', '*The Evening News*', 'Bismarck and Burton', 'Marriage and Politics', 'Tennyson and Thomson'. Some of the writing had become striking and one description of London was moving and beautiful. In another attempt to justify the outpourings of the earlier volumes, Harris fell back, in Volume Three, on quoting Anatole France:

'I want Venus from head to foot. Her face is good enough for relations and friends and children, and the husband, but her body must be ready for caresses. For I hope you are not

[1] Frank Harris, *My Life and Loves*, Vol. 2, p. 449.
[2] Ibid., p. 450.

one of those fools who would limit the lover to a kiss on the face . . . Lovers can claim all the unedited places. . . .

'People praise my learning: I only want to be learned in the things of love. Love is now my sole and particular study. It is to love that I devote the remains of my continually diminishing powers. . . .

'Make love now, by night and by day, in winter as in summer . . . You are in the world for that and the rest of life is nothing but vanity, illusion, waste. . . .'

Volume Four was short. Chapter headings like—'How I Began to Write', '*The Saturday Review*', and 'The Jameson Raid', quickly gave way to more personal matters and there followed a description of Lesbian love which achieved considerable beauty. This last volume ended on a religious note. Harris claimed that he was an agnostic and still believed that the sordid competitive scramble which made up our culture could give way to a higher and nobler way of life where Man would not be driven by mean and petty motives.

However one reviled these 1300 monumental pages of fact, fiction and obscenity, or exclaimed at a life given up to ravishment and pleasure, there remained a concern with the kind of community in which we lived, breaking through like a guilty conscience time and again. In one sense it was almost as if he hinted—had the world been different—I might have been different too.

The results of the publication of his Autobiography were devastating. A long series of letters reveal the horror which overtook him and the fresh hardships into which, he said, it plunged him. He had written to Upton Sinclair—an old friend who had praised his earlier work—about *My Life and Loves*. Sinclair replied: 'I have your letter telling me that you are sending me Volume II of the autobiography, and asking that my wife will let me tell you what I think of it. My wife does not prevent my saying what I think. . . . It is the vilest book I have ever laid eyes on: I think it absolutely inexcusable . . . poisonous!' Sinclair Lewis later wrote: 'A senile and lip-wetting giggle of an old man about his far distant filthiness. . . .' The *New York Evening World* published an editorial on the book in August 1926. 'Having put himself in the class of street walkers [Frank Harris] is entitled to no sympathy. The Frank Harris of years ago died long ago, and it is his cadaver that has been writing recently. The odor proves it.'

The odor even penetrated the august meetings of the American Senate. Senator Cutting, from New Mexico, was supporting an amendment to a bill which would have liberalized the censorship laws, when Senator Smart, a dour champion of puritanism, challenged him. 'I could take two of the books referred to and if I should read them to the Senate I do not believe there is a Senator who would dare to vote for his amendment.'

Senator Cutting demanded to know the titles of the two books. Senator Smart replied: *Lady Chatterly's Lover* by D. H. Lawrence and *My Life and Loves* by Frank Harris. Even Cutting did not want to be mixed up in quite such vile company and he replied, with indignation: 'If the Senator can point out any place where I referred to either of these books I will withdraw my amendment right now!'[1]

Nellie Harris, herself, was in great distress about *My Life and Loves*. She wouldn't read the first volume, fought bitterly with Harris over its publication and at one point, in a passion of disapproval, threatened to leave him at once if it ever achieved publication.

The history of the distribution of *My Life and Loves* is not fully known, but some of the details make fascinating reading. A series of mysterious people were involved in equally mysterious smuggling activities intended to distribute the first volume throughout France, England and America. There were several techniques. Scores of copies were covered with jackets which read—*A Tale of Two Cities* by Dickens, or *Old Goriot* by Balzac, and sent through the post. In France this method worked reasonably well. For America, copies were packed beneath equal numbers of Harris' life of Oscar Wilde and at least four hundred carefully crated in this manner. A Mrs. V—z, whose husband smuggled drugs, said she could easily get the crates into the United States. She did indeed arrive with the crates but a long silence followed and when Harris wrote

[1] A. I. Tobin and E. Gertz, *Frank Harris*, p. 314 (Madelaine Mendelsohn, 1931).

pressing for news, she informed him that all four hundred books had been seized. Harris at once demanded the return of the four hundred copies of *Oscar Wilde* and was furious to receive the reply that these were to be kept to cover her expenses.

There were many agents, methods, feuds and disappointments. B. operated in Chicago, a Dr. G. in New York and Mrs. M. L. S. and R. from varying bases. At one stage Harris conceived the idea of establishing supply centers in Canada, where a thousand copies would be stored. People were to be invited to send $15 (approximately £4) by mail, and they would receive a carefully packed copy in return. Alternatively, single copies were posted at the rate of one a day from France to Dr. G. in New York to be distributed privately. Later, what Harris referred to as the 'naughty' chapters, were separated from the French printings and sent independently to America to be re-bound into the original.

Evidence about the actual sales of the first volume is deceptive. It seems that over a thousand copies were sold, which at an average figure of $10, would yield £2,500, but there are many contradictory witnesses. Some years after Tobin and Gertz had published their biography of Harris, one of the directors of the Fortune Press wrote to Gertz: ' . . . Frank Harris misled you when he told you that from 1924 he had been living in poverty and we cannot understand your believing such a story. You say "Harris lost his savings, his health, his last bit of property through the publication of his life . . ." We happen to know that what you say is not in accordance with the facts. Harris did not lose money over his life. The first two volumes showed a handsome profit. . . .'

Whatever the precise extent of the royalties, before much of the money actually reached Harris, trouble arose with several of his agents. One was suddenly scared by a brush with customs agents and went into temporary retirement; S. gave up altogether when he became fully aware of the risks involved, and then followed a shattering blow of quite different proportions. In September 1925, a Mr. Sumner, Secretary of the Suppression of Vice Society, seized and confiscated a thousand copies of Volume Two at the American binders, and Harris' chief agent in New York was summarily arrested. Harris poured out letters explaining the disaster to his few remaining friends and there were pages full of pathetic appeals for help and money. In the middle of the new crisis, his secretary left him and his letters had to be hand-written. Suddenly and not unexpectedly his nerves were badly strained. Sometimes when he tried to write in the morning, his hand shook so much that only his wife could decipher what he had written, and letters were presently left until the afternoons. Fear of himself being arrested grew on him, and he hurriedly arranged for compromising letters to be addressed to a Mrs. Farnell Scott, c/o American Express, Nice. There were frequent visits to the pawnbroker, his wife sold her jewels, and he asked one person after another to lend him money. Quarrels with Nellie once more reached breaking point, and presently anxiety reached that pitch where life became sheer misery. 'It was,' he said to Buckland Plummer, 'all sick, grey and horrible . . . and painful . . . so painful I wonder sometimes why I haven't done away with myself.'

In debt to the extent of $3,000, what he did was to launch into another literary project far less pornographic but not less wild. Half-way through the third volume of *My Life* and inspired by hatred of Shaw's play, *St. Joan*, he determined to write a far better play about the same woman. He did, in fact, rush extravagantly into the play and immediately it was finished sent one copy to Shaw and another to Max Reinhardt. Shaw replied on May 20th, 1926: '. . . I always want to make a drama of a subject, the bigger the better. You always want to make a short story of it, the shorter the better. My making a drama of Joan enraged your instinct: you felt you must do something quite different with her; and you did not understand that the something was a short story and not a drama—the result is a shocking hybrid. Why not throw it on to the fire and write your story?'

In May 1926, his new secretary B. D. Kenet was writing to R.: 'Mr. Harris had been and is *very ill*; over-work and financial worries I think (confidential) together with a malicious cold which he doesn't seem to be able to throw off; but I feel sure that he will come out all right if Max Reinhardt should take his play. Personally I think such a ray of hope for a way out of his financial worries is all he needs and I know you pray for this as much as any and all of his devout admirers; and no one can work with or for him without desiring to do his or her utmost to help Mr. Harris in his splendid work. I boil with rage to think he must suffer what he does and that those who could and should give a helping hand are perfectly indifferent to his situation. He surely appreciates what you and Mr. L— have done and are doing for him. (This is confidential but I couldn't help from saying a word, for his condition does worry me: he doesn't seem to be able to get hold of himself—almost a general breakdown—but it isn't hopeless for I know any ray of hope will help him and I am earnestly hoping that Reinhardt will send him a favourable word soon.)'

It never came. Nothing seemed to go right. The play was a dismal failure and editors now rejected even the most carefully written articles, afraid to be associated with the author of *My Life and Loves.*

Meanwhile complications, even in France, for the distribution of each successive volume of *My Life* grew. Harris had developed the habit of collecting and storing fresh copies as they came off the presses, himself. He would hire a taxi, park it in a side street, bring out small parcels enclosing not more than twenty copies, conceal them as best he could and drive to his home where the books were carefully camouflaged and stored in the garret.

If these devices seemed extravagant in emancipated France, events quickly justified Harris' caution. One sunny morning, when the sheer beauty of the weather had momentarily revived his spirits, there came a knock on the door. Nellie answered it and returned to her husband in considerable distress. 'The police', she said and Harris leapt out of his chair, half in fear, half in fury. How dare they? What did they want hammering on his door in this fashion? He would have the law on them. It was outrageous.

The police officer showed a search warrant and two implacably silent gentlemen began to ferret and burrow in every cupboard, bookcase and portmanteau. They tilted up the beds, tapped the floorboards and asked for the keys to a locked cupboard, while Harris never ceased talking. He had to talk to cover his nerves. He put his hands in his pockets to hide their shaking, and stalked behind the police, with an air of someone grossly outraged. They did not find the carefully hidden books. Harris jeered at them as they left, and for a moment, it looked as though he might be arrested on a quite different pretext. Then he slammed the door behind them, embraced Nellie and sank into a chair, pale with relief.

The police had already visited the printers and found nothing. Now they went to every bookseller in Nice and cross-examined each in turn. Had Harris or one of his agents delivered copies of *My Life and Loves* and had they been exhibited for sale? Against the advice of French friends, convinced that in France a prosecution for such a book was impossible, Harris, with fresh cunning, had distributed the books to friends only, and had insisted that they should not be exhibited for sale. In consequence *The Authorities*, as he called them with fierce emphasis, once more drew a complete blank.

It did not stop legal action. The second volume had been printed in France, and that, finally, was pretext enough. One day Harris received a summons to appear before the local magistrate on a charge of giving an offence against public morals, and the whole of that morning he seemed stunned, hardly saying a word even to Nellie. In the afternoon he began furious letter writing, burst into forceful telephone calls, sent Nellie off on a round of visits, and launched a campaign to enlist the aid of Barbusse, Morand, Rolland and others.

When Harris finally appeared in court [1] he looked an old man. His face was haggard, his eyes dulled, and his voice carried the suspicion of a croak. Occasionally he flared out at the magistrate, echoes of the old Harris breaking through, but a new circumspection informed his whole manner and there was even the suspicion of a cringe.

He had to make two appearances in court. Meanwhile, that bush telegraph of intellectual indignation—which any attempt at literary suppression automatically set off in the France of those days—had steadily intensified; and protest after protest was voiced. Statements were signed and distributed; Barbusse

[1] 1926.

and Rolland wrote to the national press; a whole ferment of activity culminated in a considerable outcry.

Shaw was asked to sign one such protest and replied: 'This is calculated to damage Harris to the utmost possible. To address it to the judge is not only an impropriety which may, for all I know, be a punishable offence in French law . . . It draws attention quite unnecessarily to *My Life and Loves* . . . All the stuff about France and art and freedom is enough to make any lawyer sick. . . .'

Very inadequately he went on: 'I have not seen the volume in question: but Mr. Harris is in possession of my view as to how the first can be defended: that is, not as a work of art but as a document. As an invention or as a display of art for the sake of art, it is clearly a contravention of the laws against indecency. . . .' Even the devoted Shaw, who remained loyal to Harris long after everyone else had deserted him, was not prepared to whitewash a work which he regarded as a rather uninspired piece of pornography. He did not sign the protest.

Suddenly, at its height, because of the campaigns on Harris' behalf, the prosecution was called off. In the rush of relief Harris almost forgot the web of debt and suspicion which still entangled him, but presently its suffocating presence became, once more, all too clear. Violent fluctuations of mood occurred. In March 1926 he was joyfully working again, but by April of the same year everything had collapsed in misery once more. For one spell of two and a half months he simply remained in bed too sick, depressed and worried—if not frightened—to do more than turn to Nellie for reassurance. He wrote nothing, he ate little, and once in the middle of the night he woke shouting for Nellie, almost in terror.

When, at last, he had completed three-quarters of the third volume, he wondered what in heaven's name he could do with it when it was finished. And then at last came a break in the clouds. A German publisher decided to launch a German translation of *My Life and Loves* and to pay well for it. Harris did not hesitate to spend the money at once. In the worst extremity he would have no truck with bourgeois caution about money. 'I must live well or not at all,' he constantly repeated, and it was one of the few of his boasts which had any reality. Attemps to live within limited means at once drove him to thoughts of suicide, and poverty was as sordid to him as lust was to other people. He had to entertain lavishly, he must give each guest a whole bottle of personally chosen wine and provide rare delicacies and liqueurs, whenever he had the money.

But bursts of ecstatic spending would send him down to the gloom of poverty and unpaid bills with great consistency, until the cries of a man outraged that his genius could be so neglected, became a request for a loan of fifty dollars.

In 1927 there were good and bad periods and he was much more active. By January of 1928 his eyes and his memory were troubling him. As always he wrote about these new signs of age with a vivid nostalgia which became, at its best, very moving and conveyed depths of awareness so sadly lacking in other sides of his life. '. . . my eyes get blurred very quickly with reading and above all my loss of memory is a curse to me. I pick up a book and I am half way through before I remember that I have read [it] before already. . . . Still beautiful days are there and the sunshine, but I am old and the end is near and the conviction is with me all the time, paralysing me. . . .'

Sometimes he concealed his worries and anxiety; sometimes he was frank about them. Whenever he chose, in public, he could still summon up his old confident self. Many distinguished people came to call upon him in the South of France and sometimes he would put up a wonderful front. Sometimes, too, he still mustered enough money or credit to entertain in the style which he thought his place in the world demanded.

Emma Goldman, the American anarchist, arrived one hot June day and found him in very good form. She later wrote: 'The Harrises were marvellous hosts sparing no pains to surround me with care and help to restore my health and cheer. I had spent many interesting hours with Frank before, but never enough to see more than the artist, the man of the world, the interesting *causeur*. . . .'

Shaw, who had just finished *The Apple Cart*, came south for six weeks' holiday and agreed, by letter, to visit his old friend Harris for lunch. Then, on August 10th, 1928, he wrote from

Cap d'Antibes: 'My dear F. H. I can't come tomorrow. Yesterday I was smitten with the most undignified form of *maladie du pays*. My interior became a mere cave of the winds and waters: and I lay about unable to keep on my legs longer than ten minutes at a time . . . I therefore propose Wednesday instead of tomorrow. By that time I shall be either quite well or dead.

Ever G.B.S.'

There was something odd about this letter. When Harris hurried over to see Shaw he found that he had gone out for a car ride. Conceivably, his wife, who loathed Harris and had deliberately burnt two volumes of *My Life*, persuaded G.B.S. that at least he must delay meeting Harris until he could do so without her. Harris left a message and dejectedly set out for home again. Shaw read Harris' message when he returned and at once wrote: 'It was most kind of you to come all that way . . . For the moment I cannot fix a day because I have given an open invitation to Troubetsky to rush over from Lago Maggiore . . . my telegram, despatched last night, can hardly take more than a fortnight to reach him . . . and when he is disposed of I will fix a day for Cimiez.'

Maladie du pays had become a prior engagement. Eventually Shaw did drive over one day. Emma Goldman was still with the Harrises when he arrived and Frank introduced Shaw to Miss Goldman. She makes no reference to this meeting in an autobiography comprehensive enough to include far less significant moments. According to Harris, Miss Goldman told Shaw the story of how, as an anarchist, she almost became, on one occasion, a prostitute in order to raise the price of a revolver.

Another visitor at this time was Hugh Kingsmill. He had made several attempts on behalf of Harris to persuade certain English publishers that the expurgated edition of *My Life* was well worth publishing. No one believed him, but it seemed to give him excellent credentials for calling on Harris. In the South of France for a holiday, he made his way to Nice and took a taxi to the Villa Edouard Sept. As he came within sight of the villa he saw Harris, immaculately dressed, sitting bolt upright in a car between two ladies. Hastily paying his own taxi, Kingsmill rushed across and was astonished to see Harris' face go very tense. It was one of those moments when Harris identified an impetuous stranger with a possible agent of the police. Kingsmill thrust his head into the car, called a greeting and suggested visiting him next day. Still uneasy Harris murmured, 'Surely—surely,' in the vaguest possible way. The car drove off. A moment later, a bull-like roar echoed down the road, and the car jerked to a standstill. Kingsmill walked after the car to see Harris leaning out of the window his face wreathed in smiles. 'I didn't recognize you, Kingsmill,' he said. 'But my wife knew you. You've changed a lot.' Kingsmill gently reminded him of the ravages of war and said that he would call tomorrow.

The meeting was hardly memorable. He later wrote that he was 'glad to see the old ruffian again'. 'He certainly didn't look 72', Kingsmill added, but he felt that his 'force was nearly gone'. [1] It seems to have been a bad day. Whenever the situation demanded it, Harris could still summon up some of the rugged power which had once made him the lion of Fleet Street, and in the presence of company of consequence he usually made an effort: but the day Kingsmill called he had an attack of phlebitis and lay on a couch from which he made no attempt to rise.

'He talked away as of old, though without the old animation, and on less exalted topics than I had been accustomed to from him, speaking affectionately, and at length of . . . Horatio Bottomley.' It did not matter to Harris that Bottomley had once described him in print as 'a scoundrel who must not be allowed to pollute the soil of Britain'. 'That's nothing . . . nothing at all,' he now said, 'the man has brains. Real brains. I rate him far above the Asquiths and Churchills. . . .'

'Winston Churchill,' Kingsmill said, 'told me he could not forgive you for going to America and writing against England.'

'What, Churchill! A man who changes his party whenever it suits his convenience!'

'I suppose,' said Kingsmill, 'he distinguishes between

[1] Hugh Kingsmill, *Frank Harris*, p. 170 (Jonathan Cape, 1932).

crossing floors and crossing oceans. Though the principle seems the same.'[1]

George Sylvester Viereck also left Paris for the South to see Harris. He asked a number of unbelievably inane questions but found Harris, carefully posed beside the sea in his smartest clothes, ready to answer anything.

'What,' Viereck enquired with wonderful naïveté, 'is the meaning of life?' And Harris sensibly replied, 'I am doubtful whether life has any meaning.'[2]

* * * * *

In the next few months his troubles thickened appallingly. Among many new schemes he thought wildly of going back to the United States for an American lecture tour. This, he suddenly believed, might recover his fame and fortune, but the police had become an ugly ghost haunting every scene and once more he was warned of the possibility of arrest.

Harris now seemed to be 'wanted' in a number of countries. Writing to Vyvyan Holland, Lord Alfred Douglas said: '. . . You are . . . quoted as saying that Harris cannot come to England for political reasons! But perhaps you do not even know that what prevents Harris from coming to England is nothing to do with politics. He is "wanted by the Police". There is at least one warrant for his arrest which would be put into force the moment he landed in England. . . .' [3]

If he tried to enter the U.S.A. directly the police were there, waiting; if he travelled via Canada, the English authorities would ask the most difficult questions; the route through Mexico to America offered the greatest security but was very expensive and long drawn out. Yet Harris suddenly and desperately desired to escape from that warm, sunny country which had once been his spiritual home and now had become, in monotonous line of repetition, a concentrated hell of materialism where it was no longer possible even to borrow money.

Accident took him first not to America but to Germany in November of 1927. The *Berliner Tageblatt* had praised the

[1] Hugh Kingsmill, *Frank Harris*, p. 171 (Johnathan Cape, 1932).
[2] G. S. Viereck, *Glimpses of the Great* (Duckworth, 1930).
[3] Vyvyan Holland, *Son of Oscar Wilde*, p. 265 (Rupert Hart-Davis, 1954).

translation of the first two volumes of *My Life and Loves* in ecstatic terms: 'A work which overwhelms the reader with its monumental spiritual significance, with the fearlessness of its confessions, and with the intensity of its creative power.' Probably as a result of this, the Lessung-Hochschule invited Harris to visit Berlin and lecture about a trio which only Harris' genius could have brought together: Shakespeare, Shaw and Frank Harris.

His not inconsiderable reserves of optimism at once revived and within twenty-four hours he was roaring about the house making preparations with all his old arrogance, like a forgotten actor who had suddenly been given the lead in Hamlet. Everything went very well in Germany. Opening his lectures in reasonable German, Harris occasionally broke into English, but the audience was sufficiently enthusiastic not to mind what language he essayed to master.

The night before he left, a dinner was arranged and the distinguished guests included Albert Einstein. Harris made a forceful, eloquent speech, and returned to France with his new optimism undiminished. It looked as though the renaissance which he had so long craved was about to become a reality. A new briskness informed his step, the clouded eyes brightened, and Germany took the place occupied in succession by England, America and France as the cradle of culture and Harris' spiritual home.

Alas, it did not last. Harris discussed with Fischer, his German publisher, the publication of the third volume of *My Life* and when the terms had been agreed, Madame Vallentin went to work on the translation. Harris waited expectantly in France for another large cheque from Germany which would once more buy off the ravening hordes of creditors, but Fischer made the mistake of having the translation edited before sending it to Harris.

'Now what do you think this editor did?' Harris said to Tobin in New York the following year. 'He cut out completely the Heine and Jesus chapters! Think of it—the Heine and Jesus chapters completely cut out!' Harris' eyes blazed.

'I wrote to the editor that he had blotted out the two best chapters of the book. Imagine my surprise when a little later I got a reply from him informing me that the reason he had cut out the Jesus chapter was because I said nothing new in it. Immediately I challenged him to find a single reference to anything I had written about Christ . . . Talk about German stupidity!'

Whether Fischer thereupon refused to pay Harris the advance is not clear, but finances quickly became complicated once more, the trip to America was revived, and Harris decided to test the dangers and possibilities by sending his wife to the States first.

While he waited impatiently, back in the Villa Edouard, for news from Nellie, an American who had known and admired him in his *Pearsons'* days, called upon him suddenly. In the talks which followed, the American said that he himself would pay Harris a large sum to lecture in the United States. On his own testimony this mysterious American, represented under the initial N., owned a number of oil wells in Texas and had an astronomical income, but Harris, shrewd at detecting his own faults in others, quickly became sceptical of the whole scheme.

When Nellie at last returned from the United States she brought assurances from highly placed American officials that her husband would not be molested if he chose to land in New York. Almost simultaneously, to his astonishment, Harris received $1,000 for immediate expenses from N. Suddenly he bounded with enthusiasm again. Plans were made to leave for New York as soon as possible. The last attempt to retrieve a fortune thrice lost was about to begin.

CHAPTER NINETEEN

DESPITE the reassurances which Nellie had brought, the return to America deeply disturbed Harris, and as the ship approached New York he spent many worried hours arguing with her. At the age of 73 he was determined not to be arrested and imprisoned, but doubts about his reception troubled him, and he went over in detail, with Nellie, the results of the enquiries she had made. Twenty-four hours before the ship was due to arrive, a radiogram reached Arthur Ross, Harris' New York attorney, saying that Albert Ballin (alias Harris) was ill on board the ship and would like to be met. Hospitals were telephoned, a specialist summoned, and when the ship arrived two attendants walked down the gangway carrying a stretcher—but it was empty. Three minutes later, arm-in-arm, Frank and Nellie appeared, heads held high, step brisk, to all intents and purposes a happy pair. Nellie wore an elegant if somewhat faded black coat with an elaborate hat, and Frank—Frank had taken out of the moth preservers a coat of black seal-skin which might have belonged to the Bismarck he so admired, a coat so long that it threatened to trip him up. His suit was startlingly brand new, his Eton tie brilliant, his hat a big dove-grey fedora. As he left the ship he smiled and nodded to left and right at a purely imaginary audience, his cane swinging acknowledgments. It was difficult for a man famed in four continents as the author of *My Life and Loves* to believe that, of the crowd gathered to meet passengers that day, very few had read his great work; it was even more impossible for his insatiable egotism to accept the fact that only a handful of the people present were genuinely interested in this moment of his return to America.

'Hallo—hallo—everybody,' he called, beaming round on the impassive faces of strangers. 'It's wonderful to see all my friends again.'

Within a few days cold reality broke in. The lecturing which N. had promised did not materialize; the radio talks which—with his wonderful voice still intact—were to bring him thousands of dollars, never came off; and no one seemed interested in the articles he was prepared to write, or the receptions he was ready to grace. Worse, the danger of arrest still haunted him. When Tobin expressed the view that perhaps it would be better not to lecture in public whatever offers might be made, Harris snapped back: 'I'm well prepared for them. They'll never get me alive!' He tapped his vest pocket significantly. If he had stopped there his words might have carried conviction. Audacious, impulsive, given to grand gestures, a spectacular suicide by poison when at the point of arrest would have been one logical outcome of the way of life to which he had committed himself; but when, within a few seconds, he added, 'I always carry two kinds of poison with me and either one of them will do the trick,' the whole thing became wildly theatrical. Perhaps it was just another role in the myriad repertoire of his acting. Nothing was so dramatic as the threat of taking one's own life by poison.

There were many heart-felt confessions to Tobin in the next two or three weeks: 'Oh, they have been dreadful these past five years . . . I'm not used to this poverty and really I'm not a spendthrift. I want little; just enough for bare necessities so that I can finish my work.'[1]

Still capable of a very perverse form of logic, he said one day, 'I've often asked myself why it was that I couldn't join the ranks of the despoilers instead of the despoiled. And the only answer I could find is that my physical and mental structure could never be adjusted to the easier ways of life. To me the hardest way has been the only way,[2] Where once, some

[1] A. I. Tobin and E. Gertz, *Frank Harris*, p. 14 (Madelaine Mendelsohn, 1931).

[2] Ibid., p. 18.

207

subtle inflexion in the voice gave this ironic undertones, now it was delivered with the full force of a melancholy truth, but there were times now when he seemed to know that he could not escape the consequences of the evil trail he had left, and in another quite different mood, he would regard what had happened in the past six years as inevitable retribution.

His loss of memory troubled him deeply. 'I remember when I first got out of bed [and] tried to recall something and suddenly found I couldn't remember names and dates as I used to. And it has become worse and worse until today I can't remember a thing.' [1] As Tobin and Gertz remarked, his memory was worse than even this frank confession made clear. Tobin asked him, one day, why he had never interviewed Mrs. Parsons, the widow of one of the men hanged for throwing the bomb, when he was writing his novel *The Bomb*.

'Mrs. Parsons?' Harris repeated, 'Mrs. Parsons? Who is she?'

'Why Albert Parsons' wife,' Tobin answered, but this still did not connect in Harris' mind. Tobin at last explained the reference in detail. Harris looked appalled. 'Ah,' he said, 'my memory's gone—completely gone,' and a note of desperation came into his voice.

He was 73 now, and the world about him the harsh indifferent world of New York City; 73 and a bewildering rush of motor-cars, cinemas, sky-signs and noise left him tired by the sheer speed and sound of life; 73 and the need to match this brisk, forceful city a considerable effort. His face had hardened into a reptilian scaliness, and the nose, broad and pitted stood out with unmistakable Semitic thrust. Sustaining the role of the famous man, unchanged by the years, in conversation with comparative strangers he sometimes achieved a tremendous animation, but the effort was exhausting. His hair, still thick, owed its apparent youth to a hair pomade plastered on both sides, and the moustache, desperately trying to droop, was disciplined to fierce ends by wax. The hands, wrinkled and blue veined, were treated with cream to soften their surfaces, and the stomach pump continued to solve increasing digestive troubles.

[1] A. I. Tobin and E. Gertz, *Frank Harris*, p. 290 (Madelaine Mendelsohn, 1931).

But the array of artificial aids could not control those considerable stretches when, with close friends or alone, gaunt realities broke through. The chest was still magnificent, the shoulders broad, the poise only a little stooped, but there were moments when his face would suddenly collapse inwards, his skin would sag, his mouth fall half open and a 'look of haunted terror would stare from his eyes'.

In the day he continued walking the streets of New York, meeting people and lunching. He went, one day, to look at the old premises of *Pearsons Magazine*. He stood outside the building viewing it from all angles, a full five minutes, and when he walked away, tears were in his eyes. He went to the house in Washington Square where he had once lived, he visited an old crony from the advertising world, he made a handful of romantic trips to familiar places, but nobody noticed, and very few people seemed to remember him.

Within a few weeks what had long been his main fear became a certainty. The recovery of his fortune in New York was a dream and a delusion. After nine weeks he knew that he would have to return to France; there was nothing else to do. In the tenth week he stood, with Nellie, at the rail of the liner, watching the skyline of New York sink lower and lower on the horizon. His eyes were brimming, his voice hoarse, because he knew, as never before, that this was the last time he would ever see the lights of New York go down into the Atlantic.

*   *   *   *   *

It was snowing when they reached the South of France again. That sun-soaked coast where beautiful day followed perfect night and the air left a gentle intoxication in the senses, was blurred under drifting snow-storms which bleakened the lines of the coast and darkened the seas to black. Harris could not bear it. The house in the hills outside Nice seemed freshly cold and dull, and the people of Nice took no more notice of his return than the people of New York. Within a very short time he fell ill. Whether mysterious germs did, in reality, invade his system, or the black horror of decay and penury drive him to take refuge in imaginative illnesses, is not clear. He called it the grippe. People in fear sometimes suffered from something described, in those days, as the grippe, but now the reality of bronchitis followed; bronchitis and arthritis which left his bones chilled and sometimes twisted with pain. Presently he began the habit of sleeping in heavy woollen underclothes and pyjamas to keep the cold at bay.

Nellie found herself in a desperate situation. N., their American friend, had promised to send money on their return to France, but it did not arrive. According to Tobin and Gertz, Harris had left his priceless collection of letters from a whole gallery of famous people, with N. to be disposed of at the highest price, but there is some evidence to show that Harris had already sold these letters and spent the proceeds. Ill herself, weak and worried, Nellie continued to nurse Frank devotedly, uncertain where the money for the next month's rent would come from. The possibility of death was no longer a theatrical illusion. Her husband's boasting and arrogance had vanished, there were times when he seemed almost spiritless and he began to speak openly and frequently of death.

Something quite new broke in within a few weeks. He was attacked by an unpleasant form of hiccoughs which slowly increased in intensity until they were continuous and violent. Harris was like an old fighting cock, with scrawny throat and sagging comb, in the grip of a deep, retching hiccough, which went on from morning till night. Nothing seemed to stop it and the doctors were baffled. Food would not stay down, sleep became very difficult and all work ceased. On the fourth day, Harris lay back against the pillows, his face haggard, his eyes closed, and his body shook as the awful sounds went on and on. Wherever she went in the house Nellie could hear them. She used to cover her ears with her hands, raise an anguished face to the ceiling and pray that it might cease . . . soon . . . soon . . . or she would go mad. By the fifth day, the doctors did not think he would live. By the sixth day, he seemed to have fallen into a coma. And then, miraculously, with no apparent explanation, on the eighth day the hiccoughs stopped. For a few weeks Harris came back to life again.

By early July he had collapsed once more. This time he reached a stage where he no longer recognized visitors and Nellie, sleepless, despairing, wrote distraught letters to friends in England saying that she did not know how it was all going to end. . . . It was terrible, terrible.

An X-ray revealed serious stomach ulcers and an immediate operation was advised. Always a person to flourish in opposition, even in this extremity, Harris seemed to recover new strength in order to stop the doctors operating. It carried him along for another few weeks, and then, once more, he began to get better in all reality.

*   *   *   *   *

By 1930 everything had changed. He was up and about, some of his old confidence had returned, his books were beginning to sell once more, and the glimmerings of yet another possible renaissance set him panting and coughing round the house, his rheumy eyes occasionally lit with a glint of their old passion. Fischer, in Germany, had overcome his hatred of Harris, and published the German translation of the third volume of *My Life*; the Bodley Head in England republished two volumes of short stories, *Montes the Matador* and *Elder Conklin*; an invitation came for Harris to lecture to the English Literary Society in Monte Carlo and a book long rejected by one publisher after another, was at last produced under the title *Confessional*. The Panurge Press followed *Confessional* with *Pantopia*, a novel which Harris had developed from the short story, *Temple to the Forgotten Dead*. Much of this sudden upsurge of published material was old stuff, but *Pantopia* had been written over a number of years, and now appeared for the first time.

It was at this point that the American journalist Frank Scully came into Harris' life. The precise nature of their first meeting is not recorded, but Harris had become an *habitué* of the Palais de la Méditeranée, where Scully frequently went, and it was inevitable that two men professionally concerned with writing, should want to know each other. Soon they were meeting frequently. They would sit at the tables of the Palais de la Méditeranée talking about life and literature, exchanging every kind of reminiscence, discussing the books they would write and the schemes which would one day make them rich. Within a few weeks these speculations took a more serious turn. It was a book they finally concentrated upon, yet another book, but this time, of a quite different calibre from anything which had gone before, and said, originally, to have been suggested by Nellie herself.

Long after Harris' death and the publication of Tobin and Gertz's biography, Scully gave an account of a remarkable collaboration which, he said, began with Harris' book *On the Trail* and developed into a biography destined to become famous. For now, these two men suddenly decided that the book for which the world waited, with possibilities of becoming a best-seller, was a biography of Bernard Shaw by the man who clearly knew him better than anyone else in the world—Frank Harris. They wrote post-haste to Bernard Shaw in the hope that he would make certain material available and Shaw replied with equal alacrity that he wanted nothing whatever to do with it:

'. . . You have a right to make your own confessions, but not to make mine. If, disregarding this obvious limitation, you pick up what you can from gossip and from guesses . . . what will happen? Your publisher, believing me to be fabulously rich and an ill man to cross, will send me the MS. and ask me whether I have any objection to it. Unless it is a Morley-Gladstone *Who's Who* job, I will say that I have every possible objection and will assuredly not hold him guiltless that taketh my name in vain: and I will point out that, even if I consented, I could not prevent the other persons concerned from seeking their legal remedy. And then where would you be . . . ?'

Shaw explained that he had once given some autobiographical material to an Irish-American professor who proceeded to write a book which described his mother as an adultress and his father a ruthless fortune hunter. Harpers, the publishers, had to have Shaw's consent to the biography and he refused to give it point blank '. . . so the unfortunate author died of disappointment, aided by pernicious anaemia, cursing me for ruining him. . . .'

It was not a very propitious start, but Scully bore a two-year-old grudge against Shaw, and determined to fight his way through. Thus began one of the most extraordinary literary collaborations in the history of biography, a collaboration which, if one accepts Scully's account without reservation, has startling implications.

Scully pressed Harris to write to Shaw again. Roused by Shaw's refusal, Harris sent off a letter saying that whether Shaw liked it or not, they had decided that the biography would be written. Under Scully's influence, Harris smelt big money in the book and believed that an old pen portrait of Shaw which had appeared in Volume Two of *Contemporary Portraits* could easily be expanded into a biography.

On January 18th, 1930, Shaw replied:

'My dear Frank,
    You really are a daisy. You put six questions to me, the replies to which would be the book; about a year's work, which you would then decorate with nonsense about impulses and resolutions and high purposes and all the rest of the literary junk. . . .
    The odd thing about you is that though you can write, you have all the credulities and illusions and innocences of the amateur and the collector. I won't have you write my life on any terms: Nellie would do it far better. You made Shakespeare a cross between a sailor in a melodrama and a French criminal invoking the memory of his sainted mother. What you would make of me not even God knows. You haven't the very faintest notion of the sort of animal I am. If I had time I would tell you the facts just to see how utterly they would disconcert you: but I haven't so you must drop it. . . . Ever, G.B.S.'

Harris wrote back belligerently. They were not going to be intimidated. Anger, avarice, and the hope that perhaps this book had the power denied every other scheme to recover Harris' reputation as a writer, re-invigorated his aged frame. Momentarily the sparks flew, Harris thundered and his letters came alive.

Astonishingly, within six months Shaw had not only capitulated; he had written in pencil, with his own hand, his unabashed sex credo, and one morning Scully arrived to find Frank bursting with new enthusiasm. There it was in cold blood. Shaw's sex credo, with permission to print it. Clearly no one who had read *My Life and Loves* could feel safe against the wildest exaggeration of any sexual material which might fall into Harris' hands; clearly Harris was quite likely to convert Shaw into a monster of sensuality, or represent him, as Wells had once represented him, as a sex-less biped. Perhaps that was why Shaw decided to spike Harris' guns with the truth. Whatever the reason, Shaw's confession put quite new life into the collaborators. Scully immediately wrote a letter to M. Lincoln Schuster, president of Simon and Schuster, then staying in Paris, explaining the situation, and Lincoln Schuster came hurrying down to Nice.[1] The proposition of a biography of Bernard Shaw by Frank Harris with Shaw contributing a highly personal chapter was irresistible. Scully made elaborate preparations for Schuster's arrival, re-typing the old portrait from the *Contemporary Portraits*, writing a new twelve-page introduction and collecting all the letters which Shaw had written to Harris.[2]

'After looking over the various exhibits and having one delightful afternoon with Frank Harris (who picked up marvellously for the occasion, like the dying embers of a once great fire), Max Schuster cabled his partner Dick Simon, endorsing the project.'

Schuster then turned to Harris and asked him when he could have the manuscript ready and Harris calmly announced, 'Oh—in about a month. It's more than half ready now.' Only a very long training in journalism kept Scully's face impassive during this revelation, but they all parted cordially with the assurance that a new and important mine of wealth and prestige was about to be tapped. Presently Victor Gollancz agreed to publish the book simultaneously in England and to pay part of the considerable advance of $7,500 (in those days about £2,000), and everyone sat back expectantly.

How to share the spoils became a considerable haggle between Harris and Scully. 'Harris said he couldn't possibly pay me the 30 per cent—I didn't get on the cowboy book, as this

[1] According to Tobin and Gertz it was Harris' friend and lawyer, Arthur Leonard Ross, who arranged publication in America with Simon, Schuster. They added: 'When the final history of Frank Harris is written, it will be found that to few men does he owe more than to Arthur Leonard Ross.'

[2] Frank Scully, *Rogue's Gallery*, p. 214 (Murray and Gee, 1943).

time he would have to pay his New York lawyer, 10 per cent. He said he couldn't pay me more than 20 per cent. I pointed out that in that case I would be paying his lawyer . . . We argued a bit and finally I agreed to the arrangement—only to discover when I got home that we had signed a contract that gave me 80 per cent and Harris 20 per cent.' Scully sadly reversed the percentages and the contract was re-signed.

It remained to write the book. Confronted with the reality, Harris began to hedge, complained of the heat and suggested that they should move up into the Vosges Mountains where the air made 'thinking in depth' possible. Anyone less flamboyant than Harris might have hesitated to substitute a taxi for a fifteen hour train journey when money was hard to come by, but Scully claims that Nellie and Frank solemnly summoned a taxi and set out for the hotel in the Vosges Mountains which their ex-secretary had selected. He, meanwhile, went by train.

'The Harrises arrived in pouring rain and had scarcely sat down two minutes when Frank was ordering cognac and soda to allay his ague. . . . The *femme de chambres* not being fast enough in their service, got their *derrières* pinched, and were urged to hurry. . . .' It was a bad hotel. The gong for meals had an annihilating boom, the food was poor, and freight cars began unloading nearby as early as six in the morning.

'For the next five days Harris shivered and pinched all bottoms within reach, finding brandy and overcoats no protection from the frigid rain.'[1] In the end he could bear it no longer and one particularly cold, wet day, he decided to hurry back to his beloved Nice—by train.

While Scully settled down, in the rain, to write, analyzing and ordering the mass of material which he had accumulated, Harris sat in the long cool apartment of number 9 rue de la Buffa, carefully turning and re-turning the sixty-five worn pages of his original manuscript, or sipped apéritifs in the Café de la Mediterranean. Habit soon came close to ritual. He would sit huddled over the sixty-five pages, his brow furrowed in concentration for hours. He no longer knew where the information which the manuscript contained had come from and was convinced of one thing only—its originality. There were even

[1] Frank Scully, *Rogue's Gallery*, pp. 216–17 (Murray and Gee, 1943).

days when he thought that this fumbling through a threadbare manuscript would, by some mysterious means, help to organize the multitude of facts which had to be mastered before the biography of Shaw could come within reach of reality.

An advance royalty cable came from New York to the hotel in Vittel where Harris had been staying and Scully at once forwarded it to Nice. He expected his share of 20 per cent within a few days. 'Instead of $500, a thousand francs (or about $39) did arrive—with the explanation that only $2,000 had come through, as the lawyer had extracted $500 for past debts before cabling the money from New York.' Scully sighed and pressed on with another chapter. While he hammered his material direct to the typewriter, Harris continued to saunter and reflect, and disappeared into reveries which gradually developed in length and density.

It was about this time (1929) that J. MacLaren Ross went to visit him and left a remarkable picture of the encounter. An invitation to lunch at the Villa Edouard Sept, had arrived via an archaeologist friend, and one hot June day they set out together by taxi to keep the appointment. On the way, the archaeologist friend, Amberley by name, said that there was something he wanted to say about Frank Harris . . . 'You know he was very sick last year—had hiccups for over a week, something to do with his stomach: they thought he'd peg out but in the end he fooled them once again—and then of course he's been short of cash lately, though his new book ought to remedy that: he's pushing on with it all he can, but it seems G.B.S. is being bloody difficult about the whole affair; I wish to God *he'd* die, don't you? So you see Frank's got a lot to try him at the moment, and I hope you won't take offence if he seems a bit abrupt at first. . . .'

MacLaren Ross had other, far more serious worries. He was suddenly concerned about the elegant clothes he wore, in case the ex-cowpuncher mistook him for a fop and first impressions wrecked the whole luncheon. His *crêpe de chine* shirt and white mess jacket splashed by the single brilliant carnation might pass muster—'but why, for Heaven's sake, had I chosen to gird my white drill trousers with a crimson sash instead of an ordinary belt, and why co-respondent shoes? The sash, it's

216

true, could not be seen unless I removed my jacket: the shoes would, with luck, be hidden below the table, and my gold-topped malacca cane could be given up swiftly to a servant before the host had a chance to see it.' [1]

They duly arrived. A swarthy major-domo in a beautiful striped waistcoat opened the door and—tremendous relief—took the stick. They were shown into a long, low-ceilinged room, cool and dark after the glare outside, and there was the great man waiting to receive them. Ross, expecting the notorious handgrip to crush his fingers, instead found himself crushing Harris' now enfeebled hand.

Harris' voice, reduced to a whisper, wheezed, 'Aren't you Bertie's nephew?' Presently, leaning forward confidentially, the vitreous eyes brightened and Harris said: 'They used to talk about me—but Bertie . . .' A sweeping gesture conveyed an illimitable prospect of wickedness and Harris' hand slapped down hard on his thigh, but the sudden roar of laughter was strangled into a spasm of coughing which turned his face purple and set the old eyes bursting out of their sockets. A huge handkerchief engulfed his face and head, the splutterings slowly subsided and a muffled voice said, 'Blasted bronchitis. Won't even let a man bloody well laugh.' And then the stooped form came close in greater confidence and the voice continued: 'Look here, my boy . . . phlebitis, neuralgia, rheumatism, bronchial asthma . . .' A long pause '. . . Ulcers! Here, in the belly! How's that . . . ? But I'll beat 'em yet—you wait and see—the bloody lot!'

Harris suddenly snapped at the major-domo the single word, 'Drinks.'

'I was now led on to the verandah and presented to his wife . . . Mrs. Harris [was] of a fair height and handsome with burnished hair, aged about forty to my eighteen-year-old eyes . . . [She] introduced me . . . to a rather dim English couple . . . and to a man tanned the colour of chocolate, whom Harris said, with his gusty, whistling laugh was a fellow Scotchman! "McKay's not merely a writer," Harris told me, "He's something much more important," he drew a deep breath and hissed with extraordinary venom: "A *publisher*!" But his animosity

[1] *The London Magazine*, pp. 58–9, June 1955.

seemed directed at this profession in general rather than its present representative for he simultaneously clapped Mr. Kalnay (his pen name was McKay) upon the shoulders: "And President of the International Writers League. Do you belong to the International Writers League, Ross? No? Well, we'll have to make you a member . . . This young man has written a book," he continued, pointing at me; to my horror I felt a deep flush overspreading my face and threw a baleful glance at Amberley, who smiled imperturbably back: "But we'll talk about that later, see what we can do." Harris picked up a glass and drained it at a gulp. "Now for some lunch"!' [1]

The lunch went reasonably well. The food was excellent and each guest had his own bottle of Camp Romain in a separate ice bucket. The first rumble of thunder came when MacLaren Ross asked about the biography of Bernard Shaw, and Harris at once snapped—'Don't talk to me about bloody Bernard Shaw.' The second outburst occurred when he referred to Harris' Autobiography.

'How did you get hold of that?' Harris demanded and Ross explained. '. . . Pure filth . . .' Harris commented, 'not fit to be in the hands of any decent person. . . .' He croaked up the table towards his wife for confirmation: 'Isn't it, my dear . . . pure filth?'

'What's that, my dear?'

'My Autobiography of course. Pure filth.'

'Well, not all of it, Frank . . . The parts about the Wild West . . .'

'Ah—yes—but the rest's just dirt.' He turned back to Ross: 'I'd give my right arm not to have written that first volume. . . .'

It was all a question of money, he said. He needed money desperately at the time, but did he make any money—great heavens no: 'That book did me more harm than the pox . . . a bloody black harvest, me boy. . . .'

The crisis which Ross had anticipated now arrived. Two guests removed their jackets because of the heat and Nellie pressed Ross to remove his. Resisting at first, under renewed pressure there seemed to be no choice, and there, suddenly, in full view, was that brilliant crimson sash round his waist like a

[1] *The London Magazine*, pp. 61–2, June 1955.

cummerbund. His worst expectations were at once realized. About to pour from a bottle, Harris held it suspended in mid air, and blinked and peered across the table, suspicion gathering in his old eyes. Without further preliminary, he suddenly shot out:

' "Are you a sodomite?"

' "I beg your pardon?" [MacLaren Ross] stammered, seeing out of the corner of [his] eye Mr. Kalnay suddenly pause . . . .

' "Are you a B – – R?" This time it came loud enough for all to hear.

'Mrs. Harris called "Frank!" sharply down the table.

'Harris turned slightly in his seat, "It's all right, my dear," he said testily, "I'm just asking Ross a civil question—nothing to be alarmed about . . . Not offended, are you, me boy—don't mind me asking eh?"

' "No," I said, "Not at all."

' "And you're not a sodomite now, are you?"

' "As a matter of fact no."

' "You see, Nellie," Harris called triumphantly up to his wife, "He isn't one at all, what'd I tell you? And now," glancing for approval at his guests, "let's have something more to drink." ' [1]

Before MacLaren Ross left, Harris promised to read every word of his novel and to find a publisher for it. The parting was accompanied by much hand-shaking, protestations of eternal fellowship and some talk of meeting again. The following Monday morning a messenger called on MacLaren Ross to return the parcel containing his manuscript, and it was quite evident to his practised eye that the string and brown paper were intact. It had never been opened. A letter from Harris said that he had greatly enjoyed reading the novel but pressure of work on his biography of Shaw prevented him from finding the publisher he had promised.

MacLaren Ross saw Harris once more. It was six months later. Harris was hunched up over an apéritif with Nellie by his side at the Casino de la Méditerranée. She sighted MacLaren Ross, plucked her husband's sleeve and smiled acknowledgement at the young author. Swivelling in his chair Harris stared

[1] *The London Magazine*, June 1955.

glassily in his direction, but before he had a chance to discover who this stranger might be, MacLaren Ross 'bowed frigidly—to Mrs. Harris—and passed on.'

* * * * *

The biography of Shaw became steadily more tormenting. Time and again Harris struggled to put something fresh down on paper, only to exhaust his inspiration within a few pages; time and again he sent messages to Scully, still away in Vittel, asking when the devil he was coming back, because he now knew with appalling certainty, two things. He could never complete the Shaw biography without Scully's help and his own powers of writing were threatened with total collapse. His memory reduced to a shambles, his health failing again and his spirits depressed, he still clung to the certainty that the book was his and that he must at any cost finish it; but he needed help. Still he sought every morning to resurrect himself, to dress to perfection, to fill out the hollowed voice, to speak with authority.

At last Scully returned. He came madly through the rain by car, driven by a man wanted for uttering a worthless cheque, and the wild gallop down from the mountains shook off the trunk containing all the Shaw material. It was hit by a car travelling in the opposite direction, but it survived the encounter and Scully read this as a good omen for the book. He brought with him a number of completed chapters, unaware of the shocks that awaited him.

First—he claims[1]—it became clear that Harris had hardly written more than a few extra pages, and second and far worse, he had already sent off certain material to the publishers. This consisted of the 'sixty-five page fragment . . . in appalling disorder, and not five of them written since the contract.' The sixty-five pages, he had told the publishers, was his first instalment. The contract laid it down that $2,500 were due on signature, a fresh $1,000 on completion of each 25,000 words and a final $1,000 on publication day. By sending the ancient sixty-five pages as the first instalment, Harris had been able to claim and receive another $1,000. An explosion followed. When the report on Harris' first instalment arrived from the

[1] Frank Scully, *Rogue's Gallery* (Murray and Gee, 1943).

publishers, it was searing and 'made no bones about how badly they had been rooked'.

Scully saw that something dramatic had to be done, because, by now, they were within four months of the date when the biography was due to be completed. He went to work with a will. A number of un-named helpers were organized to carry out intensive research into musty old magazines, periodicals, newspapers, books and letters, distilling all those quotations which were vital to any biography of Shaw. The letters were copied, sent to Shaw, and his permission to quote sought. Meanwhile the farcical routine on the sixth floor of 9 rue de la Buffa was solemnly played out morning after morning. Scully arrived to begin work at ten, found the woollen underclothes and pyjamas drying on the radiators, and waited for Harris to appear. Unaware, in the early stages, of the elaborate dressing and the consideration of the straightened shoulders in the mirror which preceded his entrance every morning, Scully did not realize that at least an hour must elapse before Harris felt himself ready to face the world.

Facing the world quickly took the form of the visit to the Palais de la Méditerranée, followed by lunch, and the sleep in the early afternoon. The strain of the morning, needed the relaxation of the drive by taxi round the hills of Nice in the afternoon. In the evening there were more apéritifs and sufficient reading to satisfy a man of culture.

Somewhere in the background, Scully continued to work, plotting the book, laying out chapters and 'Whenever I was short of material on Shaw using more interesting material from the life of Harris. It would be, in short, a battle of giants and if it turned out to be more Harris than Shaw, what of it?'

Fresh trouble suddenly developed when Shaw wrote on September 18th, 1930: 'Dear Frank Harris, An American firm is advertising your biography as being authorized and as containing fifteen thousand words by me. I have written to them to say that no biography of me except Henderson's is authorized and that yours is especially deprecated . . . You are personally capable of writing a worthy successor to the Wilde biography without quoting a single word from my accounts of myself;

and I shall do everything in my power to force you to do so.'

The publishers did not like this letter, but the joint authors remained undisturbed. Scully, in particular, was quite undaunted. True, Henderson's biography had been fully authorized but who on earth ever bothered to read that twin monument of pedantry and dullness? He suggested to Harris that the publishers should take a 'strongly negative line' with their own book, and describe it as 'unauthorized but authentic'. Finally he hit upon the phrase 'unauthorized but written from voluntarily supplied documents'.

By November 3rd, 1930, Shaw seems to have changed his mind again. He wrote: 'I sent the letters back to you yesterday in a hurry. One of them contains, I regret to say, the improper expression "permanent whore". Change the second word to "mistress!" Our forecastle style will not do on the quarterdeck.

'I give you a free hand as to the letters, but they are so condensed and so dependent on the context of our personal relations that expatiation may be better than quotation. I again urge that it must be your book. You must not let me play you off the stage.

'Your publishers protest that all the announcements to which I took exception came from Nice, and that they are entirely guiltless. I have told them not to be alarmed; that I will see you through with plenty to quote. G.B.S.'

Within a month of his return to Nice, Scully claims that he had completed 28,000 words, sent it to the publishers, and received the following reply:

'Dear Frank Scully,
    The first 28,000 words received in good order and I congratulate you and Frank Harris on the job. With some qualifications the material is well-organized, well-paced and well-written. If the rest is as good or better, it will be a grand book.'

Scully described what followed:
'I went on at a mad writing pace, while the Harrises taxied around the hills of Nice, dropping in every now and then to plague me as to when the next instalment would be ready.

They badly needed money, they told me, and at one time remarked they had only ten francs in the house. This may have been true, but there were treasures all over the flat. . . .' [1]

Three months went by. Harris alternated between a fever of anxiety about the book, long periods of gloomy reverie beside an apéritif glass, attempts to catch on paper memories of Shaw, and fights against the doctors who warned him that he must take care and not strain himself.

According to Scully, within four months, he had himself completed no less than 150,000 words, sent them to the publishers, and received a request to cut at least 65,000. The final version was at last approved and Scully called upon Harris to re-arrange their financial agreement. A long tussle ensued. In the end it was agreed that he should get another 10 per cent bringing his 20 per cent up to 30 per cent. Scully wrote: 'They begged me not to say what I had done as it would hurt the book. . . . In fewer words, I was supposed not even to say I was working with Harris, much less doing the whole job, and for keeping quiet I was not to be paid adequately because association with him would be pay enough.' [2]

It was Scully's last interview with Harris. Something quite final intervened between that interview and publication of the book, but publication set off endless repercussions. In the first place the book was dedicated to: 'Frank Scully who goaded me into undertaking it and then wouldn't let me have a minute's peace till it was completed.' Scully regarded this, in cold print, with ironic amusement. He claimed that he himself had written the dedication, 'figuring that there must be some way I could take a bow without causing the whole delicate structure of literature to tumble.'

The book was widely reviewed and very successful, not least because the two chapters headed, 'Experiences with Actresses' and 'Shaw's Sex Credo' were swiftly scanned by hundreds of people who never troubled to read the rest of the book. The first chapter entwined the alien spirits of Frank Harris and Bernard Shaw, with Harris a little more in evidence than Shaw, but subsequent chapters gave Shaw considerable attention.

[1] Frank Scully, *Rogue's Gallery*, p. 229 (Murray and Gee, 1943).
[2] Ibid.

Time and again Harris could not stop himself bursting into the book which confirmed Scully's plan of relying on the life of Harris when the life of Shaw proved comparatively paltry. If there is very little resemblance between the style in which Scully wrote his 'exposure' of the biography, and that of the biography itself, as a skilled journalist, Scully could have disguised his own style or imitated that of Harris.

There was no need for imitation with 'Shaw's Sex Credo'. Shaw had practically written the whole chapter himself. It opened with the question Louis Wilkinson had once put to Bernard Shaw: 'What do you consider the greatest obstacle to the emancipation of women?' and Shaw dramatically answered 'Lust.'

Later in the chapter came the letter in which Shaw lifted the veil on his private life. Dated June 24th, 1930, it began:

'First, O Biographer, get it clear in your mind that you can learn nothing about your sitter . . . from a mere record of gallantries.[1] If I were to tell you every such adventure that I have enjoyed you would be none the wiser as to my personal nor even as to my sexual history. You would know what you already know: I am a human being. If you have any doubts as to my normal virility, dismiss them from your mind. I was not impotent: I was not sterile: I was not homosexual: and I was extremely though not promiscuously susceptible.

Also I was entirely free from the neurosis (as it seems to me) of Original Sin. I never associated sexual intercourse with delinquency. I associated it always with delight, and had no scruples nor remorses nor misgivings of conscience. Of course I had scruples, and effectively inhibitive ones too, about getting women into trouble (or, rather letting them get themselves into it, with me) or cuckolding my friends; and I understand that chastity can be a passion just as intellect is a passion: but St. Paul was to me always a pathological case. Sexual experiences seemed a necessary completion of human growth; and I was not attracted by virgins as such. I preferred women who knew what they were doing. . . .'

[1] In the original the word 'gallantries' read 'copulations'.

224

So the letter ran on, obligatory reading in those days when Shaw's fame was at its peak and very little known about his sex life. He even hinted at what has only become evident in recent years: that the affairs which preceded his marriage did not lead to a physically passionate relationship with his wife but instead to total abstinence, the marriage never reaching consummation. 'I found sex hopeless as a basis for permanent relations, and never dreamt of marriage in connection with it.' But sexual intercourse in the early affairs he liked 'because of its amazing power of producing a celestial flood of emotion and exaltation of existence which, however momentary, gave one a sample of what may one day be the normal state of being for mankind in intellectual ecstasy. I always gave the wildest expression to this in a torrent of words, partly because I felt it due to the women to know what I felt in her arms, and partly because I wanted her to share it. . . .'

Something equally interesting occurred at the end of the book in the form of a postscript by Shaw. It talked about Harris himself, and suggested that the real Harris, hidden fathoms deep behind the adventurer, was not a tough, hard-bitten rogue at all '. . . but a man of immense sensitivity. Instead of showing his sensitiveness he made everyone believe that he was as tough as hickory.'

And there it was again. Could it possibly be that the real Harris still lay quivering behind a ten foot thick wall which had taken him sixty years to erect, and was the tough exterior a carefully built up deception made necessary by a brutal world? Or was it that his acting powers never failed when confronted with the need to fulfil one role or another, and he could still run the whole gamut from the highly sensitive to the brutally tough, with the tough generally in the ascendant?

Perhaps that was the real key to Harris. He was a man without a core. Born a sensitive boy, he had first tried to outdo the toughness imposed by a disciplinarian father and thus overcome the punishments he suffered. Later, he found that he could act all the roles—lover, politician, poet, blackmailer, seducer—and he played them for all they were worth, reaping the easiest and richest rewards. In the end it destroyed that mysterious—something—which holds a personality together and makes it consistent at a deeper level. He became an acting machine, giving the response which would bring the desired reward in the shortest possible time. Hence there were no scruples, no core, nothing which could be said to reconcile the dozen parts he played. When the pressures built up around this vacuum and threatened a breakdown—as in the prison episode—he suddenly threw all his acting powers into believing himself a Messiah. Paranoia, which had its seeds in an attempt to outdo his father, was reinforced by his marvellous acting powers and reached a pitch where he thought himself into the part of the prophet. As a prophet he achieved the final end. For a time he replaced the missing core.

*　　*　　*　　*　　*

Harris never lived to reap the rewards of the Shaw biography. Everywhere people talked about it. On the day of publication in London it sold 21,000 copies, in America it entered the list of best sellers, and was praised by British and American critics from the *Daily Telegraph* to the *New Yorker*. A considerable skirmish over filchings from the official biography by Archibald Henderson developed and died away again, but not before Henderson complained that 113 separate items had been 'taken' from his book. Shaw believed that Harris had never even troubled to read the official biography, but Scully found Harris' copy of Henderson's Life and recorded that many pages were bent down and some passages marked. Troubled as he then was with a very eccentric memory, Harris may have absorbed what he wanted from Henderson, forgotten its source, and repeated the material to Scully as his own.

Worse trouble supervened when the Paris correspondent of *Variety* printed a story hinting that Scully's part in the biography had been much more important than anyone knew. According to Scully he at once received an hysterical telegram from Nellie demanding that he immediately deny the story. 'Failing to get the kind of response she wanted by telegram,' she 'rushed to Paris and then to London to defend what . . . she mistook for Frank Harris' honor.

'The story, she assured me, would do the book no end of harm: the publishers would suffer vast losses. Frank's reputa-

226

tion would be ruined, and all that. If I would write them a denial, she ended, everything would be straightened out.'

But all Nellie's persuasions—and eventually she was reduced to tears—did not change Scully's attitude. 'She continued to burn with a slow indignation over the statement she had failed to get from me.'

In the end Scully's evidence made it all very difficult. It would be poetic justice in overwhelming force if the fame for the biography of Bernard Shaw, written on the brink of the grave, turned out to be false.[1]

[1] It remains to add that at least two persons in the United States who knew Harris well, regard Scully's account as seriously exaggerated, hold firmly to the belief that Harris wrote the greater part of the Shaw biography himself and point to the style of the book, as in their eyes, conclusive evidence.

CHAPTER TWENTY

O_N his seventy-fifth birthday there was a party, small beside those he had once given in the old Café Royal. He spoke suddenly of the Café Royal days and recalled those heady years when he had edited the *Fortnightly*, half literary London came to his luncheons and everyone knew him. No one cared very much now. England had almost forgotten him. In France he was an old eccentric unknown to the new generation of writers. His name no longer appeared in the newspapers. On his seventy-fifth birthday, suddenly aware of his age in a new and deeply depressed way, he ate steadily through several courses, drank deeply of wine and liqueurs, suddenly turned green and hurried from the room. 'Five minutes later he returned to the party . . . smiling again. . . .' The stomach pump was still working its miracles, but he was old in a different way and he knew it.

One golden day with blue skies gave place to another and the steadily more drawn-out morning rituals were followed by afternoons of near sleep. Intermittently his leg swelled with the agony of phlebitis, his lungs wheezed with the remnants of bronchitis, his heart weakened, and his eyes . . . When he managed, sometimes, to get down to the Café de la Mediterranean, he sat stooped over an apéritif, his eyes on the shady patch thrown by the umbrella because the sun made them sore. One particularly golden day when the bay was vivid blue, the sea lazing over the rocks in gentle foam, the air cooled by the subtlest breeze from the mountains and the boulevards gay with beautiful women, he saw, walking past, a girl of Junoesque proportions in a bathing costume which made more evident every voluptuous line. His eyes momentarily lifted towards her and fell again. He muttered something and Nellie said, 'What was that, Frank?' 'Nothing—nothing,' he wheezed, emptied his glass and lay back in his chair.

The voice was changed now out of all recognition—'a muffled whisper wheezing in his larynx'. His eyes were old, his hair, plastered down, achieved the effect of a wig, and his shoulders had sunk forward in a more pronounced stoop. The ulcers in his stomach, the phlebitis, the lung trouble and a heart weakened by extravagant living, had combined their forces for two years in an attempt to kill him. Dr. Hort did not understand why he was still alive. He should have died, he said, at least two years before, but the cannon-pulse which had driven him so greedily into life sustained him now in near death.

Few people visited him. Correspondents fell away. There were long desolate evenings when he sat opposite Nellie, neither said a word and both desperately hoped that tomorrow someone would write, call, or telephone.

His health grew worse. Soon there were days when he stayed in bed all day. Sometimes he spoke of Monsignor Barry Doyle who lived twenty miles away at Menton. It was almost as if he discerned such horrors in the mists coming up to encompass him that his pagan soul groped in the dusk for the image of the Holy Church.

On August 25th, 1931, he passed a very restless afternoon. And then, at five o'clock, some instinct seemed to tell him that the end was near and in that moment the old swashbuckling Harris came struggling back to life again. Death in bed . . . that was for respectable people; that was mean, petty, bourgeois. He struggled to a sitting position, he thrust his legs over the side and stood half propped by the bed. Then his shaking hand tried to fill an empty glass; he drained it, took the glass and with a last burst of strength dashed it against the wall. Nellie heard the crash, came rushing in and was appalled at what she saw. The gaunt, shaking Harris, half standing against the bed, his eyes momentarily demonic. But the last defiant gesture had been made. She settled him, swearing, back into bed.

suited to his purpose and in two or three stories he employed his crisp evocative language to write narratives which still grip the attention and compare, in one or two cases, with some of Maupassant's work.

As a short story writer he matured comparatively late and he was advanced in years when his book *Undream'd of Shores* revealed his powers at work to write the savage little vignette *A Fit of Madness*, in which a husband goes mad, imagines his wife a stranger and makes love to her as he did when they were first married. Recovering from his madness he treats her coolly and carelessly again and his wife bursts out, 'My God! It's terrible to think you're cured so soon.' A not unexpected blend of cynicism and sentimentality, brutality and tenderness marked these stories. On the surface, nothing could have been more Hemingway in its detachment than the cool representation of violence in *A Chinese Story*, but if one read carefully, echoes of a crudely concealed enjoyment came up to mar the detachment. Nothing could have been more sophisticated than the woman—loved by the narrator, in the story *Central Africa*—enjoying for dinner, part of the smoked thigh of a young girl of 13 killed in an accident, but once again, the narrator's revulsion rings false. Many kinds of horror are let loose in these stories, and several remain, underneath, sensual indulgences. It was Harris finding fresh ways of stirring his jaded appetites. He had always hoped that he would write a love story with the delicacy of Turgenev, or a piece of realism equal to Maupassant's *Bel-Ami*. It did not happen. But there were stories which at least bear some comparison with the lesser works of these masters—like the *Miracle of the Stigmata*.

As a person . . . the inevitable concomitant of virility and toughness showed itself in his personality as a form of sentimentality. The roué had to romanticize the object of his appetites and Harris' apparent cynicism—especially with women—sometimes became sentimental. There was also the falsity of a man frequently acting the emotions he dare not, or could not, experience in reality, but his personality developed through many phases and it was only in young manhood that the unscrupulous opportunist showed the first seeds of what was to become a scoundrel. He did not desire to become a scoundrel because he enjoyed the experience of being one. He became a scoundrel because that was a short cut to the success he craved. Happier sides of his nature were frequently obscured by sheer gossip and notoriety.

He had known the experience called love, he had on occasion been generous, he did sometimes tell the truth devastatingly, and it needed great courage to face up to and survive the censure which his conduct inevitably brought down on his head. But, alas, nothing in the end could justify the life he led; not even the fact that he was a considerable writer, because in the end he wasted his talents on the tawdry, the sordid, and the second-rate.

So many of his talents were squandered. A man who could enthral Oscar Wilde, Bernard Shaw, Max Beerbohm and—sometimes—H. G. Wells with his talk, was no mean fellow. Developed and applied to different ends the combined abilities of Harris might have carried him to fame instead of notoriety in some very high places. Fate—and Frank Harris—decreed otherwise.

A biblical grandeur broke through his own last words: 'There is an end of time and an end of the evil thereof; when delight is gone out of thee and desire is dead, thy mourning shall not be for long . . . Yet the adventure of life was glorious and the magic of moments of love and pity and understanding beyond description or thanks.' [1]

In those words he had written the epitaph which he himself would have preferred.

[1] Frank Harris, *Undream'd of Shores*, p. 297. 'My Last Word' (Brentanos, 1924).

BIBLIOGRAPHY

Books by Frank Harris:

Elder Conklin and Other Stories, Heinemann, 1894.

How to Beat the Boer, Heinemann, 1900.

Montes the Matador, Grant Richards, 1900.

The Bomb, John Long, 1908.

The Man Shakespeare and His Tragic Life Story, Frank Palmer, 1909.

Shakespeare and His Love, Frank Palmer, 1910.

The Women of Shakespeare, Methuen, 1911.

Unpath'd Waters, John Lane, 1913.

Great Days, John Lane, 1914.

The Yellow Ticket and Other Stories, Grant Richards, 1914.

England or Germany, Wilmarth Press, 1915.

Contemporary Portraits, Methuen, 1915.

Love in Youth, Doran, 1916.

Oscar Wilde, His Life and Confessions, The Author, 1916.

Oscar Wilde, His Life and Confessions, with Memories of Oscar Wilde by G. B. Shaw, The Author, 1918.

Contemporary Portraits, Second Series, The Author, 1919.

Contemporary Portraits, Third Series, The Author, 1920.

Contemporary Portraits, Fourth Series, Brentanos, 1923.

Undream'd of Shores, Brentanos, 1924.

Joan La Romee, Nicaise, 1926.

Latest Contemporary Portraits, Macaulay, 1927.

On the Trail, Being My Reminiscences as a Cowboy, John Lane, 1930.

Confessional, Panurge Press, 1930.

Pantopia, Panurge Press, 1930.
Bernard Shaw, Gollancz, 1931.
Bernard Shaw, with a Preface by Shaw himself, Gollancz, 1938.
My Life and Loves, Four Volumes, Various private publishers, 1925–1929.
Mr. and Mrs. Daventry, Richards Press, 1957.

Other Books Consulted:
Anstey, F., *A Long Retrospect*, Oxford University Press, 1936.
Arliss, George, *Up the Years from Bloomsbury*, Little Brown, 1928.
Arrest and Escape of James Stephens, Privately published, 1866.
A Young Scholar's Letters, Being a Memoir of Byron Caldwell Smith, Putnam, 1897.
Beerbohm, Max, *A Christmas Garland*, Dutton, 1925.
Brome, Vincent, *H. G. Wells*, Longmans, Green, 1951.
Brown, Ivor, *Shakespeare*, Collins, 1949.
Carrel, Frederic, *The Adventures of John Johns*, Bliss, Sands and Co., 1897.
Crowley, Aleister, *The Diary of a Drug Fiend*, Dutton, 1923.
Cumberland, Gerald, *Set Down in Malice*, Brentanos, 1919.
Douglas, Lord Alfred, *Without Apology*, Martin Secker, 1929.
Drew, Elizabeth, *James Welsh and Jane Carlyle*, Harcourt Brace, 1928.
Ensor, R. C. K., *Oxford English History*, Oxford University Press, 1936.
Froude, J. A., *My Relations with Carlyle*, Longmans, 1903.
Garnett, Edward (Editor), *Letters from Joseph Conrad*, The Nonesuch Press, 1928.
Goldman, Emma, *Living My Life*, Duckworth, 1932.
Goldring, Douglas, *Odd Man Out*, Chapman and Hall, 1935.
Halliday, J. L., *Mr. Carlyle, My Patient*, Heinemann, 1949.
Hare, Kenneth, *London's Latin Quarter*, John Lane, 1926.
Henderson, Archibald, *Playboy and Prophet*, Appleton, 1932.
History of the Fabian Society, Edward Pease, 1925.
Holland, Vyvyan, *Son of Oscar Wilde*, Rupert Hart-Davis, 1954.
Hyde, Montgomery, M.P., Preface to *Mr. and Mrs. Daventry*, Richards Press, 1957.

James Stephens, Fenian Brotherhood, 1866.

John, Augustus, *Chiaroschuro*, Jonathan Cape, 1952.

Johnston, Sir Harry H., *The Story of My Life*, Bobbs-Merrill, 1923.

Kingsmill, Hugh, *After Puritanism, 1850–1900*, Duckworth, 1929.

       Frank Harris, Jonathan Cape, 1932.

Lunn, Hugh, *The Will to Love*, Chapman and Hall, 1919.

Mencken, H. L., *Prejudices*, Third Series, Knopf, 1922.

Mes Souvenirs, Arthur Symons, 1931.

Mordell, A., *Frank Harris and Haldemann-Julius*, Haldemann-Julius, 1950.

Murry, J. Middleton, *Between Two Worlds*, Jonathan Cape, 1935.

Ould, Hermon (Editor), *The Book of the P.E.N.*, 1950.

Pearson, Hesketh, *Modern Men and Mummers*, Allen and Unwin, 1921.

       Ventilations, Lippincott, 1929.

       Thinking It Over, Hamish Hamilton, 1938.

       Bernard Shaw, Collins, 1942.

Pennell, E. R. and J., *Life of J. M. Whistler*, Lippincott, 1911.

Pound, Reginald, *Arnold Bennett*, Heinemann, 1952.

Root, E. M., *Frank Harris*, Odyssey Press, 1947.

Roth, Samuel, *The Private Life of Frank Harris*, William Faro, 1931.

Rothenstein, William, *Men and Memories*, Coward McCann, 1931.

Savage, Henry, *Richard Middleton*, Small, Maynard, 1929.

Scully, Frank, *Rogue's Gallery*, Murray and Gee, 1943.

Shepard, R. H., *Bernard Shaw, Frank Harris and Oscar Wilde*, T. Werner Laurie, 1937.

Smith, Gerrit and Mary Caldwell, *Lies and Libels of Frank Harris* (Arguments by Kate Stephens), Antique Press, 1929.

Stokes, Sewell, *Pilloried!*, Appleton, 1929.

Symons, J. S., *Thomas Carlyle. The Life and Ideas of a Prophet*, Gollancz, 1952.

Tobin, A. I. and Gertz, E., *Frank Harris*, Madelaine Mendelsohn, 1931.

Viereck, G. S., *Glimpses of the Great*, Duckworth, 1930.

Ward, S. C., *Bernard Shaw*, British Council, 1951.

Wells, H. G., *Experiment in Autobiography*, Gollancz and Cresset Press, 1934.

West, Geoffrey, *H. G. Wells*, Gerald Howe, 1930.

Whyte, Frederick, *Life of T. W. Stead*, Jonathan Cape, 1925.

Williams, H. L. Llewellyn, *The Fenian Chief*, Privately published, 1865.

Among the periodicals consulted were:

English Review, June, 1911. 'Thoughts on Morals' by Frank Harris.

Spectator, June 10th, 1911. 'The Great Adult Review.'

Spectator, June 17th, 1911. Comment by editor and letters from Austin Harrison, Arnold Bennett and R. A. Scott James.

Spectator, June 24th, 1911. Letters from Henry Newbolt, Ford Maddox Hueffer and May Sinclair.

Mercure de France, July 1st, 1911. 'The English Review and the Spectator' by H. D. Davray.

Bookman, September, 1911. 'Mrs. Grundy Again.'

English Review, November, 1911. 'Frank Harris and his (Imaginary) Talks with Carlyle' by A. Carlyle, with Harris' reply.

New Statesman, June 19th, 1915. 'The Adventure of Frank Harris.'

New Statesman, June 26th, 1915. G. B. Shaw replies.

New Statesman, July 31st, 1915. Frank Harris replies.

New York Morning Telegraph, August 27th, 1926. 'Once Too Often Frank.'

Mercure de France, February 1st, 1929, 'Oscar Wilde et Alfred Douglas.'

Mercure de France, March 15th, 1929. A reply by Frank Harris.

The New York World, January 20th, 1929. 'An Hour with Frank Harris.'

The New York World, March 30th, 1930. 'Frank Harris at Home.'

Bookman, April–May, 1930. 'Oscar Wilde's Unwritten Play' by T. H. Bell.

Bookman, November, 1931. Harris replies.

Nation, December, 1931. 'Frank Harris.'

Literary Digest, September, 1931. 'Brilliant Ruffian.'

Bookman, November, 1931. 'Frank Harris.'

Bookman, October, 1931. 'Sir Hall Caine and Frank Harris.'

Nation, December, 1931. Harris Versus Shaw.

Nation, May, 1932. Harris Versus Shaw.

Fortnightly Review, January, 1932. Frank Harris: Bernard Shaw.

New Republic, February, 1932. Frank Harris on Mr. Shaw.

American Mercury, February, 1932. Harris on Shaw.

Catholic World, December, 1932. 'Recollections and Impressions.'

Bookman, October, 1932. 'Tempest in a Bookshop.'

Bookman, February, 1933. 'Chapters from an Autobiography'.

London Magazine, Volume 2, No. 6, June, 1955. 'A Visit to the Villa Edouard Sept.'

Letters consulted:

I have read and consulted over 1,000 letters from Harris, some unpublished, some partly published:

Correspondence between Harris and B., 1925–1926. Unpublished.

Correspondence between Harris and his secretary Bell, 1901–1904. Partly published.

Correspondence between Harris and Arnold Bennett, 1908–1910. Privately published.

Correspondence between Harris and Jack Carney, 1917–1919. Unpublished.

Correspondence between Harris and Davray, 1899–1905. Unpublished.

A long correspondence between Harris and Hesketh Pearson, 1915–1926. Partly unpublished.

Correspondence between Harris and R. and Mrs. R., 1923–1926. Largely unpublished.

Correspondence between Harris and Blanche and Arnold Rittenberg, 1921–1924 and 1926. Unpublished.

Correspondence between Harris and G. S. Viereck, 1915–1926. Unpublished.

Correspondence between Harris and Percy Ward, February
1920–May 1921. Unpublished.

A letter from Harris to Lord Alfred Douglas, December
16th, 1925. Unpublished.

A letter from Harris to H. L. Mencken, 1922. Part published.

Letters from Harris to Middleton Murry, 1900. Unpublished.

Two letters from Harris to Lady Welby, September 6th and
14th, 1892. Unpublished.

A letter from Hugh Kingsmill to Enid Bagnold concerning
Harris, 1914, unpublished.

A letter from Oscar Wilde to More Adey, April 12th, 1897.
Partly unpublished.

Letters from Oscar Wilde to Robert Ross, 1898–1900. Partly
unpublished.

Two letters from the Fortune Press, February and March,
1939. Unpublished.

Letters from Middleton Murry to the author, 1957. Unpublished.

A letter from Mrs. Harold Weston to the author, September
14th, 1956. Unpublished.

Notes provided by E. Gertz on two meetings with
Gwladys Price-Williams, Frank Harris' niece, in 1929.
Unpublished.

Very interesting quotations from the following letters were
given in the catalogue of Autograph Letters and Manuscripts
issued by Charles S. Boesen.

R. D. Blackmore. Two letters to Frank Harris, August 12th
and September 23rd, 1896.

Oscar Browning. Seven letters to Harris between September
25th, 1919 and May 1st, 1921.

Mrs. Patrick Campbell. A letter to Harris, September 7th, 1900.

Lord Randolph Churchill. A letter to Harris, November
17th, 1909.

Winston Churchill. Eight letters to Harris between July
22nd and November 27th, 1905.

John Davidson. A letter to Harris, undated.

Eugene Debs. Two letters to Harris, January 28th, 1918 and
October 14th, 1920.

Lord Alfred Douglas. Three letters to Harris, September 4th and December 10th and 27th, 1925.

Theodor Dreiser. Eight letters to Harris between April and July, 1918.

Max Eastman. A letter to Harris, June 29th, (?).

Mary Garden. A letter to Harris, February 25th, (?).

Emma Goldman. Four letters to Harris between May 14th, 1924 and February 3rd, 1926.

James Hureker. A letter to Harris, November 22nd, 1920.

Thomas Huxley. Three letters to Harris, June 2nd, 10th and 12th, 1891.

Arthur Machen. A letter to Harris, June 3rd, 1903.

Henri Matisse. Two letters to Harris, March 23rd and 24th, (?).

Texiera de Mattos. A letter to Harris, July 11th, 1911.

Robert Ross. Three letters to Harris, September 6th, 1913, November 27th, 1916, and February 3rd, 1917.

G. W. Russell. Seven letters to Harris between February 4th, 1921 and August 14th, 1923.

Edgar Saltus. Three letters to Harris, undated.

Olive Schreiner. Letter to Harris, undated.

Upton Sinclair. Twenty-three letters to Harris between 1916 and 1925.

W. B. Yeats. A letter to Harris, December 23rd, (?).

Oscar Wilde. Three letters to Harris, undated.

INDEX